THE
VIRGINIA WAY

THE
VIRGINIA WAY

DEMOCRACY AND POWER

AFTER 2016

JEFF THOMAS

THE
History
PRESS

Published by The History Press
Charleston, SC
www.historypress.com

Front cover: Governor Ralph Northam and Dominion Energy CEO Tom Farrell onstage, August 2018. *Office of the Governor of Virginia*.

Back cover: George Mason Elementary School bathroom, Richmond, July 2018. *From the* Richmond Times-Dispatch; Theresa "Red" Terry surveys pipeline damage on her family's property, Bent Mountain, August 2018. *Courtesy of Mara Robbins*; Richmond mayor Levar Stoney pitched a 1.5 percent meals tax increase for schools as "less than these two pennies I have in my hands," January 2018. *From the* Richmond Times-Dispatch.

First published 2019

Manufactured in the United States

ISBN 9781467143684

Library of Congress Control Number: 2019937048

In The Virginia Way, *Jeff Thomas takes an uncompromising look at how Virginia's economic and social hierarchy maintains control. He examines in detail a series of contemporary issues, consolidating research in ways that the state's small, economically constrained journalistic community often cannot do. Whether Virginia is more subject to concentrated economic control than other states may be debated, but the way in which the entire dynamic is cloaked in gentility is distinctively Virginian. The author opens the curtain on persistently powerful interests seldom exposed or contradicted. His account is not the only truth— but it is the part of the truth that is rarely identified. This is an important, knowledgeable, disturbing, carefully researched book.*
—The Reverend Benjamin Campbell,
author of Richmond's Unhealed History

Jeff Thomas has again hit pay dirt with this neatly written, deeply researched look at how a narrow group of oligarchs runs Virginia despite its conceits of being the birthplace of American democracy. This up-to-date account explains questionable gas pipelines, laissez-faire political donations and an arrogant electric utility.
—Peter Galuszka,
author of Thunder on the Mountain: Death at Massey and the Dirty Secrets of Big Coal

Jeff Thomas writes with compelling, methodical, deft outrage. The Virginia Way *is lucid and solidly researched. Grab this tool and go fix Virginia.*
—Stephen Nash, University of Richmond,
author of Virginia Climate Fever

For the people

The man who is possessed of wealth, who lolls on his sofa or rolls in his carriage, cannot judge of the wants or feelings of the day laborer. The government we mean to erect is intended to last for ages. The landed interest, at present, is prevalent; but in process of time, when we approximate to the states and kingdoms of Europe; when the number of landholders shall be comparatively small, through the various means of trade and manufactures, will not the landed interest be overbalanced in future elections, and unless wisely provided against, what will become of your government? In England, at this day, if elections were open to all classes of people, the property of the landed proprietors would be insecure. An agrarian law would soon take place. If these observations be just, our government ought to secure the permanent interests of the country against innovation. Landholders ought to have a share in the government, to support these invaluable interests and to balance and check the other. They ought to be so constituted as to protect the minority of the opulent against the majority.
—James Madison

The strong do what they can and the weak suffer what they must.
—Thucydides

CONTENTS

THE VIRGINIA WAY

Power concedes nothing without a demand. It never did and it never will.
　　　　　　　　　　—*Frederick Douglass*

No event better illustrated the state of Virginia politics and government in the early twenty-first century than a sixty-one-year-old grandmother who confounded governors, CEOs, and the federal government when she was charged with trespassing on her own property. The most pressing issue on the minds of those officials in April 2018 was probably not Theresa "Red" Terry and her family's cabin at the end of an unpaved road in Bent Mountain, Virginia. But it soon would be.

They hoped the Mountain Valley Pipeline would one day carry natural gas from Pennsylvania and West Virginia fracking operations to international export through ports on Virginia's coast.[1] The 308-mile pipeline was not popular among Virginians whose land would be seized, uprooted, and polluted so that investors could send out-of-state gas to India.[2] Adding fuel to the fire was an unusual amendment to the Virginia Constitution that prohibited corporations from using eminent domain to take people's land for private gain—corporations, that is, except for utilities.[3] The Virginia legislature had been complicit in this land grab, from passing a 2004 law that guaranteed that "gas companies have the power to enter property without permission," as Bart Hinkle of the *Richmond Times-Dispatch* put it, to twice passing the above amendment, as required by the state constitution, before sending it to the voters for final approval in 2012.[1] For opponents, then, stopping the pipeline was no longer a matter of legislation but of justice.

The centuries-old farm had been in Red's husband's family since before the Revolutionary War, and she would be a witness to crews despoiling it with chainsaws and bulldozers.[5] It was fair to call her headstrong when her husband nailed a stand and tarp thirty feet up a tree on their property, and she climbed it with little fanfare in late March 2018. When she began her vigil, nobody seemed to care, and construction crews felled the forest around her. "My daughter is also in a tree and had them on all four sides of her," Red said. "She cried all day."[6] A local radio station covered her plight two weeks later, and on April 17, the state's leading Democratic blog, *Blue Virginia*, published an activist's video that drew thousands of views from the sort of people who followed politics every day.[7] Red peered out from her stand and told a videographer, "I will come out of the tree when these people get off my land." The next day, lawmakers from the area and northern Virginia held a press conference at the state capitol to express concerns over myriad issues with the pipeline, from contaminated water to eminent domain abuse to the treatment of Red and her daughter.[8] One Nelson County resident said that the cooperation between rural and urban lawmakers was "very important. They have a lot of votes and a lot of swagger behind them that maybe those of us in rural areas don't have." Red responded that she was thankful for the attention, but she would prefer it be focused on the pipeline rather than her.[9]

That same day, "a Roanoke County magistrate was signing their arrest warrants for trespassing and obstruction of justice."[10] The story went viral when reporters and readers heard a mother and her daughter were about to be arrested for "trespassing" on their own property. "They're not taking my property without a fight," Red said.[11] Even more troubling were conflicting reports that they were being denied food and water and that local police told her husband that "he could leave food for his wife at the bottom of the tree, but she would have to come down to get it." "They're violating her basic human rights, by not letting her have food or water should she ask for it, or a hot meal should she ask for it," her husband said. "You put someone in prison you feed 'em. Usually when you get to prison you've been tried and convicted. And she has neither been arrested, tried or convicted." The spotlight swung over to the Roanoke Police Department, and its tactics put its leaders on the defensive.[12] The *Washington Post* soon picked up the story under the headline "Perched on a Platform High in a Tree, a 61-Year-Old Woman Fights a Gas Pipeline."[13] The clickbait proved irresistible, and Red was the lead story on that paper's national website on Sunday, April 22, 2018.

When I visited Red on April 23, 2018, her civil disobedience may have seemed much like she looked to those below: lonely, desperate, and doomed, but also inspiring, courageous, and just. A closer look revealed even more. To scan the crowd of fifty or so surrounding Red was to see how dire the situation was becoming not for the lone prisoner, but for the power brokers in Richmond and Washington who made the decisions that drove her there. There was a group of young and radical environmentalists who had at the beginning of the vigil erected a base camp around her. They ran the show, and nobody else would have been there without them. But among the crowd were photographers, civil rights attorneys, and Delegate Sam Rasoul of Roanoke speaking to a television crew. Staffers of Delegate Lee Carter and Senator Chap Petersen were there, and Jennifer Lewis, candidate for Congress and leader of an anti-pipeline group, was moved to tears. A newcomer to the crowd asked a series of bold questions of the organizers. "Who are you?" one finally asked him. "I'm Henry Howell. Do I need to say anything more?" said Henry Howell III, pugilist lawyer and son of the great politician who had come closest of any populist in the twentieth century to winning the Virginia governorship.[14] In addition to the activists, who could be dismissed by those in power, the presence of the lawyers, media, and politicians personified the structural crisis facing the operation of Virginia politics and government in the second decade of the twenty-first century. Put simply, it was bad for business to raise electricity rates in order to bury explosive hazards throughout hundreds of miles of public forests and private land. Whereas a few days earlier, the Roanoke Police had been using hunger as a weapon to speed Red Terry's arrest, that day, officers personally delivered her pizza and sandwiches.[15]

"Appalachian politics are more eclectic than what the national headlines would suggest," and an even deeper examination fleshed out the nature of the motley group.[16] Professor Rhiannon Leebrick of Wofford College, whose research focused on social change and environmental issues in South Central Appalachia, noted that, contrary to impression, the "young and radical" organizers of environmental justice movements in rural Virginia possessed social networks, political sophistication, and economic capital that could be brought to bear on local governments and nongovernmental organizations to influence public policies.[17] "The activists" had turned a small vigil into an international media scrum within a week.[18]

In a system of government like Virginia's where the laws were largely written by and for the powerful, lawyers would be key. Red's civil disobedience, and the efforts of thousands of others who toiled without recognition, catalyzed the legal activism of those who knew that though the law had once worked for the pipeline, it could now be put into service against it. "My name is Henry Howell, Bar number 22274. Write that down!" he told a National Forest Service officer surveilling him with a telephoto lens, as he escorted Senator Petersen to other pipeline protesters that Petersen would soon file suit to protect.[19] "All these brave, courageous, intrepid tree sitters must be wondering where their Governor and Attorney General are, as the economic powers of interstate, out-of-state pipeline companies are using *our government* to enforce a federal judge's order for private companies to profit by taking people's land," Howell III wrote, as he outlined a case for court action.[20]

Red came down after thirty-five days, but the truth was, she won the longer war.[21] In August, the state capitol's newspaper of record reported on the fusillade of legal skirmishes that had begun since Red's last stand.

> *In Virginia and West Virginia, Mountain Valley has been put on notice six times since April that its measures to control erosion and sediment were failing, with muddy water sometimes flowing from work zones into nearby streams. Then in late July, a federal appeals court invalidated permits allowing the pipeline to cross through the Jefferson National Forest, faulting the U.S. Forest Service for not pushing for tougher erosion controls.... Then, the Federal Energy Regulatory Commission ordered a stop to all work on Aug. 3. The commission also this month ordered work to stop on the Dominion Energy–led Atlantic Coast Pipeline.*[22]

In an extraordinary series of events on December 7, 2018, the Fourth Circuit Court of Appeals issued a stay for Atlantic Coast Pipeline construction; the Virginia State Corporation Commission, for the first time in history, rejected as not in the public interest the Dominion monopoly's integrated resource plan for future infrastructure; and Virginia's Attorney General Mark Herring sued Mountain Valley Pipeline alleging more than three hundred environmental pollution violations.[23] Reflecting a heretofore unimagined political reality, Herring also chose this day to announce that he would seek the governorship in 2021.[24] Days later, he pledged that he would never again accept any money from Dominion or its executives.[25]

Red Terry surveys pipeline damage on her property. August 2018. *Mara Robbins.*

The years 2016 to 2019, from President Trump's election through the aftermath of the 2018 midterm elections, represented both populist and elite backlashes to the operation of the so-called Virginia Way, the corporate-centric philosophy by which state government had been run since colonial times. The internal contradictions of this system had come to harm not only the working and middle classes, as the Virginia Way always had, but also the ruling class itself. Dominion Energy, which had ruled the roost as Virginia's most powerful corporation for generations, was facing the most serious challenges in its history, from people who could not and would not be ignored. Virginia's political class was facing the greatest upheaval since the days of Henry Howell Jr.—and perhaps since Reconstruction a century before that.

THE BIPARTISAN CONSENSUS

The modern Virginia political system was Senator Harry Byrd's machine turned bipartisan. Harvard political scientist V.O. Key presciently noted that Byrd's hegemony over Virginia politics in the middle of the twentieth century had instituted "an autocratic machine that may long outlive him."[26] Virginia did not share West Virginia's history of New Deal populism and labor organizing, except in the far southwest, resource-extractive areas.[27] North Carolina had embraced forward-looking education and business policies in the decades after desegregation, especially at the University of North Carolina and in cosmopolitan Charlotte.[28] Virginia instead pursued a bipartisan economic consensus more comparable to the reactionary Deep South, just with more money and less overt racism. Robert Caro wrote:

> *"The Byrd machine is genteel,"* the liberal Reporter *magazine had to admit. "There are no gallus-snapping or banjo-playing characters in Virginia politics." Its hallmark was courtliness, not the demagoguery prevalent in other southern states. "Virginia breeds no Huey Longs or Talmadges," John Gunther wrote in* Inside U.S.A. *"The Byrd machine is the most urbane and genteel dictatorship in America." "He hated public debt with a holy passion,"* [U.S. Senator Paul] *Douglas was to write of Byrd. "With little or no sympathy for poor people, and instinctively on the side of the rich and powerful, of whom he was one, he nevertheless had a certain rugged personal honesty and a genial air of courtesy towards*

his opponents, except when severely pressed." While he ran the [Senate Finance Committee] *graciously, however, he ran it unyieldingly. "He had a habit of slapping" a fellow senator on the back and laughing, "as if they were both enjoying a good joke," while he was denying a request....His economic philosophy was a businessman's philosophy. No one ever called him a reader or a particularly deep thinker, or even a man with more than a surface understanding.*[29]

The Byrd machine's paternalism and even its mannerisms were easily recognizable in Virginia's political circles well into the twenty-first century. The state followed this well-worn path even as Democratic Party hegemony bifurcated and evolved into what was effectively one-party dominance with a Republican and Democratic wing.

Key and others contended that Byrd's political organization practiced relatively clean government and was not known for graft. However, Brent Tarter, founding editor of the *Dictionary of Virginia Biography*, pointed out that the machine was so efficient that its practitioners "did not need to steal money because they had already stolen something a lot more valuable: they had stolen democracy." Outright graft was less common in Virginia because its politicians controlled public policy so thoroughly that they could just write the laws to directly benefit themselves.[30] The constitutional amendment permitting gas companies to legally trespass on people's land while labeling its owners as trespassers was a quintessential example.

The Virginia political system in the twenty-first century was as deeply entrenched as the Byrd dynasty from which it descended. In the two-party era, since the civil rights movement secured voting rights for the disenfranchised 20 percent of Virginians, Virginia politics and government had operated with bipartisan consensus. There was division on social issues, such as abortion, gay marriage, and gun rights, but on the economic issues that mattered to businesses and the bottom line, there was and always had been unity among the parties, with rare exceptions. For a long time in Virginia, it did not really matter whom citizens voted for on economic issues, because both parties would give them the same. As the descendant of a system in which the powerful wrote laws to benefit themselves, state politics still reflected the will of business and campaign donors. The most incisive way to cut through the daily noise and truly comprehend Virginia politics and government was to understand that politicians were doing what their donors wanted and donors got what they paid for: low taxes, underfunded public services, hostility to workers and unions, low public welfare and high corporate welfare. The Virginia Way was not broken; on the contrary, it worked exactly as it was designed as a way for politicians and donors to maintain their lucrative, symbiotic monopoly on power.

Political scientists often argued for a median voter theorem in which elections and policy were determined by the midpoint of a bell curve distribution of voters.[31] In this theory, politicians moved to centrist positions to capture the largest share of the electorate. In Virginia, this mode of electioneering only existed with social issues and minor controversies, which were given disproportionate weight by antagonistic reportorial styles and partisan electioneering that accentuated wedge issue conflicts. The political and economic affairs of the state were bimodal, and Republican and Democratic politicians were on the same side, generally opposed to the public. For example, the business-political class got what it wanted with electoral and fiscal policies, even though measures like expanding voting rights and increasing the minimum wage were supported by a substantial majority of the population (69 percent and 74 percent, respectively, in February 2018).[32] A corollary was that the bipartisan consensus meant politics was commodified: for sale to the highest bidder. Thus, there was little difference in the economic programs of the two parties because they were both beholden to the common interests of their donors. With the exception of Reconstruction, there was, and always had been, a bipartisan economic consensus supporting the Virginia Way.

Even into the twenty-first century, the real work of government was largely predetermined; the bipartisan consensus gave voters the illusion of choice at the polls. Virginia's budget changed little when a governor from one or the other party came into office. The economic programs of Democratic governors like Doug Wilder, Mark Warner, and Tim Kaine were indistinguishable from their Republican counterparts, or from Dwight Eisenhower's, for that matter. Kaine was considered the state's most liberal U.S. senator since Reconstruction; nevertheless, when he ran for vice president in 2016, he was criticized as too moderate by many national Democratic groups.[33] In 2018, the president and editor-in-chief of *Virginia Business* magazine wrote:

> *As governor, Kaine supported spending for mass transit, highway construction and education. He struck a centrist note in supporting a coal-fired power plant in Wise County that was opposed by environmentalists, while backing tighter restrictions on mountaintop removal mining. As a senator, Kaine again has struck a centrist note, aligning himself with*

Virginia's living governors at the Governor's Mansion, December 2018. Not pictured: Linwood Holton, Tim Kaine, Mark Warner, and Doug Wilder. *Office of the Governor.*

issues and bills supported by the U.S. Chamber of Commerce, the Virginia Chamber of Commerce and other business advocacy groups. His voting record has been pro-business on immigration, health-care reform, free trade, military spending and investment in infrastructure projects....A vote for Kaine is good for business and good for Virginia.[31]

Whether voters faced a promise-breaking regressive tax increase to pay for transportation and infrastructure under Warner in 2004 or Republican Bob McDonnell in 2013 was mostly arbitrary and was determined more by legislative leaders' personal psychodramas about which executive they happened to like. In one glaring example, Democratic governor Terry McAuliffe, a hard-charging New York transplant, unsuccessfully worked the Republican legislature for four years to accept the 100 percent federal funding available to expand Medicaid health insurance for the working poor, a measure that was supported by business interests in Virginia. He was succeeded by Democratic governor Ralph Northam, a soft-spoken doctor and son of a Virginia judge, and within the first six months of his term, the Republican legislature accepted now-diminished 90 percent funding for

Medicaid expansion, with Virginia's 10 percent contribution coming from raising taxes on hospitals.[55]

In a two-party society, there was no way to vote against policies on which the parties aligned. It was not a coincidence that Barack Obama and Donald Trump had both run as outsiders trying to clean up Washington, and their slogans reflected a poll-tested yearning of Americans for political change. Increasingly, during the years covered in this book, disaffected voters from all sides of the political spectrum attacked the sclerotic Virginia Way. This precipitated a grassroots backlash on the progressive and Tea Party sides of the Democratic and Republican Parties in which activists increasingly shared the same language and even the same goals. Attendees at political events and consumers of grassroots media would notice a surprising overlap in rhetorical frames among members of progressive and Tea Party groups that both criticized establishment politicians for wasting taxpayer money on projects that benefited donors primarily. More than rhetoric, the specific issues on which these groups organized were sometimes entirely in accord. It may have surprised members of both groups to learn that Activate Virginia, created by former Bernie Sanders national delegate Josh Stanfield to oppose Dominion's legislative influence, and the Virginia Tea Party, which was so strongly opposed to Dominion that the company's 2018 bill was one of just two the group marked on its legislative scorecard that year, were working toward the same goal and offered the same critiques of that company's political power. At the same time, Virginians were living in a country increasingly divided along political, media, and social media lines. As a consequence, practical efforts toward common cause that honest people could find as a solution to the Virginia Way were almost nonexistent. As much as donors and their political power were uniform across the parties, the activist groups in Virginia remained partisan and siloed, to the continued benefit of the bipartisan consensus.

THE VIRGINIA WAY IN 2020

Followers of current events may have had the impression that the biggest stories in Virginia politics were the 2017 and 2018 "blue wave" elections. These were undoubtedly important, but the biggest story in Virginia politics in the first two years of President Trump's administration was not the backlash to him but the backlash to the Virginia Way.[36] This anti-democratic bipartisan consensus was lauded, for example, by former state senator John Chichester:

> *In large part, the "Virginia [W]ay" is rooted in the deep sense of responsibility that goes with occupying the space of our founding fathers—those who shaped this great nation with a bold vision that continues to inspire the world....We can take comfort in the lessons of Virginia history. At those crucial points in our journey, Virginia's political leaders will reach deep and find fortitude and courage. They will coalesce and make that unpopular choice, if it truly is necessary to preserve the treasure that is our Commonwealth.*[37]

It was rare to see an American politician so openly bash democracy in favor of elitist rule. The more accepted stance was to pay rhetorical homage to "all men are created equal," and this was even exaggerated in Virginia, where native son Thomas Jefferson designed both the state's capitol and first university. While all are indeed created equal, another truism was that "different interests necessarily exist in different classes of citizens," as written by native son James Madison.[38] The Virginia Way called back not to Jefferson but to Madison, who further argued at the Constitutional Convention:

> *The man who is possessed of wealth, who lolls on his sofa or rolls in his carriage, cannot judge of the wants or feelings of the day laborer. The government we mean to erect is intended to last for ages. The landed interest, at present, is prevalent; but in process of time, when we approximate to the states and kingdoms of Europe; when the number of landholders shall be comparatively small, through the various means of trade and manufactures, will not the landed interest be overbalanced in future elections, and unless wisely provided against, what will become of your government? In England, at this day, if elections were open to all classes of people, the property of the landed proprietors would be insecure. An agrarian law would soon take place. If these observations be just, our government ought to secure the permanent interests of the country against innovation. Landholders ought to have a share in the government, to support these invaluable interests and to balance and check the other. They ought to be so constituted as to protect the minority of the opulent against the majority.*[39]

The money that flowed to politicians and the hubris that they were "occupying the space of our founding fathers" when they did something "unpopular" conflated to make the Virginia Way a seductive ideological space. Virginia politicians passed no state laws beyond disclosure to guard against unethical behavior. "Virginia is the only state where lawmakers can raise unlimited campaign donations from anyone, including corporations and unions, and spend the money on themselves," a reporter noted.[10] What did this temptation invite?

The legislature was, as Madison wanted, the most powerful branch of government, and the leaders of the Virginia House and Senate represented its apotheosis.[11] Senate Democratic leader Dick Saslaw expressed his perceived role in a debate with his Republican counterpart as if they were in a contest: "Go ask Dominion, go ask any of these companies—beer and wine wholesalers, banks, the development community—every one of them will tell you, they will tell you I'm the most pro-business senator."[12]

Senate Republican leader Tommy Norment took things a step further and was literally in bed with a lobbyist; his long affair with one was disclosed only when a former client filed an ethics complaint against him.[13] During the time in which he was committing adultery, itself a Class 4 misdemeanor in the state, Norment not only failed to recuse himself from voting on lobbyist Angela Bezik's bills but also was the leading sponsor of two of them.[14] The FBI interviewed Norment, who was represented by Richard Cullen, former U.S. Attorney for the Eastern District of Virginia, but the current U.S. Attorney for the Eastern District of Virginia declined to press criminal charges.[15] When the scandal broke in 2015, Norment claimed that he and his wife "were able to work through our issues including me having to share with her some of my misbehaving which was painful but necessary for a reconciliation. We are doing quite well now without any issues."[16] Norment soon divorced her. On June 16, 2018, he announced that he was engaged to Bezik, who was still employed as a state lobbyist.[17]

On the same day as Norment's engagement news, Speaker of the House Bill Howell announced that he was taking a job at McGuireWoods, Virginia's most powerful lobbying firm. "Although state law forbids Howell from lobbying his former colleagues in the General Assembly for one year, Howell started a job Monday in a non-lobbying capacity as a consultant with McGuireWoods Consulting," Patrick Wilson wrote. "A weak definition of lobbyist in Virginia allows Howell to advise clients on how they can influence his former colleagues, and allows him to call former colleagues in the legislature to request appointments for clients."[18] Howell was reportedly "the first former House Speaker" in Virginia history to turn to "consulting."[49]

Norment and Howell knew very well what was moral; in fact, they had publicly written about their vision of good government and the perils of corruption in a joint essay just a few years earlier:

> *Public service requires loyalty—not to a party or an ideology, but to those we serve. Public service also requires sacrifice. While that sacrifice is often measured in time away from family, it is more than that. It is an unconditional and unequivocal promise to place the best interests of the commonwealth before oneself. Public trust and the integrity of elected leaders are essential to the success of representative democracy. When the public loses confidence in those processes and those entrusted with significant responsibility and power, the system can crumble.*[50]

It was disconcerting in the state that was "the birthplace of the constitutional right to a free press" to see the contempt of the people and the press evidenced so brazenly in Norment and Howell's simultaneous statements; Norment's story was eclipsed by Howell's.[51] It well illustrates a common theme in Virginia: the vast disconnect between words and actions in service of the Virginia Way. Some people chose to believe the words; some people looked at actions.

The true meaning of the Virginia Way was clear for those concerned with reality rather than ideology. Robert Zullo left the *Richmond Times-Dispatch* in 2018 and formed the *Virginia Mercury* with three other political reporters. He shared his motivation in "Meet the Mercury: A New Look at the Virginia Way":

> *For his enthusiastic support of the "big boys," other delegates in the House jokingly branded the amiable* [Delegate Terry] *Kilgore a "reverse Robin Hood" and gifted him with a trophy stuffed with fake cash and festooned with corporate logos in a surreal scene that might have managed to capture everything wrong with how business is done at the Capitol. "It's all in good fun," Kilgore said. Sit through enough legislative committee meetings and you'll see a steady stream of common-sense bills that could benefit regular people swatted down like flies day in and day out during the session. Generally, their fatal flaw is that they might make a business, insurance company, landlord or other entity with a powerful paid lobbying organization do something it doesn't want to.*[52]

House of Delegates colleagues awarded Terry Kilgore "a trophy stuffed with fake cash and festooned with corporate logos" for his work during the 2018 session. *From the* Richmond Times-Dispatch.

A poll showed that just one in three Virginians felt that Virginia politicians were "exceptionally" or "mostly" honest. "Clearly, the idea that Virginia has an exceptionally ethical and honest political culture is a figment of the imagination," said political scientist Quentin Kidd. "The public simply doesn't buy it."[53]

GOVERNOR MCDONNELL'S LEGACY

Crises create opportunities for reform, and in the five years after Governor and First Lady McDonnells' corruption scandals in 2013–14, there was a moment for honest reassessment that could have fixed many of the problems of the Virginia Way. The McDonnells had been caught taking bribes from Jonnie Williams, a cartoonish con man who "cooked tobacco in microwaves from Wal-Mart, packaged it in candy-like lozenges and tried to turn Virginia's oldest cash crop into an elixir for old age."[54] Williams received immunity, and the McDonnells were convicted of nearly a dozen felonies each. They seemed destined to spend a year or two in prison, and it is often assumed that they were found not guilty on appeal. In fact, the U.S. Supreme Court ruled that the jury instructions had been too broad and sent the case back to the Fourth Circuit of Appeals, but President Obama's Justice Department decided not to push the matter further.[55] One of McDonnell's notable legacies was that the governorship was not mired in further corruption scandals after he left.

The administration of Governor Terry McAuliffe, who was sworn into office just ten days before the McDonnells were indicted, reflected a time when Virginia politicians faced an existential moment.[56] Should they continue business as usual, or should they change the Virginia Way? The system continued onward, but only for those who had been immersed in it; for others, the McDonnell scandals shattered the myth.[57] Governors McAuliffe and Northam were two very different people, and McAuliffe in particular had a checkered past growing wealthy in the gray area between business and politics, but, as of this writing, it appeared that neither McAuliffe nor Northam had succumbed to the temptation of monetizing their office for private gain.[58]

Running against the Virginia Way proved a successful political strategy for legislators, too, and voters increasingly elected people who rebelled against the pay-to-play system of the state's politics. The Virginia Way was effective at reconstituting itself, but self-aggrandizement was far from sufficient. Entrenched power also relied on anti-democratic principles. For the first time in the long history of the state, in November 2015, every politician who ran for reelection won, an incredible 122 out of 122. The fact that 2017 witnessed a landslide election for Democrats, but the House of Delegates remained precisely equally divided, showed the continuing power of gerrymandering. Virginia was changing, but the political and business elites were still the descendants of the tobacco planters who ruled a government "of the businessmen, by the businessmen, and for the businessmen."[59]

CRISES OF POWER

In Dominion Energy, the intersection of money and politics was at its most egregious, and it was worth examining as a window into Virginia government. Dominion was essentially a state monopoly electric utility held within an investor-owned natural gas corporation; it could not fairly be called a private company, because two-thirds of its revenue and four-fifths of its cash came from the state monopoly.[60] Virginia lawmakers guaranteed the utility a rate of return of roughly 10 percent that flowed to executives, Wall Street, and politicians. Despite this guarantee, Dominion had made a practice of overcharging Virginians by tens of millions or even hundreds of millions of dollars every year. The State Corporation Commission, tasked with regulating state monopolies and power rates, had never once found that Dominion had charged fair rates. After a 2007 biennial refund law was enacted, more than $700 million was refunded to Virginians in 2010 and, in 2012, more than $70 million. Dominion passed a bill in 2015 that ended these refunds and consequently raised electricity rates on more than two million people and tens of thousands of businesses. The fact that Dominion's interests in high electricity rates ran counter to not just ordinary citizens' but also small and large business interests may have seemed befuddling to some in this ostensibly pro-business state. But the paradox was resolved when one saw that Dominion was the state's most profligate campaign contributor, and therefore, its lawyers wrote Virginia's energy policies.

For the first time in history, in 2017, there was a true grassroots campaign in Virginia politics to elect people who pledged to never take campaign contributions or "gifts" from Dominion. Thirteen candidates who made this pledge won election. A bloc that large was significant, could sway votes, and could not be ignored. Because of the power of incumbency, some of these thirteen people would serve in office for many years. Dominion was the most powerful company in state politics precisely because it was the largest donor, and upstart politicians had little to lose and lots of good press to gain by pledging to not take Dominion's dirty money. Activate Virginia and many others understood that giving money to politicians was the root of so many of the problems affecting state government, and the power of the idea was spreading throughout Virginia's political system like a genie that could not be put back in the bottle.

For the first time in history, again in 2017, two contenders came within a hair's breadth of winning their party's nomination for governor without the support of the business community. Both Democrat Tom Perriello and Republican Corey Stewart ran on anti-Dominion platforms only to narrowly lose their primaries by 10 percent and 1 percent, respectively, to establishment candidates who supported Dominion and other corporate priorities.

If the Virginia Way was "a euphemism for corruption," then politicians with integrity were a foundational threat.[61] The people in power never admitted to being swayed by activists or so-called ordinary citizens, but they always listened to criticism and protest. Always—because it affected the bottom line. In 2015, Dominion spokesperson David Botkins "could not name a piece of legislation in the past five years in which Dominion did not get what it wanted from the General Assembly."[62] But by 2017, "after two years of defending a controversial law that froze base rates for Virginia's two largest electric utilities as a hedge against carbon regulation, Dominion Energy officials said Monday that it's 'time to transition away' from the 2015 rate freeze."[63] By 2018, for the first time in history, Dominion could not get everything that it wanted. The backlash was too great; the threat of democracy was too real.

Dominion was extreme, but not unique. The business interests of Richmond-based cigarette giant Altria (formerly Philip Morris) in addicting customers to poison harmed the addicts, their friends, and families, and all citizen and business taxpayers footed the bill through Medicare, Medicaid, emergency room subsidies, and higher insurance premiums. The direct healthcare costs to Virginia government from tobacco were estimated at $1.92 billion in 2009, and it was not an exaggeration to say that Altria killed more Virginians than it employed.[64] How did the corporation's leadership get away with running a business that actively harmed the economy and our people, while being taxed at the rate of fiftieth out of fifty-one states, plus D.C.? Altria was the state's second-largest campaign contributor; therefore, its lawyers wrote Virginia's tobacco policies.[65]

Were these two companies out of the ordinary? An audit of the Virginia Economic Development Partnership, the corporate subsidy organization of the state, found that it had given away $400 million over the last ten years without any accountability or oversight and even gave money to companies that did not exist and were created only on paper to get these subsidies.[66]

THE PURPOSE OF WRITING HISTORY

There had been a long campaign to convince voters and scholars of the Virginia Way myth of clean government in which examples of corruption were usually dismissed as deviations from a glorious history stretching back to Lee, Jefferson, and Jamestown. The "deviations" were really the main story. Virginia politicians ignored plain facts and evident consequences in service of a Virginia Way ideology that just so happened to benefit themselves.

The Virginia Way was most pernicious not in its clearly self-serving corporate and government public relations functions, but in the insidious dissemination of a false ideology that was and always had been central to the identities of many well-meaning, well-educated Virginians. The history of Virginia as the birthplace of democracy and "great men" was subject to mythmaking and historical revisionism from those who possessed the intellectual gifts and freedom to know better. James Southall Wilson had attained the highest honors as the Edgar Allan Poe Professor of English at the University of Virginia, and in 1930, he reviewed *The Virginia Plutarch*, a collection of essays on thirty-two men and one woman whom the author, Philip Alexander Bruce, felt had the greatest impact on Virginia history. Wilson wrote that Bruce

> *is himself one of the highest and most exquisite illustrations of the civilization of the old South. He belongs to a generation close enough to the Virginia that ended with the War between the States to know its soul and to be touched with the savor of its tradition, and he comes of a family that was of the bone and sinew of the old aristocracy, and that through ties of blood or of courtesy was linked with the great men of whom he writes. No one less to the manner born could fittingly have lifted a mirror great enough to give the true reflection of Virginia's Great Tradition, nor could anyone bred in a later generation have felt instinctively the code and the spirit in which his heroes act.*[67]

Compare this with the *Richmond Times-Dispatch* editorial board's "salute" of Congressman Eric Cantor in 2014 after he was so despised by his constituents that he became the first House Majority Leader to lose reelection in American history:[68]

> *Today's Op/Ed page features an extraordinary column by an extraordinary human being. Rep. Eric Cantor (R-7th) uses the space as a platform to announce his resignation from the House of Representatives....Cantor has drawn comfort and strength from sacred texts. "I seek refuge in You, O Lord; may I never be disappointed. As You are beneficent, save me and rescue me; incline Your ear to me and deliver me. Be a sheltering rock for me to which I may always repair; decree my deliverance, for you are my rock and fortress," the Psalmist says....Cantor came to the political world naturally. His gifts were displayed early as though he were to the manner born. Young Eric Cantor saw rainbows; throughout his life he has pursued them. We salute him.*[69]

The editorialists did not mention that Cantor's wife was on the board of directors of the company that owned the *Times-Dispatch*.[70]

Or witness the 2018 op-ed from nephew of a state senator and former Dominion employee Gordon Morse titled, "Bill Howell: An Honorable Servant of Virginia," penned after the former Speaker of the House took his non-lobbying job at McGuireWoods.

> *Howell took over as speaker (greatness was thrust upon him, for all intents) at a time of political turmoil and uncertainty, when the commonwealth might well have slipped backwards, sideways and over itself, riven by partisanship....Howell's easy wit made him good company. That helped in many ways. After all, you cannot equitably preside over a disputatious room of elected egos without a high measure of amity and patience. Howell unfailingly provided....In Howell, McGuire Woods* [sic] *will get an experienced personality more given to managing than being managed. He will tell them what he thinks and where the lines are drawn. He has been living within those lines all his life. His influence might be as much internal as external. In a nutshell, the idea, thus advanced, that Howell simply took this new job to "cash in" is offensive.*[71]

The "great men" view of history advanced in the preceding examples is standard in Virginia history, though things have begun to change as old assumptions are battered against the rocks of serious scholars who were not "to the manner born."[72] Tarter found that "an unexamined reverence for the [Virginia Way] that Douglas Southall Freeman, Virginius Dabney, and others propagated in the twentieth century allowed a mythic version of the past to constrict the range of options that the state's political leaders contemplated. That reverence, more importantly, either blinded them and the larger public to the undemocratic features of their government or allowed them to ignore or accept those features as if they were part of the inevitable natural order of things." The bipartisan fake history of the Virginia Way was just as damaging as partisan fake news stories. It affected what men whom "greatness was thrust upon" thought of our present society, the responsibilities of government, and the possibilities for public policy and reform.[73] If everything was fine, as they were taught in school and believed as adults, then why change?

Ben Campbell, Rhodes Scholar and author of *Richmond's Unhealed History*, said that "because our history has been lied about for so long, we can never get to the point where the truth gets told, so we act as if injustice were an *exception* to our situation. The fact of the matter is things are not right; they did not start right; they have never been right. If we can start from there, then maybe we can make them right. That is the challenge of our time, and that is why history has to be properly told."[71]

But the books of the past century lived on in the dogma of this century. How did this happen? In "Making History in Virginia," Tarter relates how the reality described by Campbell and contemporary journalists coexisted with the ideological predispositions of Virginia Way apologists. "Beginning with the original narratives of 1607 and for the next three centuries, the writers who interpreted Virginia's history were the same people who made the history…so infecting historical writing that much that issued from the book publishers in the guise of history was really fiction in disguise." Virginia students had always been taught the "Moonlight and Magnolias" history of Freeman, Dabney, and other Virginia Way historians. "Those were the books that the supporters of massive resistance read when they were in school," and one of many consequences for the overwhelming majority of Virginians was the barbaric discrimination that shaped that society and echoed to the present.

In the 1950s, a committee of politicians rather than historians edited the mandated textbooks on Virginia history for public school students. The legislators "were not so much attempting to live in the past as acting on and celebrating what they had been taught and had read about that past and what they therefore believed was the truth. Such was the influence of the textbooks and the historical literature that it reinforced in a select population of powerful public persons what they wanted to believe about themselves and their heritage."[75] Fred Eichelman explored this case for his dissertation and later wrote:

> One of the authors informed me that she was told not to be concerned with exposing myths; that was the job of college teachers. An author for the high school textbook told me he was forced to put little emphasis on Native Americans and not mention any plights they may have had due to colonial rule. A whole chapter he devoted to them was deleted. He was also forced to deradicalize Nathaniel Bacon, Thomas Jefferson and Patrick Henry. Any attempt to humanize Jefferson or relate how he was concerned that slavery would divide the nation would be an attack on the aristocracy. In relation to government there was to be no mention of the Byrd Organization or Machine and no mention of poverty or the poor. The Republican Party was to receive little mention with the exception of Abraham Lincoln who triggered the War Between the States. A Democrat commission member admitted that he personally wrote the government section.

CHAPTER 29

How the Negroes Lived under Slavery

SLAVE LAWS NOT STRICTLY ENFORCED

EARLY in Virginia's history the General Assembly made laws closely controlling the Negroes. However, the laws were not fully enforced. Many slave masters did not like to have the state government meddle in what they considered their private business. They managed their servants according to their own methods. They knew the best way to control their slaves was to win their confidence and affection.

Many Negroes were taught to read and write. Many of them were allowed to meet in groups for preaching, for funerals, and for singing and dancing. They went visiting at night and sometimes owned guns and other weapons. The

368

A page from the textbook *Virginia: History, Government, Geography*, which the state government mandated in public middle schools from the 1950s through the 1970s.

These textbooks, which can only fairly be described as government propaganda, were used in Virginia "from 1957 into the late 1970s."[76]

Learning selective history holds particular power over young minds, for the worldview of youth can blind and bind the subconscious of all that follows.[77] In an insightful book from the University of Virginia Press, Charles Dew movingly examined his own Virginia upbringing in *The Making of a Racist*. "My training as a Confederate youth had pretty much been completed when I was in my early teens," he lamented. "Everything I had learned growing up pointed in exactly the same direction.…[A]nyone who thought otherwise was either an arrogant, or ignorant, Yankee or certifiably insane." We know that learning is natural when we are young—indeed, children cannot *not* learn—and requires more effort as the years go by. "I could have stopped at this point and remained warm and content in a cocoon," Dew wrote.[78] Satirist James Branch Cabell pinpointed this mindset in the character of Senior, *Let Me Lie*'s graying bloviator: "That which, incessantly, we were taught before reaching manhood we must continue to believe forever in our hearts; so that even should our reason be convinced that some of if not all this teaching was incorrect, our hearts simply do not honor the argument with their attention."[79] The "great men" view of history thus became so central to the identities of many Virginians who grew up during the mid- to late twentieth century that in 2018, someone as smart as Morse did not merely object to the notion that the former Speaker's move to the state's most powerful corporate lobbying firm was not in the public interest—a clear enough proposition—but found statement of the idea "offensive." The Virginia Way presumes politicians' purity of motive even in the face of countervailing evidence.

Historical mythmaking and revisionism still did not fully explain what Virginians faced well into the twenty-first century; the reception of another remarkable book shone a mirror on Virginia's character better than anything else. Published in 2010, it told the story of Richmond's dysfunctional public schools more thoroughly and poignantly than any work ever had or likely ever would. It was as if James Ryan was genetically engineered to write about the problems that ailed Richmond. The son of an adoptive family, and a first-generation college student, he had won a full scholarship to Yale and another to the University of Virginia Law School, where he graduated first in his class, then returned as a professor for fifteen years after clerking for Supreme Court Chief Justice William Rehnquist. He followed this with service as dean of Harvard's Graduate School of Education. He examined Richmond's Thomas Jefferson and Henrico's Douglas Freeman public high schools as the foundational case study for America's modern education system in his first book, *Five Miles Away, A World Apart*.[80] His sublime description of Richmond's battle for freedom and justice diagnosed the failure to integrate the city as the preeminent factor in what Frederick Law Olmsted had called Richmond's most memorable trait, its "failure…in the promises of the past."[81] Ryan was not a partisan, and he was open to and supportive of solutions ranging across the ideological spectrum.

What was so unusual about this book was that unlike some of the other major works discussed in this chapter, Ryan found an acolyte in Todd Culbertson, who spent forty years, in his own words, "inflicting opinions on readers" as an editorialist for the *Richmond Times-Dispatch*.[82] The hagiography of former congressman Eric Cantor quoted earlier evinced Culbertson's typical method, but Culbertson praised *Five Miles Away* in ten editorials between 2010 and 2013, writing, for example, that it "belongs on the required reading lists of public officials and private citizens seeking to comment on the state of the schools."[83] After a time, Culbertson understood as well as anyone that his wide audience could not have missed mention of the book in the city's only daily newspaper. He penned an unforgettable editorial, "Education Book: Vanishing Act":

> *We hoped that "Five Miles" would capture the local imagination. This is a compelling book about local institutions and local conditions published by Oxford University Press, an unsurpassed academic house. Ryan reports evidence and offers ideas crucial to the education debate not only in Metro Richmond but also throughout Virginia and the entire United States. Ryan has spoken at Virginia Commonwealth University and next month will appear at the University of Richmond. Interested individuals have contacted him. Still, he and his book deserve far more play than they have received. The region's school officials and other political figures should have welcomed the opportunity to embrace "Five Miles" or to refute it. They did not—or have not done so with sufficient visibility. The book also seems to have eluded the grasp of many private groups and people identified with the promotion of good schools. All of central Virginia should be talking about "Five Miles." The absence of vigor dismays—and fails to flatter the establishment.[84]*

The paper's editorials quickly became conventional wisdom among the tens of thousands of Richmonders who read the paper every morning with their coffee—but in this case, the editorials were repeatedly ignored, as the book was, and continues to be. Ryan was, in a word, beloved, and as a measure of his brilliance and integrity, in 2018 he returned from Harvard and assumed a post as the ninth president of the University of Virginia.[85] Even Ryan's appointment to the most meritocratic position in the state had no noticeable effect on Richmond's education conversation. The most momentous book ever published about Richmond elucidated the city's most pressing problems, and knowledge of the work and its importance were spread in the most public way to the city's citizens. The book did indeed hold a mirror to our society: the lesson was that the people in Virginia's capital who read these editorials and actually could have done something about the problems collectively decided to decline this unprecedented opportunity in thousands of individual, independent decisions.

The legacy of the Virginia Way was much deeper than portraying or perceiving historical falsehoods as facts. The most profound finding from Eichelman's study was that "one former commission member admitted to me that the goal of the seventh grade book was to 'make every seventh-grader aspire to the colonnaded mansion; and if he can't get there, make him happy in the cabin.'"[86]

There was a purpose to Virginia Way history: it was designed to instill among the population rose-colored reverence for the Founding Fathers and the Civil War in order to ingrain docility about their current society by repressing the natural human drives for creativity and freedom. Reverend Campbell said after his lifetime of service in Richmond that "what I have encountered is this tremendous sense of passivity before human change. I have this image of Patrick Henry standing up in the middle of St. John's Church in 1775 saying, 'Give me liberty, or give me death!' And everybody else goes back and says, 'Well, I think we'll just stay a British colony.'"[87] Cabell wrote:

> *The well-born Virginian of our era is not, and has never been, able to look forward. He has not even looked, with any large interest, at his current surroundings. For we were always taught to look backward, toward the glories of which we had been dispossessed at Appomattox....The dream is the one true reality.*[88]

Virginians lived in a free society, but they were uncommonly burdened by an unseen force in the freedoms they chose to exercise. In 2019, most Virginians, perhaps almost all, may have felt not just that the state's past was a certain way, but also that they did not have full agency in their own lives to do something about it. When their individual actions added up to a society, the Virginia Way was not "history" as past events: it was a living history and collective unconscious that actively constrained Virginia's potential in the present.

1

CORPORATE POWER

DOMINION'S HEGEMONY

"It was considered suicide to even speak against Dominion [three years ago],*"
said Sen. Chap Petersen, a Democrat who added that he recently received a
standing ovation at a town hall when he previewed a bill to ban public service
corporations like electric utilities from making political contributions. "First time
in 21 years of public service."*

*From a conservative standpoint, what bothers me here is the cronyism, one, and the
further deviation from something approaching free-market pricing as we can achieve.
It hurts everybody—it hurts the poor, it hurts business, it hurts opportunity.*
—former Virginia Attorney General Ken Cuccinelli

Few people would have considered a twenty-eight-year-old living with
his mother as a serious threat to the most powerful corporation in
Virginia. But such was the power of Josh Stanfield's idea that its
spread represented the direst challenge to Dominion Energy's decades-long
reign as the state's legislative hegemon.

In Virginia's donor-controlled government, Dominion's legacy as the state's
largest campaign contributor produced extraordinary dividends. Free market
capitalism did not and, by law, could not exist in Virginia's electricity industry.
No business except Dominion could produce and sell electricity in two-thirds
of the state, and Dominion was guaranteed to make money off its monopoly.
It was even more unusual that Dominion was allowed to use its government-
guaranteed money to buy political influence. Such an arrangement would not
be permissible at the national level: both corporations and federal contractors

were barred from donating money to congressional candidates.[1] In Virginia, too, the state liquor monopoly was prohibited from donating to Virginia political campaigns, as were its executives and their family members.[2] There were other socialist monopolies in Virginia, which many paid homage to when they drank tap water or flushed a toilet. City water and sewer systems were not perfect but were run like true public utilities, and nobody ever claimed the head of the local water treatment plant was buying elections.

Nor were they buying private jets, like Dominion's 2013 Gulfstream G280, 2014 Gulfstream G28, and 2017 Gulfstream G450 (tail numbers N603D, N604D, and N607D, respectively), the latter of which alone cost about $40 million up front and $2.5 million per year to operate.[3] As another measure of skewed market incentives, Dominion CEO Tom Farrell was the highest-paid utility executive in the United States, while Dominion was the nation's second-least energy-efficient utility, ranked between Alabama Power and Entergy Louisiana.[4]

Dominion consisted of a government electric company held within a private natural gas corporation. The socialist component, in which the government compelled more than two and a half million homes and businesses to buy electricity only from Dominion, was guaranteed a rate of return by the government of about 10 percent.[5] Other ventures received higher payouts: with the Atlantic Coast Pipeline, Wall Street Dominion could charge its captive electric Dominion customers up to a 14 percent return on investment.[6] Despite these guaranteed profits, Dominion stock over the five years between 2014 and 2019 had far underperformed the S&P 500.[7] Dominion the private company was far less profitable than Dominion the government-guaranteed monopoly; in fact, the latter had spun off and subsidized the former. Dominion tried to pretend it was a capitalist company, but when the parent corporation tried to take over the much larger socialist utility in 1994, the utility "generated more than 90 percent of shareholder profits." The "merger" was consummated in 1997, and generous taxpayer-guaranteed profits had subsidized and allowed the conglomerate to expand risk-free for decades.[8] Today, "the monopoly still accounts for about 65 percent of Dominion's revenue, but most importantly, it generates almost 80 percent of the corporation's cash."[9] The relationship between the two entities was inherently conflicted, to Dominion's tremendous benefit. The "private" Atlantic Coast Pipeline, for example, would be substantially paid for by tacking an additional $2.3 billion onto its monopoly customers' power bills—while the company publicly said the pipeline would save its customers money.[10] American taxpayers subsidized this when the company somehow managed to pay no federal income taxes on about $3 billion in profit and even received a rebate in 2018.[11] All in all, it was an impressive marketing feat to see Dominion portray itself as a private company.

Dominion was not only guaranteed a rate of return by the government, but it also wrote the laws that politicians voted on and always passed. In the late 1990s, "a deregulation wave for setting electricity rates was sweeping the country and Dominion asked to be part of it," wrote energy journalist Peter Galuszka, who had worked as Moscow bureau chief for *Business Week*. "But a few years later, Dominion realized that dereg[ulation] wasn't working quite to their advantage, so they got the General Assembly to change it all back again to regulation….[At the end of the 2007 session], '(State Sen.) Tommy Norment just reached into his drawer and pulled out a re-reg bill,'" he wrote, quoting former Virginia Sierra Club lawyer Glen Besa.[12] The bill passed easily, and thus was instituted the modern framework in which the state guaranteed Dominion its roughly 10 percent rate of return.

An overearnings provision that required refunds when Dominion charged above this generous rate of return benefited the public but was an obstacle to even more lucrative electricity rate hikes.[13] In the 2015 legislative session, Dominion set its sights on canceling these refunds under the pretense that Dominion needed them to pay for President Obama's Clean Power Plan. "In an Orwellian turnabout," reporters uncritically adopted Dominion's language that this was a "rate freeze," "when in fact the only thing frozen is base rate cuts and consumer refunds," a journalist noted. "The lock-in established a floor for rates, but no ceiling."[14] Senator Frank Wagner was the lead sponsor of the bill, which he openly admitted Dominion lawyers wrote.[15]

At the time, Dominion spokesman David Botkins "could not name a piece of legislation in the past five years in which Dominion did not get what it wanted from the General Assembly."[16] Unsurprisingly, despite an enormous public outcry, Dominion passed this bill as well.[17] "Dominion writes utility legislation in Virginia," said Senator Chap Petersen. "They do it to make more profit."[18] Time quickly bore that out: in the next year, Dominion overearned an estimated $426 million.[19] "This bill was all about Wall Street versus Main Street, and basically they wanted to make sure that the Wall Street analysts for their stock were not continuing to ding them because of the uncertainty associated with their profit margins," said Besa.[20] A reporter found that "the new law has been good for company shareholders, who faced a risk of losing 40 to 60 cents per share if the constitutional challenge had prevailed and Dominion's profit margin were lowered to the levels allowed in most states, according to an analysis by Goldman Sachs Equity Research in June."[21]

(Left to right) Senate Majority Leader Tommy Norment and Senator Frank Wagner listen to Dominion lobbyists Bill Thomas, Daniel Weekley, and Eva Teig Hardy, February 6, 2015. *From the* Richmond Times-Dispatch.

As national political events had influenced earlier fights for de- and re-regulation, Donald Trump's 2016 election affected the permissive climate surrounding the conflicted relationship between Dominion and Virginia government. Most importantly, President Trump quickly scuttled Obama's Clean Power Plan and thus negated Dominion's oft-stated rationale for taking hundreds of millions of additional dollars from Virginia citizens and businesses even above its overly generous, guaranteed rate of return. Second, a new wave of Trump- and Bernie Sanders–style populists were redefining the boundaries of acceptable policies and behaviors for political candidates on the right and left nationwide. Third, the backlash to President Trump and the traditional seesaw dynamics of midterm elections augured Democratic waves in Virginia's 2017 state elections, 2018 federal elections and potentially beyond. Lastly, and harder to quantify, was corporate hubris: Dominion had overextended its hand with the 2015 rate hike bill and cross-state pipelines. The civil disobedience of ordinary people like Red and Minor Terry could not have come at a worse time for Dominion.[22] They symbolized that the checks and balances that had long been embedded in America's broader democratic mosaic, like the judiciary, the free press, and civil society, were beginning to view Dominion as the head of the snake of a deeply corrupted establishment. It became difficult to find an article, group, or politician praising Dominion that the company had not paid for itself.

Josh Stanfield had two insights into this new political environment. Dominion faced the political reality that socialist monopolies were antithetical to democracy and capitalism, so to maintain its favored position, its business model relied on legally bribing establishment legislators through Virginia's "wild, wild West" system of campaign contributions.[23] Therefore, politicians who refused to take money from Dominion were an existential threat to Dominion's Virginia Way. Stanfield theorized that challengers in races against incumbents could gain positive press coverage for refusing money from Dominion, which would fail to recognize the evolving political dynamic and invariably support the incumbent. In the absence of a co-opted legislature, Dominion would be a ripe target for politically popular refunds that would boost the economy and turn out votes as effectively as any tax cut. Though the incumbent political system favored Dominion because of its campaign contributions, the political pull of giving refunds to constituents would eventually be unassailable. "How many times as a politician can you get a check to every single constituent?" Stanfield asked.[24] He reached out to all Democratic challengers for the 2017 House of Delegates races (the Virginia Senate would not hold elections until 2019) and secured the pledges of an astonishing seventy-six challengers to never take money from Dominion. "We're lucky in Virginia that we have a common villain with Dominion Energy," he said. "Dominion is trying to build the Atlantic Coast pipeline, so we have a lot of pipeline fighters who hate Dominion for that. They buy out our legislature; a lot of people hate that. They've got coal ash all over Virginia; everyone hates that. It was so easy to build a coalition against them."[25]

The first indication of electoral trouble for Dominion came when former congressman Tom Perriello launched an anti-Dominion, Sanders-style campaign for governor focused on the company's pipelines and influence-peddling.[26] "In an era of deep partisanship in Richmond, the only truly bipartisan consensus is taking money from Dominion," Perriello noted.[27] His campaign, getting a late start against an establishment frontrunner who had cleared the field, quickly gained momentum and gave an unexpected, serious challenge to Virginia's political order.[28] For his part, Ralph Northam promised to set a $10,000 cap on individual donations and ban corporate campaign contributions.[29]

Anti-Dominion platforms were politically popular, and as long as President Trump remained in office, the state would continue to have blue waves that required Republican politicians to move left, right, or anywhere except for establishment centrism.[30] So Trump-aligned Republican gubernatorial candidate Corey Stewart also fought against Dominion. "Dominion had no idea what it was in for when it picked a fight with the Carver Road community" over eminent domain rights, Stewart said. "If I were to choose an enemy, [Dominion] would be the one I would have chosen."[31] Libertarian gubernatorial nominee Cliff Hyra also opposed Dominion's pipelines.[32] Stewart and Perriello narrowly lost their primaries, but all three Democratic lieutenant governor candidates also refused to take money from Dominion, and Justin Fairfax went on to win election in November 2017. "The only strong conclusion you can draw from this primary is that refusing Dominion money didn't noticeably hurt, and might actually be helping, Democratic candidates," Stanfield noted.[33]

The House of Delegates' challengers' surprising new platform was hardly a shock to the system: in the 2015 elections, every single incumbent who sought reelection that November won, a flawless and historically unprecedented 122 out of 122.[34] However, political operatives and commentators failed to anticipate the scale of the 2017 Democratic landslide elections. Whereas in 2015, Senate Majority Leader Tommy Norment had stated, "never in the remainder of our chronological life [*sic*] is the House of Delegates going Democratic," after the 2017 elections, the House was as close to evenly divided as possible.[35] The Republicans held on to 50 seats, the Democrats captured 49, and the remaining seat that would determine the balance of power went through recount after recount until the Board of Elections stunningly declared that the final vote count was an exact tie. As dictated by Virginia law, the winner in this last race was picked at random, and in a surreal scene, control over the House of Delegates for the 2018–20 session was determined by drawing a candidate's name from a bowl. The Republican happened to win, so his party controlled the House, 51–49.[36]

The 2017 Democratic wave thrust into office a dozen politicians who had pledged to never take money from Dominion. A thirteenth, incumbent Sam Rasoul, had taken the pledge and won reelection.[37] This was a significant bloc of power in a body where Republicans held onto the slimmest majority and shuddered to consider what might happen in 2019. While Dominion from time to time had swatted away upstart challengers from the populist left and right, in 2017, politicians had challenged the Virginia Way and won—exactly the wrong lesson to be learned, if, like Dominion, you relied on campaign contributions to secure political fealty and the money you needed to pay Wall Street.

The counterargument was that the Democratic wave would have happened even without the anti-Dominion pledges, but it was hard to give that much credence because of one race in particular in which the winner ran away from the Virginia Democratic Party. Lee Carter ran his race in Manassas with what many politicos assumed was a political suicide wish as he proudly extolled his admiration for democratic socialism. His opponent, House Majority Whip Jackson Miller, had been in office for over a decade and had access to all the money and endorsements he could ask for, which he used liberally to inform his constituents how much Carter resembled Mao and Stalin. The Democratic Party of Virginia, itself flush with cash, did not support Carter's campaign after the former Marine made it clear that he did not agree with some of the Party's methods. Carter made a pro-worker, anti-Dominion message the centerpiece of his campaign, and the only press that Carter could get was as a political oddity. Patrick Wilson wrote that "people within the Democratic Party would have preferred I not write about him." But Carter won his race by nine points after he took the anti-Dominion pledge, and won a 2019 primary challenge, despite being all but disavowed by Virginia Democrats.[38]

While awaiting the next blue wave in 2019's state races, things got even worse for Dominion. Nominees for Congress from both parties refused to take Dominion's PAC money in every seat not held by an incumbent Democrat in the 2018 midterms.

District	Candidate (Party)
1	Vangie Williams (D)
2	**Elaine Luria (D)**
5	**Denver Riggleman (R)**
5	Leslie Cockburn (D)
6	Jennifer Lewis (D)
7	**Abigail Spanberger (D)**
8	Thomas Oh (R)
9	Anthony Flaccavento (D)
10	**Jennifer Wexton (D)**

Virginia's 2018 congressional candidates who refused campaign donations from Dominion's PAC. Districts 3, 4, 8, and 11 were represented by incumbent Democrats; bold indicates winners.

Vote counters realized that, if and when it was put to a vote in the Virginia legislature after a potential 2019 blue wave, the Democratic Party would likely vote to ban Dominion's campaign contributions. Even more striking was that Stewart, Riggleman, and Oh were harbingers that indicated not only Democrats but also the Tea Party, non-establishment Republicans, and moderate Republicans in Democratic districts might also vote to prohibit campaign contributions from the socialist monopoly.

This political evolution took place as the sources of wealth and power in America continued to shift away from heavy industry to tech and finance. Dominion was weathering a pincer movement from the left and right and facing a frontal assault from far wealthier national groups that became engaged when Virginia was a leading swing state in 2016, and then a year later when it held the first competitive elections since Trump's victory. Dominion's supporters, such as blogger Jim Bacon, who was paid a "five figure" sum annually by Dominion for the three years ending in June 2018, were quick to label those who had criticized Dominion's influence peddling as hypocritical for the much more subdued coverage of the environmentalists' money.[39] The issue got some traction in the media.[40] Environmental groups like NextGen Climate Action and the League of Conservation Voters outspent Dominion in those two years, but they lacked the legislative focus, lobbying muscle, and long game that Dominion had perfected over generations.[41]

When Charlottesville-based major donor and former Goldman Sachs executive Michael Bills promised to financially support those who took the politically popular position of standing up to Dominion, it blunted the California carpetbagger charge.[42] His money would go to a Clean Virginia Project explicitly aimed at Dominion. "Confronting the dominant financial influence of Dominion's executives, lobbyists and allies on Virginia's representatives, Clean Virginia will shine a light on the price of legalized corruption in terms of lost jobs, lost business opportunities, and lost rebates in past overcharged electric bills, totaling up to $1 billion," the group promised.[43] The transformed financial landscape was a sea change and heralded a potential win-win for populist and establishment politicians who wanted to avoid charges of corruption. It was hard to criticize the donations of a Virginia businessman who had no self-interest at stake while defending campaign contributions from a socialist corporation.

As with the pipeline fight, Dominion was now a wedge issue that had caused a split in the aristocratic class that ruled Virginia. "Those who hope for reform could hardly invent a better nemesis than Dominion," a reporter noted.[14] "Lawmakers, lobbyists and others at the General Assembly say there's been a noticeable change in attitude toward the company this year compared to three years ago, when Dominion had little trouble passing legislation that has yielded a significant windfall for the company," wrote Associated Press reporter Alan Suderman. "'It was considered suicide to even speak against Dominion,' said Sen. Chap Petersen, a Democrat who added that he recently received a standing ovation at a town hall when he previewed a bill to ban public service corporations like electric utilities from making political contributions. 'First time in 21 years of public service.'"[15]

THE SOUTH CAROLINA WAY

With its transactional political-business model under threat, Dominion had to expand the Virginia Way to other markets and in January 2018 announced an offer to purchase the South Carolina utility SCANA, which served 1.1 million customers.[16] Like Dominion, SCANA was a publicly traded natural gas company with a subsidiary government-guaranteed electric utility, and as in Virginia, the South Carolina legislature had long regulated the utility. Within two days of the announcement, Dominion added a stable of lobbyists, including former South Carolina governor Jim Hodges, to its payroll.[17] It also launched a "blitzkrieg" of "television, radio, internet and print" ads that one legislator likened to a presidential primary.[18]

When Virginia legislators raised rates on their constituents in 2015, they also passed a resolution honoring Dominion and resolving that "the Clerk of the Senate prepare a copy of this resolution for presentation to Thomas F. Farrell II, chair, president, and chief executive officer of Dominion Resources, Inc., as an expression of the General Assembly's gratitude and admiration for the company's commitment to service."[19] It would have been inconceivable for them to imagine the scenes that would unfold in South Carolina in a legislature that was not co-opted.

Unlike the obsequiousness that always greeted Dominion in the Virginia legislature, the company's promises were met with bipartisan incredulity in the South Carolina legislature. A special Senate committee was set up to examine the merger, and Farrell was called to testify about it in a hearing just two weeks after the bombshell announcement. Democratic Senator Mike

Fanning "asked every utility official in the room to stand so the lawmakers could recognize them. After some reluctance, dozens of lobbyists, lawyers and utility staffers stood. 'This is what the people of South Carolina, the ratepayers, are up against right here,' Fanning said. 'It's only going to get bigger and worse as it goes on.'"[50] "It was literally 80 of the 110 people in the room," Fanning told a reporter. "I wanted to call attention that the Good Ol' Boy system is still in force"[51] "Thank you for recognizing them," Farrell said sarcastically.[52] Farrell testified that if the legislature did not let Dominion charge customers the 10.25 percent rate of return on a failed nuclear plant that the company was accustomed to in Virginia, then SCANA would go bankrupt. "You walk in here this morning, and now I feel like I've got a gun to my head," Fanning said. "There is no gun here," Farrell replied. "The cries of bankruptcy have to be looked at," Republican Senate Majority Leader Shane Massey said. "I think it's a bluff."[53] Dominion understood the logic of refunds—not for Virginians, whose refunds it had canceled, but for South Carolinians, to whom Dominion promised refunds of $1,000 to sweeten its takeover of SCANA.[54] Massey compared the $1,000 refund "to a payday loan, where customers get a benefit up front but end up paying more in the long run."[55]

In a hearing the following month, the bipartisan leaders of the Senate attacked the foundation of Dominion's business model in Virginia. "Why is it fair that customers have to pay more than the debt, more than the interest, so that shareholders will get even more money?" Massey asked Farrell, who claimed it was a fair rate of return. Democratic Senate Minority Leader Nikki Seltzer said that "the amount that SCANA has paid their stockholders and the money their institutional investors are going to get out of this is really questionable. I don't know why that money couldn't be directed to ratepayers instead of these out-of-state investors."

Massey asked how much money Dominion would make.

"We believe it will add to our earnings," Farrell said. "It depends on a lot of assumptions how that will turn out.…There's no good way to answer that question. We do expect Dominion to earn profits on the purchase, yes, sir."

"No question about that," Massey countered. "I want a number. Y'all have got a number. I mean, you've run the numbers. You wouldn't have come up with this particular plan over 20 years and these particular rebates unless you've got a number on how much you stand to make."

"Don't have a number, sir," Farrell dissembled. "We don't run numbers out 20 years."[56] In fact, for the $1,000 "payday loan," Dominion would receive $4,000 from the average consumer over the next twenty years.[57] Energy analyst Hugh Wynne argued that it would be a far better deal for ratepayers to finance bonds to pay for the failed nuclear project. The lower interest rates would save them more than $150 million per year for twenty years.[58]

In a scene that would seem like *The Twilight Zone* in Richmond, in the face of dubious warnings by Dominion, South Carolina passed a measure 37–2 in the Senate and 109–4 in the House in early 2018 to cut electric rates by 15 percent.[59] The bill also "create[d] a state consumer advocate's office to fight for ratepayers against utility rate hikes" and made "the state Office of Regulatory Staff, which police[d] utilities, a tougher watchdog by giving it subpoena power over utilities and removing part of its previous mission, which required it also to look out for utilities' financial interests." Governor Henry McMaster vetoed the bill that summer not because the legislature did not do Dominion's bidding, but because he wanted the legislature to cut rates even further. His veto was overridden "within minutes" by 110–1 in the House and 39–0 in the Senate.[60]

The imperious Farrell, whose mask quickly slipped off in the rare cases where he did not get his way, issued a hyperbolic and ironic statement claiming that "the South Carolina Legislature is playing a high-stakes game where they are gambling with the money of customers and taxpayers" and "promoting continued turmoil for South Carolina's energy and business future."[61] It later came out that Dominion had offered to increase the refund to $1,500 if the rate cuts were scuttled, further indication of how valuable the higher rates really were to the company.[62] Analyst Wynne said that Farrell was "like Br'er Rabbit after he's punched a tar baby. He's stuck and he realizes he can't win and now he's looking for a face saving way to get out."[63]

Nobody could seriously accuse South Carolina of harboring anti-capitalist sentiment; South Carolina lawmakers simply had not been bought off and used their common sense to see that cutting electricity rates was the same as cutting taxes. In 2019, it was still too early to see what the merger would entail in the long term—skepticism is certainly warranted—but when it finally went through, electricity bills were cut by 15 percent, and the average SCANA customer would save about $5,700 over twenty years compared to the status quo.[64] The Virginia Way stopped at the border.

DOUBLING DOWN

To fight the continuing crisis of democracy in Virginia, Dominion undertook multipronged public relations and electoral strategies. In early 2017, the company changed its logo from something that "look[ed] like the hand of Michelangelo's Adam receiving life from God" to something more abstract resembling Adidas's branding.[65] It also changed its name from Dominion Resources to Dominion Energy and excised the ambiguous word *Power* from its socialist utility subsidiaries in Virginia and North Carolina in favor of the more benign *Energy*.[66] Just before the gubernatorial primaries, Farrell sent a thinly veiled letter to employees and shareholders asking them to "take time to review the candidates' positions and see how they stand on critical projects such as the Atlantic Coast Pipeline" and then "exercise your constitutional right to vote."[67] Then, Dominion hired away the *Richmond Times-Dispatch*'s editorialist Bart Hinkle, a self-styled libertarian who began his new venture untroubled by the irony of going to work for an anti-capitalist machine that he had for years railed against in principle, if not always in practice.[68]

After the 2017 wave elections, Dominion announced that it was "time to transition away" from the 2015 rate hike bill that had raised electricity prices on millions of involuntary customers.[69] Dominion was acutely aware of the shift in public opinion, but this announcement was indicative of a public relations strategy more than any serious policy change. In an audacious play, Dominion would use the 2018 legislative session to double down on its broadly unpopular 2015 rate hikes and get even more money from captive ratepayers. But for the first time in memory, in 2018, Dominion would get *almost* everything it wanted instead of everything.

There was still a bipartisan consensus favoring the Virginia Way, personified in the state senate's grandees who had not yet faced the disrupting blue wave. Many senators had served for decades and had been through an acculturation process of learning the Virginia Way. As noted in the introduction, Senate Democratic Leader Dick Saslaw had been in the legislature for more than forty years and plainly elucidated his philosophy: "Go ask Dominion, go ask any of these companies—beer and wine wholesalers, banks, the development community—every one of them will tell you, they will tell you I'm the most pro-business senator."[70] In a campaign finance environment where corporate contributions were unlimited, Dominion wined and dined and treated legislators to golf tournaments and hunting trips, while giving them tens or hundreds of thousands of dollars in cash that could be spent with no restrictions.[71] The bacchanalia had partly abated in the years since the McDonnells' corruption scandals, but the campaign money still flowed freely even to those who faced no challengers at reelection time.[72] More than ideology and corporate largesse, many legislators saw no conflict in owning substantial amounts of Dominion stock. Senate Majority Leader Norment owned between $50,000 and $250,000 worth, as did Delegate Chris Jones, chairman of the Appropriations Committee. Senator Bill DeSteph owned more than $250,000 worth, the highest disclosure level.[73]

Governor Ralph Northam, son and grandson of Virginia judges, had served as a senator and shared the disposition of the grandees.[74] He owned between $10,000 and $50,000 in Dominion stock when he was a senator and lieutenant governor. "When an issue threatens a major donor, you don't see a lot people stick their necks out," said Senator Petersen. "The lieutenant governor was no different than anyone else." Northam pledged to put his assets in a blind trust if he won the gubernatorial election.[75] His campaign promise to ban corporate contributions was immediately jettisoned after he won the election, and he did not even feign otherwise.[76] Dominion gave Northam's campaign $50,000. Governors in Virginia cannot constitutionally run for consecutive terms, so Northam would not face reelection in 2021; after he was elected, Dominion gave $50,000 to his inauguration, a bizarre practice that could only be fairly described as buying influence at the outset of each new administration.[77] Immediately before the start of the 2019 legislative session, Dominion and its law firm, McGuireWoods, hosted a fundraiser for Northam at the firm's Richmond headquarters with ticket prices ranging to $10,000.[78]

Other influence-peddling efforts generated tax write-offs. It was revealed in the summer of 2015 that Dominion had "given" more than $1 million to charity while tacking the costs of these donations onto customers' bills.[79] After the scandal was revealed, spokesperson David Botkins claimed they would stop the practice.[80] An exposé revealed what had happened in the interim. Dominion's foundation had given between $500 and $5,000 to Peter Paul Development Center, a small Richmond charity, for years, while Farrell had given a $5,000 annual donation going back at least to 2012. Yet after Peter Paul's director of operations Lamont Bagby was elected to the House of Delegates in 2015, these donations skyrocketed. In December 2015, Dominion's foundation gave the center $25,000, and Farrell committed $100,000 in June 2016. By an equally mysterious sleight of hand, Bagby was the lead Democratic House sponsor of Dominion's 2018 bill. He would be joined by Republican Terry Kilgore, who was pictured in the introduction gripping a "trophy stuffed with fake cash" on the House floor.[81]

Governor Northam and Dominion CEO Tom Farrell on stage, August 2018. *Office of the Governor.*

Another $5.1 million was offered to "divide-and-conquer" a poor African American community whose members had mobilized to oppose locating a gas compressor station for the pipeline in their neighborhood.[82] Taxpayers in essence paid these "gifts" twice over through charitable deductions.

Virginia's 2018 legislative session began with the public and most officials in the dark about what Dominion had meant when its spokespeople claimed they wanted to "transition away" from the 2015 rate hikes. Given that the 2015 hikes had been rationalized by a Clean Power Plan that Trump had repealed, it seemed natural to also repeal the 2015 rate hikes.[83] On the gubernatorial campaign trail, personification of the establishment Ed Gillespie noted the logical syllogism: "[T]he justification for that bill was the imposition of the Clean Power Plan," he said. "If the Clean Power Plan goes away, the justification for the bill has gone away." A Goldman Sachs analysis "found that overturning the law would present substantial—10 percent to 15 percent—downside risk to Dominion's earnings."[84] Yet when Senator Petersen introduced a full repeal bill, a capital reporter instantly noted that the bill was dead on arrival. Senate Minority Leader Saslaw would introduce and carry Dominion's bill, which senators seemed to consider a fait accompli despite the fact that it had not even been introduced. Steve Haner of the Virginia Poverty Law Center described matter-of-factly how legislation was written in Virginia: Dominion lobbyists were "running around the Capitol looking for allies, and they're asking allies what they need to join the team.…It's nice to see them working so hard."[85] Two days later, Petersen's bill was voted down 13–1 in committee.[86] "It's no wonder why people are frustrated," said Delegate Sam Rasoul. "It's no wonder why we can really give no other explanation than this law was a corrupt law."[87] Another Senate committee voted down a bill 12–2 that would have prohibited government-guaranteed monopolies like Dominion from making campaign donations.[88]

Dominion's bill was introduced on January 19, 2018, and it somehow employed twenty-two lobbyists to push it.[89] Even for close observers, it was "a riddle wrapped in a mystery, inside an enigma." Customers would receive a partial $133 million refund of the overearnings, while the majority would be plowed back into Dominion for various infrastructure measures over the next decade, from which Dominion would get to keep a healthy profit on top of the original profit. Rate reviews for even more overearnings in subsequent years were structured so that "it could be 2024 at the earliest before anyone gets their money back."[90] "This is the rate freeze on steroids," said Senator Petersen. "It's the deep freeze."[91] Most importantly, the bill contained a provision that would allow the utility to essentially double-charge customers for infrastructure. "If it sounds confusing, it's supposed to be," Jeff Schapiro wrote. In Virginia's short legislative sessions, Dominion wanted to ram the bill its lawyers had written through the legislature before people could understand it.[92]

In late January, Associated Press reporter Alan Suderman published emails exchanged between Saslaw and Dominion's Executive Vice President Bob Blue after the Democratic Party of Virginia excoriated a Republican for his relationship with Dominion. "'I was very disappointed to see this, especially considering how our company has supported Democrats over the years,' [Blue wrote]. 'As you know, many of us have been personal supporters as well.' Saslaw…quickly apologized and criticized the state party for not doing its 'homework' on 'how generous Dominion has been to me' and others in the party." Dominion was Saslaw's largest donor.[93] The mandate of Attorney General Mark Herring's office vis-à-vis utilities was to protect Virginia's ratepayers, and he noted that the Dominion bill would harm consumers.[94] No matter. Saslaw continued to carry the bill, and he and Republican bill lead Frank Wagner assured their committee that, contrary to independent expert reports, there was not what had become known as the "double dip" provision.[95] In 2019, Saslaw came within five hundred votes of losing his seat in a primary against two unknowns and Wagner resigned his seat.

Governor Northam stepped in and convened a secret working group to find what was characterized as a compromise. In fact, it was straight out of Dominion's playbook. In the 2015 rate hikes, Dominion had skillfully won perhaps more than $1 billion in additional rate hikes and inserted into the bill tens of millions of dollars in solar and low-income heating assistance after the original bill was introduced. It was a transparent ploy, but skillful enough that it more or less bought off a number of environmental groups that endorsed the bill. Northam's 2018 working group consisted of Dominion lobbyists, executive branch officials, and business, consumer, and environmental representatives. Tellingly, no legislators were in the group, since it was well understood that the usual suspects would advance whatever "compromise" bill Dominion told them to advance.[96]

What emerged kept Dominion's framework but, predictably, included a refund that had increased to $200 million, as well as more investments in alternative energy and low-income assistance.[97] South Carolinians instinctively understood this game, but some of the usually streetwise reporters who covered Richmond's legislative sessions began to uncritically label the bill a compromise that Governor Northam had brokered, without asking if that had been Dominion's plan all along.[98] Northam released a statement heralding the "compromise," and the main audience, essentially the inside-the-Richmond-Beltway crowd, was convinced.[99] To support the bill, Dominion asked its employees and stockholders to contact the legislature and launched a newspaper and television ad blitz that included an expensive Super Bowl commercial.[100] The League of Conservation Voters and the Natural Resources Defense Council announced their support, but Attorney General Herring reiterated his office's finding that the bill would be bad for citizens. Furthermore, the double charging remained.[101]

Legislators had access to professional analysis via the State Corporation Commission (SCC), which was set up early in the twentieth century to protect businesses and citizens from monopolies.[102] Senator Petersen asked the SCC for a report on Dominion's bill. Before the analysis was even written, the Senate committee passed the bill 10–4, two days before the SCC produced its report on February 7, 2018.[103] Like the bill, the analysis was also technical, but at twelve pages, it was digestible and helped set the terms of the debate. Most importantly, the nonpartisan analysts confirmed that there was a "double dip" provision.[104] When a reporter asked Saslaw about the analysis, he replied, "Well, the donors got some experts, too, OK?"[105] Foppish Dominion spokesperson David Botkins took the metaphor a little further and claimed, "There is no double-dip, but there is a single-scoop with whipped cream and a cherry on top for our customers, who will have stable rates and a modern, clean infrastructure improving the reliability of the energy they use."[106] With that out of the way, the full Senate passed Dominion's bill 26–13 on February 9, before the ink was dry on the SCC findings.[107] A complete SCC report would not come out until eight months later, when in August 2018, Virginians discovered that the cost of the bill would be $5.6 billion over fifteen years.[108]

Political opponents of the bill became unusual bedfellows. Herring and the SCC were joined in their critiques by former attorney general Ken Cuccinelli, whose time in office was best known for suing UVA climate scientist Michael Mann and a distinctive puritanism in which he ordered his staff to cover up the drawing of the breast on the goddess Virtus on Virginia's Romanesque state seal.[109] Cuccinelli called the bill "one of the biggest tax increases in Virginia history." He cited a report by investment bank UBS that he said "gushed over how spectacular Dominion handles the General Assembly and governors of Virginia to boost Dominion's value" [*sic*]. "Dominion spends mere millions on TV commercials, on lobbying and on political contributions to candidates and legislators and in return Dominion gets to write its own legislation that returns billions of dollars in cash and value….To use a dating analogy, if Virginia were dating utilities, her name and phone number would be on the boardroom wall of every utility in the commonwealth under phrases like 'for a good time call.'"[110] He pointed to a letter from UBS that "praised Dominion as being 'adept at navigating VA politics' and added 5 percent to the expected value of its business in expectation of the General Assembly's passing a favorable regulatory overhaul."[111] "People say this bill is pro-business," Petersen lamented. "This ain't business. This ain't the free enterprise system. There ain't no risk here."[112] Jeff Schapiro marveled at the free market taking a back seat to socialism. "Other businesses looking to grow must borrow from a bank or an investment fund, repaying those loans with interest or equity. That's an expense these utilities can avoid. Plus, Dominion and Appalachian [Power] won't need your approval to spend your money. If they turned to the capital markets, whether issuing stock or floating bonds, the companies would have to persuade doubting underwriters."[113]

POWER EQUALS ENERGY OVER TIME

The outset of this legislative session played out indistinguishably from any of dozens before it. Future Virginians will no doubt marvel at the depths of understanding among Virginia's political class, which assumed that Dominion would write and pass whatever bills it wanted, and how tenuous its grip on power really was. For the first time in memory in the 2018 session, Dominion lost a vote in the Virginia legislature on principle. The House of Delegates was newly energized by a slate of legislators who had won office on a shared anti-Dominion platform. This group of thirteen had not lived through the old senators' acculturation process. It was as if the majority of the House awoke one day to realize that voting against Dominion was good politics, and the epiphany spread throughout the capitol as quickly as news that the emperor had no clothes.

The issue of double charging became the battlefield on which both sides would fight to the end. Dominion and its allies in the Governor's Office and legislature continued to insist that double charging was not a part of the bill, but the energy experts in the SCC and the Attorney General's Office said that it was. Democratic Minority Leader David Toscano called Dominion's bluff and introduced an amendment that would negate a double-dipping provision, if it existed.[114] Dominion's phalanx of lobbyists working the amendment included people like former cabinet secretary Eva Teig Hardy who were veritably household names among the political class, and Executive Vice President Bob Blue emailed legislators just before the vote claiming the double-dip vote was "a political 'red herring' that draws attention away from moving Virginia forward and maintaining its low stable rates for a decade of investments, which in other states, have brought about large rate increases."[115] It was not reported as such, and it did not seem the groups were talking to each other, but an extraordinary cross-section of Tea Party and progressive grassroots groups in Virginia organized independently to launch social media and phone banking campaigns to influence their legislators.[116] Toscano whipped the bill, too, and on the floor, six Republicans joined all Democrats in voting for his amendment.[117] "Then Republicans who control[led] the chamber—sensing the political value of the vote—brought back the amendment, and it passed 96-to-1, with two abstentions."[118] The takeaway was not that this particular issue was politically controversial, but that Dominion had pulled out all the stops for the amendment, and its efforts failed. This was "a political earthquake" and "a public rebuke that longtime political watchers said was unprecedented."[119] "This is the first time I've seen Dominion lose on the floor. This is a game-changer," said a legislative aide. "I've never seen Dominion lobbyists look so sad."[120]

Advocates were excited in the moment, but the vote did not change the underlying rules of the game. The editorial board of the *Staunton News Leader* called it "the reality of politics in Virginia":

> *Rule 1: Dominion eventually gets what it wants.*
> *Rule 2: When someone disagrees, refer to rule 1.*[121]

The overall bill still heavily favored Dominion, and no one disputed that giving a company almost everything it wanted was still an overwhelming victory for it. Some warned that "the new legislation locks in so many regulatory carve-outs that many experts believe it is worse for consumers than the 2015 rate-freeze law."[122] Within a day, Dominion's legislators had resumed their push of the bill with the amended language. Even more surprisingly, Dominion had moved opposition groups like the Sierra Club to neutral on the bill, "but they're neutral with a big smile," noted Senator Wagner.[123] Wagner himself owned "more than $50,000 interest in a liquefied natural gas terminal Dominion operates," and "none of the major holders of Dominion Energy shares abstained" from voting on the bill, which passed easily.[124] The most egregious boondoggle was an offshore wind project that would cost $300 million, Dominion would profit from at no risk, and electricity it generated would "cost nine times more than both the [Martha's] Vineyard Wind offshore wind project off the Massachusetts coast and onshore wind facilities, as well as almost 14 times more than new solar power generation."[125] The opposition had largely burned itself out in the victory.[126] A lawyer for Appalachian Voices took a longer view: whereas the 2015 bill "passed the Senate by a 5-to-1 margin (32-6), and the House by a 3-to-1 margin (72-24), [in 2018, Dominion's] bill passed both houses by a 2-to-1 margin (Senate 27-13, and House 65-31). This is progress."[127] More ominous for the monopoly was that the majority of the Democratic caucus, including Leader Toscano, voted against the final, amended bill.[128] "This is a new dynamic right now," Toscano said. "It's a function of some of these new people and in general some of the populism of the time."[129]

Because of Dominion's machinations, the legislature was the final battleground for measures relating to utilities. Dominion had effected this transformation gradually over the last twenty-five years, when its modus operandi had been to do whatever it wanted, especially on pollution issues, and then to go to the legislature for post hoc permission. The 2015 rate hike bill had included a radical provision that the State Corporation Commission could not set electric rates despite its long-held constitutional mandate to do so.[130] Dominion had always been able to manipulate legislators, but its unrealistic numbers could not get past the professional staff at the SCC. Legal challenges to the 2015 rate hike bill argued that the legislature was usurping the SCC's role and unconstitutionally setting electric rates. The case made it to the Virginia Supreme Court, whose judges were appointed by the legislature for twelve-year terms, and the court unsurprisingly ruled in Dominion's favor.[131] The ability of the legislature to regulate the utility in a way that would maximize refunds for voters might in the future become a poison pill for Dominion if Virginia's politicians begin to have the same pro-business tilt as South Carolina's.

FALLOUT

The salutary effect of the 2018 legislative session was significant. In a situation like this in which a special interest would have liked to enforce legislative discipline, Planned Parenthood or the National Rifle Association would typically target an antagonistic politician and choose to make an example of him or her by sponsoring an opponent. Dominion had never done this at the legislative level and arguably did not have the wherewithal to do it now; it was not a Super PAC, and its contribution levels of a few thousand dollars per legislator would not be decisive. Moreover, there was not a great target. Toscano was nearing retirement but was still a leader in the House of Delegates, and attacking him or his caucus members would incur his and his caucus's wrath. The thirteen people who openly abhorred Dominion may even have benefitted from being singled out. Unlike the issue groups previously mentioned, Dominion did not have a natural constituency who believed its rights were being violated or its freedoms were under attack if the monopoly's electricity rates were not raised. Dominion could turn out some voters, as any group could, but its efforts would be dwarfed by people who were incensed at its greed and corruption. The House had ultimately voted against Dominion 96–1, and Dominion just had to take it.[132]

In March, Delegate Mark Keam announced in a *Washington Post* op-ed that he was "breaking up with Dominion." Keam was a staid former Federal Communications Commission and Verizon lawyer who had first been elected in the Tea Party wave of 2009. His objections to Dominion came down to profit-gouging and the way that Dominion circumvented the constitutionally established SCC. "Dealing with Dominion feels like Charlie Brown facing Lucy and her repeated football prank," he wrote, and he would refuse all further campaign contributions from it.[133]

Dominion really had only one sharp tool in its toolbox, and it was a testament to Stanfield that he perceived how effectively its money could be used as a cudgel against it. Disclosure forms filed in 2018 would show the corporation "spent more than $1 million on lobbyists, entertainment, meals and communications from May 2017 to the end of April 2018. That's about 10 times what the company said it spent in last year's filing."[134]

One of Dominion's allies in the fight was Appalachian Power Company, which, like Dominion, was a government-guaranteed monopoly, albeit one with captive customers in southwest Virginia and a much smaller political footprint. The no-contribution pledge applied to ApCo as well as Dominion. In June, ApCo's law firm Hunton Andrews Kurth announced that it would not give money to lawmakers who refused money from ApCo. It was curious to see the utility become involved in this way; its service territory was dominated by Republican politicians who had easily survived the blue wave in 2017. Delegate Sam Rasoul of Roanoke lived in ApCo's service territory and refused Dominion's money on principle, but his district was a tiny Democratic outpost in a sea of red that extended veritably from Richmond to St. Louis. But the company had made at least $20 million from the 2015 rate hike bill.[135] "Our state government relations practice group feels a high sense of loyalty to all of our clients," said the law firm's top lobbyist. "We have represented Appalachian Power for the last 10 years or so, and (works) [sic] with members of the General Assembly on legislation of importance to Appalachian Power as we have for a number of other clients. The unusual step of (lawmakers) automatically refusing to accept contributions from a client has caused us to hold back our contributions to those same legislators."[136]

It was as if the firm's lobbyists decided that people who had just won elections on anticorruption platforms would publicly abandon their principles at the suggestion that a giant lobbying firm would not give them money. It was foolish groupthink. The announcement had the predictable result of garnering more positive coverage for campaign finance reform and negative attention to the corrupt Virginia Way. "Anything that diminishes the influence of large corporations over Virginia politics is fine by me," Lee Carter said. "If there's one less lobbying firm giving one less dollar to one less legislator, that's a step in the right direction," Stanfield agreed. "From my point of view, it's almost like a concession."[137] "Such pronouncements from a donor to candidates are rarely made public because their rank and odor are worse than that of swamp muck," editorialized the *Daily Press*.[138] The *Lynchburg News & Advance* summarized it well: "They're evidently scared."[139] By July, the pledge to not take campaign money from state monopolies spread to West Virginia.[140]

THE ANTI-BUSINESS MACHINE

During this time, a news story broke that pro-business politicians would have closely scrutinized as a major scandal. Dominion had discovered in mid-2016 that it had overcharged an incredible 10 percent of its commercial customers, a total of twenty-four thousand Virginia businesses, for at least three years. Evidently, the company was not resetting these businesses' meters after their peak demands were read, and the total overbilling amounted to at least $10 million. This multiyear period of overcharging was never fully tabulated because Dominion claimed that it did not keep records going back more than three years. A condo owner "said bills for the building mysteriously got cut in half recently after nearly 13 years of the association complaining.…She can't prove the high bills were related to the meter reading lapses, but she said the letter she received from the [State Corporation Commission] didn't leave any doubts in her mind. 'The minute I got that letter, I said, 'Oh they finally figured it out.'" "Customers seeking compensation for over-billing that may have happened before July 2013 will have to submit their own billing records," a company spokesperson said. This wrongdoing was covered in a grand total of two pieces: once in the *Richmond Times-Dispatch*, and a one-paragraph Associated Press item picked up by a handful of outlets. No politicians ever commented on it.[141]

Virginia's purported pro-business political philosophy was jarring to witness in comparison to Dominion and the legislature's repeated efforts to raise electricity rates, and it was one reason why examining Dominion as a case study was so important. Electricity was a major cost for every business and customer; therefore, raising electricity rates was bad for business. "There's no difference between the legislature granting Dominion and (Appalachian Power) windfall profits and raising taxes," Cuccinelli noted.[142]

"It's not a tax to pay police or educate children," said former SCC judge Hullihen Moore. "It's a tax that goes into Dominion's pocket."[143] The 2015 and 2018 rate hike bills were the definition of "corporate welfare" and took hundreds of millions of dollars out of the pockets of businesses and voters.[144] South Carolina legislators understood this immediately because it was self-evident. In 2019, the largest retailers in the state—among them Walmart, Sam's Club, Costco, Kroger and Target—asked the SCC to negotiate their own electricity contracts and avoid Dominion's rate hikes; the SCC rejected their claims and forced them to buy electricity from the monopoly.[145] Microsoft, Apple, and eight other major tech companies wrote an unusual joint letter that May calling for Dominion to provide more energy from renewables and less from gas; they were ignored, of course.[146] The Virginia Way was not pro-business—it was pro-donor. There was a straight, bright, irrefutable line between Dominion's campaign contributions and writing the state's energy policies; the connection was only disputed by people who were paid to dispute it.

The Virginia Way was sold to the public as being good for business. Whether government should only exist to promote those interests was another question, but a business-centric theory of government and politics was at least comprehensible. America is, after all, a capitalist society; but the Virginia Way was about donors and politicians, and the Dominion-politician nexus functioned as an anti-business machine.

Dominion was facing the most serious challenge in its 110-year history: politicians who supported it were being voted out of office.[147] In a state that had putatively been run "of the businessmen, by the businessmen, for the businessmen" but was now run of, by, and for donors, Dominion was facing a crisis of democracy as conservatives and liberals realized independently that Dominion corrupted capitalism and government.[148] "From a conservative standpoint, what bothers me here is the cronyism, one, and the further deviation from something approaching free-market pricing as we can achieve," Tea Party leader Ken Cuccinelli told the *Huffington Post*. "It hurts everybody—it hurts the poor, it hurts business, it hurts opportunity."[149] Virginians on the left and right organizing together were an existential threat to Dominion's true constituents and their spreadsheets in lower Manhattan. "For the first time, maybe ever, or for the first time in this era, Dominion is having to answer for things it does," said political scientist Quentin Kidd.[150] How Dominion responds to democracy—and how citizens will respond to Dominion—will chart the destiny not just of that company but of Virginia politics and government for the next decade and beyond. The ultimate nightmare for Dominion was that the politicians who had done its bidding since time immemorial would come to understand that Dominion's self-interest in raising electricity rates was bad for business and hurt voters—or would come to be outnumbered by politicians who did.

THE UNIVERSITY OF VIRGINIA

AFFIRMATIVE ACTION FOR THE WEALTHY

"The father [redacted] *was killed in a* [redacted] *crash a few years ago
following a high-profile contentious divorce."*
*"This is all helpful and interesting background. Just let me know how I might
begin a relationship with the student and family as they enter into the fold."*
*—emails between Ryan William Emanuel, development staffer, and Sean
Jenkins, senior assistant to the president, University of Virginia*

The myth and reality of the Virginia Way shaped the operation of
the state's flagship university. By 2019, the University of Virginia
had publicly proclaimed in materials dating back at least a decade
that it practiced "need-blind" admissions; in reality, it had operated a secret
financial intelligence unit that reached into the President's Office in order to
help children of extreme wealth who otherwise would be rejected from UVA
gain admission.[1] Just like the political system, Virginia's government through
a state university picked winners and losers based on whether the students'
acceptances benefitted donors.

This was all the more striking for the milieu in which it occurred.
More than any other university in the nation, the University of Virginia
reached back to its founder so frequently that it was as if its grounds were
haunted by a saintly ghost. For all his hypocrisy and evil—even Monticello
acknowledged that many of Jefferson's child slaves looked just like him—he
was in many ways a radical reformer for his time.[2] The idea of white male
suffrage went hand-in-hand with his vision for what is still known as "Mr.

Jefferson's university."[3] He advocated universal education for white boys and girls, though he also harbored the prejudice that only white men would or should pursue higher education.[4]

In his foundational "Report of the Board of Commissioners for the University of Virginia to the Virginia General Assembly," Jefferson specifically addressed the counterargument that a public university was not necessary because white men were free to pursue all the education they wanted individually. Not so, Jefferson wrote, for that design for education was unrealistically "far beyond the reach of individual means, & [therefore] must either derive existence from public patronage or not exist at all."[5] Furthermore, public education for Jefferson was no less than "the key to preserving republican government."[6]

Even as the paeans to his wisdom reverberated to the present, as of 2019, the University of Virginia had been practicing an anti-Jeffersonian approach to education behind closed doors. UVA accepted students who were nearly all at the heads of their classes, but there was less than 1 percent who did not even graduate in the top half of their high schools.[7] Even if one assumed these were all recruited athletes, there were still too many to be explained by athletics scholarships, so there must have some other rare, non-academic trait that UVA valued. In response to a Freedom of Information Act (FOIA) request, the university released more than 150 pages of spreadsheets constructed over the course of a decade in which the admissions office had recorded select applicants' names, a detailed description of their family wealth or connections, and how the President's Office wanted to change their admissions statuses.[8]

The documents demonstrated that the University of Virginia had for at least ten years operated a financial intelligence unit in the offices of admissions, fundraising, and the president whose mission was to provide affirmative action to the children of wealthy or influential people. Much of the information was redacted, but some handwritten notations escaped the censors and showed what UVA had privately recorded for years but was so eager to hide from the public. For one of many examples, a note of "$500k" was coupled with the intelligence, "really need to know if get in WL—must be on WL; mother BFF w/ [redacted] and sorority sister." The next column showed that the President's Office wanted the student's admissions status changed from denied to waitlisted.

Another notation showed "$140K"; that the applicant had met with Sean Jenkins, senior assistant to the president; that admissions "could push" the applicant; and that Jeff Boyd, director of the UVA Parents Fund, wanted "at

Applicant/ Student Last Name	Applicant/ Student First Name	O.D. WL,T R	Parent Name	Parent Affiliation (Alum w/ sch & yr; Parent; Friend)	Why is this Applicant recommended?	DO	A,B, C	Preli m	Next Steps	SJ category	rank
				A&S 84	#################################	Boyd, Schutt; Woo	B	D	would have to work very hard for WL	D to WL	0
				A&S 81		Packer	B	D	rough decision for legacy ... SJ pushing for WL	D to WL	
				A&S 77, PA 13		Packer	A	HWL	would not be hard to A ... really important per MP	WL to A	2
				Friend		Gail	A	D	out-of-state non-legacy ... met with Sean Jenkins ... could push it priority	D to WL	1-5
				PA 13		Packer	A-	D	D but look exceptional ... must at lea	D to WL	5
				A&S, 73; PA 11, 12		Khan	A	HWL	out-of-state non-legacy ... did not meet with Sean Jenkins ... would have to know if UVa is 1st choice ... confirmed UVA is 1st choice	WL to A	2
				A&S 81 , LAW 84		Gail	B	D	D very low ... could try for courtesy WL if important	D to WL	2
				A&S 81		Beltridge/Wo o/Kipps	A	WL		WL to A	1-1
				PA 13		MWright	A	D	met with Sean Jenkins ... take over ... really needs good grades ... push to WL.	D to A	1-2

A redacted page of UVA's admissions list for children from wealthy families. Key: D = deny; WL = waitlist; A = accept; SJ = Sean Jenkins, senior assistant to the president.

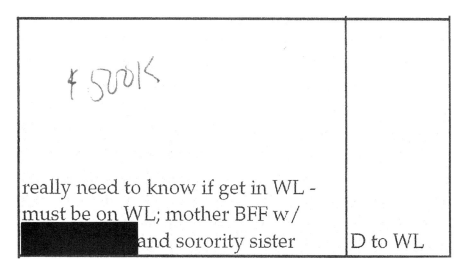

Handwritten note of $500K shows the type of information collected on wealthy applicants to UVA and how the President's Office sought to change the applicants' status from denial.

†	40 K met with Sean Jenkins … could push … Jeff Boyd says at least WL	D to A? or WL?

Handwritten note shows contribution levels, and the Office of the President and UVA Parents Fund "could push" to "at least" waitlist and possibly accept a denied applicant.

least" waitlist. The applicant was in the denied category, and the spreadsheet asked whether to change that to admit or waitlist. Such examples continued for hundreds of pages.

UVA presented a very different image to the public. Even through 2019, long after the above scandal was uncovered, the University of Virginia trumpeted on its website that "students are offered admission based on intellectual ability, academic achievement and personal qualities, regardless of their financial situation or ability to pay."[9] Similarly, its financial aid website falsely stated, "We accept students solely on their academic merit, regardless of their ability to pay."[10] UVA was acutely aware of financial need, or the lack thereof, and deliberately tasked employees to research how much money students' families had so that their admissions statuses could be changed.

UVA'S SPOKESMAN

The reaction from government officials at UVA after this admissions practice was revealed was disconcerting. Rather than admitting error and apologizing to the hundreds of students who had been rejected over the years in favor of someone who was less qualified but whose parents had more money, they doubled down. Spokesperson Anthony De Bruyn contended that the admissions office did "not coordinate with the advancement [fundraising] office about applicants during the application process." However, UVA "declined to make admissions or advancement officials available for an interview, and declined to answer written questions about specific cases in the files."[11] In a follow-up interview with Derek Quizon of Charlottesville's

Daily Progress, De Bruyn conceded that UVA kept records on wealthy children but claimed the reason was that "this practice allows development officers to serve as a buffer with those alumni, donors and friends who have provided prospective student endorsements during the admission cycle."[12]

Unfortunately, the "no coordination" and "buffer" defenses were not credible. The documents showed ten years of systematic coordination between donors, admissions, and advancement. They clearly and indisputably indicated that the President's Office used donor information to influence admissions decisions. These records did not catalogue responses to requests for information from donors; they documented how much money someone's parents had and the recommendation of the President's Office for how to change the admissions office's decisions. For example, in one applicant's case, Sean Jenkins would "try for WL," and for another, "was A and changd to WL…would be easy to move [*sic*]."[13] In fact, UVA officials explicitly noted when they were *not* trying to influence admissions decisions by noting "just tracking."[14]

Most damaging to UVA's defense was that, though spokespeople were free to dissemble with impunity, under Virginia law, public documents could only be redacted for specified reasons. The redaction of students' names and other personal identifying information like Social Security numbers was reasonable, but students' personal privacy did not extend to the dollar gift levels associated with people whose names were hidden. Despite UVA's public claims that these lists had nothing to do with fundraising, large sections of the document under the heading "Why is this Applicant recommended?" were explicitly redacted under a "fundraising" exemption.[15]

It was unusual to come across an issue on which conservative and liberal commentators universally agreed, but after the *Washington Post* broke this story, it went viral and was condemned across the political spectrum.[16] Even more unusually, it was criticized by partisans for the same reason: the practice was morally wrong. Daniel Golden, who won a Pulitzer Prize for reporting on university admissions for the *Wall Street Journal*, stated that "the mission of universities—particularly state universities like UVa—is find people with the most potential and nurture it. They're supposed to find the diamonds in the rough and help with upward mobility, rather than furthering aristocracy in this country."[17] Generally speaking, with all their advantages in private education, test tutors, summer enrichment, health, nutrition, physical activity, family environment, and all the rest, children of the wealthy were already at a substantial advantage by the time they applied to college. Wealthy children from elite private schools had nothing to blame but their own work ethic for not getting decent grades in high school, and they were the last people who needed a helping hand from the government. The *Cavalier Daily* student newspaper called it "fundamentally unfair" and "reprehensible."[18] UVA alum Jim Bacon wrote, "UVa denies it happens, but nobody believes the disclaimers."[19] The *Richmond Times-Dispatch* editorialized against "affirmative action for rich people" and pointedly concluded that "the University of Virginia would like to know who you're gonna believe: the school, or your lyin' eyes?"[20]

It was nearly impossible to find anyone outside of UVA spokespeople who defended the tawdry practice and impossible to find anyone who actually believed their explanation. The only article published on the topic in its defense was by a UVA student who took the utilitarian position that, though this was unfair, there could be a level of giving at which the benefit to society could outweigh the cost of admitting one unqualified student.[21] There were potential legal problems that would make this problematic: donors could not fully deduct donations from their taxes if they benefited from the donation. It was hard to know if this was unethical or something more sinister, but situations could certainly arise in which bribery of government officials was at issue if major donors would only "donate" if a favored candidate was admitted. With UVA's stonewalling, it was impossible for the public to know whether that had taken place. The influence peddling was so opaque that the mere hope of a donation could influence admissions decisions, yet that hope could end up being worth nothing to the university. If it were to truly work in practice, then those prices should have been advertised in a free market and sold to raise revenue just like basketball suites. This logic harshly also assumed that people were motivated to give money to universities for self-interested reasons and that their offspring were not qualified; in other words, someone would only give money if his or her child were both unqualified to gain admission and would also be admitted because of the donation. It was interesting to consider the idea, no longer hypothetical, that UVA was not just for sale, but should be; however, for many reasons, this was a provocative thesis that did not have a great deal behind it.

Spokesperson De Bruyn offered yet another purported defense by claiming to Virginia Public Radio that other schools did this.[22] To test this theory, I submitted Freedom of Information Act requests to ask five other top public universities around the state to release their own lists. A William & Mary FOIA officer wrote, "After reaching out to Undergraduate Admission, as well as the deans of our graduate programs, I can confirm that the university does not possess lists of applicants tracked for fundraising purposes."[23] George Mason responded, "I've contacted several offices at the university, including Development, the Office of the President, Government and Community Relations, and Admissions, and they have informed me that Mason has never kept such a list."[24] Christopher Newport University, Virginia Commonwealth University and Virginia Tech also said they did not have any such lists.[25]

Some schools in other states did, as De Bruyn claimed, but the reaction when similar scandals were uncovered contrasted remarkably with UVA's.[26] A scandal involving a "clout list" at the University of Illinois bore striking similarities to UVA's and was exposed in the *Chicago Tribune* in late May 2009. The governor quickly appointed an investigatory commission, and within three months, the university's president and chairman of the board had both resigned over the matter.[27] More recently, a board member of the University of Texas charged that influential individuals were lobbying the President's Office at the flagship UT-Austin for special admissions treatment. The university launched an internal investigation that confirmed these charges in May 2014, and the president was forced to resign.[28] The university subsequently commissioned an independent legal investigation by an outside law firm that confirmed the findings and reported that the university president, his administration, and other officials were fully cooperative. The essential conclusion was that the president and his office had influenced admissions decisions. There was no allegation or evidence that the Texas scandal even approached the list uncovered at UVA.[29] However, UVA not only failed to launch an investigation, but responsible officials would not even publicly comment on it.

STONEWALLED INVESTIGATIONS

Leading student institutions were essentially powerless in the matter, but they did what they could to address a problem that had denied hundreds of deserving students admission. The *Cavalier Daily* covered the topic well, and UVA's student government launched an investigation.[30] The methodology of the investigation consisted of a student representative reviewing the documents and the student council president briefly interviewing Dean of Students Allen Groves and Dean of Admissions Greg Roberts in a joint meeting. The university declined to make available any other official, such as Sean Jenkins or President Teresa Sullivan, who could have answered questions related to this. UVA also declined to release the full, unredacted documents. The nine-page final report was stymied from the beginning, but it produced a useful admission when Roberts noted that Jenkins was "the intermediary between the offices of advancement and admissions, acting as a go-between in the situations where collaboration or communication would be helpful."[31] UVA had falsely claimed to this point that the admissions and advancement offices did not work together, and the university would continue to maintain this fiction moving forward. In a meeting to discuss the investigation, student government leaders expressed concern over the lack of transparency and thoroughness of the investigation, but they understood very well that there was nothing more they could do.[32]

Normally, the Virginia Attorney General's Office would investigate the matter, but the web of conflicts was breathtaking. Attorney General Herring was an alumnus of UVA, as were the Speaker of the House and another eighteen legislators. The legislature and governor appointed the UVA Board, many of whom were among the largest political donors in the state and many of whose names were on these influence-peddling lists. UVA was responsible for tens of thousands of jobs and billions of dollars in economic output. Anybody who knew how Virginia politics and government actually worked understood that it was difficult for officials to do anything that people with money did not want them to do. Powerful UVA supporters could not impartially investigate themselves.

The reaction of the Virginia Way class was precisely the opposite of the reaction of the rest of Virginia, and even the political cultures of Democratic Illinois and Republican Texas, states not exactly renowned for clean government. In Virginia, there was no response to the scandal other than dissembling from a spokesman. No one issued an apology to the many bright and hardworking students who were denied admission because their parents could not contribute money to the university. One's alma mater has a considerable impact on future careers and earnings, and UVA's decisions would haunt innocent people for the rest of their lives.

There was one thing that changed because of the scandal. Instead of emailing, Sean Jenkins would talk to people in person so that his actions would be even less subject to accountability from the Freedom of Information Act. It was extremely unusual to see this sentiment admitted, but the week after the scandal broke, Jenkins replied to investment manager Hi Ewald's email about the scandal: "Because of FOIA requests I look forward to more in person."[33]

HOW THE SYSTEM WORKED

When publication of the "watch lists" by the *Washington Post* was imminent, Nancy Rivers, chief of staff to President Sullivan, forwarded an email to Sullivan and the president's executive cabinet firmly denying any connection between fundraising and admission. "There is a protocol by which the Office of Admission does not coordinate with the Advancement Office about applicants during the application process," Rivers wrote, quoting University Communications.[34]

Despite these assurances to the public and to high-level administrators, a new batch of more than five hundred pages of documents obtained through the Freedom of Information Act and revealed here for the first time demonstrated a multiyear operation by which the children of the ultra-wealthy received special treatment through consistent coordination between Advancement and Admissions through Senior Assistant Sean Jenkins in the President's Office.

The documents, which covered the period 2011 to 2017, showed that requests for special treatment were collected by many top UVA officials—ranging from Bob Bruner, dean of the Darden (Business) School, to James Wright, president of the Jefferson Scholars Foundation, to Athletics Foundation executive director Dirk Katstra, to Nursing School assistant dean for admissions and financial aid Clay Hysell—and run through Jenkins in the President's Office.[35] Some prominent individuals like former UVA President John Casteen, author John Grisham and former or current board members Mac Caputo, Bobbie Kilberg, and Whitt Clement reached out proactively.[36] Often, Jenkins was contacted directly by applicants or parents of applicants, and if they were wealthy or influential enough, Jenkins would add them to his list and work with staff in the Office of Advancement to track them and foster relationships. Similarly, over the course of a year, school deans and university foundation leaders would submit their own list of candidates, numbering from perhaps one to a dozen. Staff meetings would often follow to discuss the watch list, such as one in late 2015 between various development officials, Jenkins, and Ian Baucom, Dean of the College and Graduate School of Arts & Sciences.[37] Then, in meetings usually scheduled in January, March, and May, as the early, regular, and waitlist application cycles were coming to a close, Jenkins would meet with Director of Undergraduate Admissions Greg Roberts and tell him which wealthy candidates should receive admissions boosts. The system was not complicated.

Recall that the original public justification was that these lists were kept to serve as a "buffer." Ordinary applicants faced an actual "buffer" by virtue of that fact that there was nobody in the President's Office who went to the dean of admissions every spring to ask the dean to change his admissions decisions. It was not hard to comprehend that most applicants were simply not given special treatment.

Rather than admitting their error, the increasingly implausible officials' proclamations were that the annual meetings between Jenkins and Roberts were merely to *suggest* outcomes and that Roberts made the final decisions independent of any influence. This was even less believable than the buffer theory. Clearly there would be no reason to meet with Roberts in the first place to discuss this list other than to influence admissions decisions. The curation of this list was a substantial part of Jenkins's professional responsibilities and was well known by the highest officials of the university. But while UVA denied to the public that the watch list had any significance outside of donor maintenance, internal documents showed Jenkins readily admitting the importance of the watch list in influencing admissions decisions. "I'm meeting with Greg [Roberts] tomorrow, and I will go over these candidates and hopeful outcomes with him in person," Jenkins wrote to a Nursing School assistant dean, for one example.[38] In another instance, he wrote, "I can ask the student for an interview but more importantly we should put her on our watch list."[39] Getting his office involved was "better than outside recommendation letters," he admitted in a third.[40] This was only true if his office had influence over admissions.

Far from serving as a "buffer" for helicopter parents, one of the most unsettling functions of the Advancement Office was to hunt for intelligence—including highly personal details—on applicants' family wealth. "We have research on the family in progress, which I will share once it is complete," Advancement staffer Ryan William Emanuel wrote to Jenkins. "The father [redacted] was killed in a [redacted] crash a few years ago following a high-profile contentious divorce." "This is all helpful and interesting background," Jenkins responded. "Just let me know how I might begin a relationship with the student and family as they enter into the fold."[41]

The close connection between fundraising and admissions blurred other ethical lines. In one email, real estate investor Tyler Blue inquired as to a particular candidate, then wrote, "On another note with respect to putting together our real estate tour at Burning Tree do you have a preference for June or July?" Jenkins responded, "I'm happy to stay in touch" about the candidate and "I'd love to make [the vacation] happen!"[42]

From: Jenkins, Sean (skj9d)
Sent: Sat Jan 21 16:07:27 2012
To: ██████████
Subject: RE: █████ and McIntire
Importance: Normal

Not at the moment. Once her application is in I will call Carl Zeithaml and Rebecca Leonard (who handles the admission) process. They'll put her on a watch list and communicate with me throughout the process. And of course we will also strongly support her candidacy. Those steps are better than outside recommendation letters.

From: ████████████████████████
Sent: Saturday, January 21, 2012 11:46 AM
To: Jenkins, Sean (skj9d)
Subject: █████ and McIntire

Sean...is there anything I can/should do to help ██████ at McIntire other than encourage her?

Presidential assistant Sean Jenkins discusses how he will help a candidate gain admission to the McIntire School of Commerce. Carl Zeithaml is the dean.

From: Jenkins, Sean Kirk (skj9d)
Sent: Tuesday, February 23, 2016 8:32 AM
To: Emanuel, Ryan William (rwe2s); Citro, Michael J. (mjc2w)
Subject: RE: Incoming First-Year

Ryan—This is all helpful and interesting background. I'm happy to help in any way possible. Just let me know how I might begin a relationship with the student and family as they enter into the fold. Sean

From: Emanuel, Ryan William (rwe2s)
Sent: Monday, February 22, 2016 1:46 PM
To: Jenkins, Sean Kirk (skj9d); Citro, Michael J. (mjc2w)
Subject: RE: Incoming First-Year

Thank you, Sean and Mike.

Bob Sweeney received a call from Gordon Rainey today with information Gordon received from a fellow alum that the ████████████████████████████████ The father, ███████ was killed in a ████████ crash a few years ago, following a high-profile contentious divorce. ████████ is enrolling this fall at SEAS.

Emails showing the type of research on family tragedies that was welcomed by the UVA President's Office.

Also noteworthy were differences in levels of special treatment within the ranks of children of the ultra-wealthy. "We met through Joe Hall last year and my father [redacted] and I sat down with you to discuss the road ahead and my strong desire to attend" UVA, wrote one applicant. "I will be pleased to make sure you receive a close review in the admission process," Jenkins replied.[13] For another applicant, Jenkins offered to review "his proposed senior year schedule so I can sign off on it."[14] Locke Ogens, Executive Director of the Darden School Foundation, wrote of Dean Bob Bruner's enthusiasm for a candidate: "son of [redacted]...His mom [redacted] is a great UVA graduate [redacted] very engaged at Darden....I don't have grades, etc., but can easily get that for you if you need it." Jenkins replied, "Leonard [Sandridge, former UVA presidential assistant], Greg, and I met about this one two years ago. We're on top of it."[15] A more highly sought-after student received an official tour itinerary on letterhead from the Office of the President. Over the course of a planned day, the applicant met individually with both Jenkins and Dean Ian Baucom of the College of Arts and Sciences, lunched with a fourth-year student and attended a class on the news media.[16] Jenkins felt that one applicant's denial was so important that he asked Rivers to brief President Sullivan on it in an email titled "CONFIDENTIAL DONOR INFORMATION."[17] One fortunate applicant "recommended by [redacted], important UVA supporter" was deemed so critical that she or he "met personally with President Sullivan."[18]

The persistence with which UVA pursued some students was matched by the callousness with which officials regarded normal applicants. When one applicant was denied, Jenkins wrote, "There wasn't much follow through on her support. She wasn't listed as a high priority."[19] "Could [redacted] be related to [redacted]?" he asked of another.[50] "The name is unfamiliar to me which in and of itself speaks to the priority," wrote Jenkins of a third.[51]

It has also not been reported that one cold-hearted aspect of this fundraising strategy was that the "goal" of the President's Office was to change all "top early action priorities" that were initially denied to defer and that there would be "no defers to offers." In practice, only about 10 percent of "top early action priorities" had the goal of changing from "Deny" to "Defer or Admit," though the documents did not indicate the final decision. A blanket policy of changing early admissions denials of wealthy children to defer was a cynical fundraising strategy to string parents along to give more money as their children's futures remained in limbo.

Despite UVA's obstinate and increasingly blind insistence that the list and the wide-reaching system that supported it existed so that admissions

The strategy for wealthy applicants who were rejected early admission was to change their status to defer, but rarely to an outright acceptance.

decisions would *not* be affected by the development office, there were those who received no special treatment whatsoever: applicants from ordinary families. One angry alum with her daughter on the waitlist wrote to President Sullivan noting that she did not "have the resources to 'buy' her [daughter] into UVA even though I am an ardent supporter—with my time….This violates EVERY standard of conduct I associate with Virginia and I am sure that Thomas Jefferson is rolling over in his grave."[52]

THE UNIVERSITY OF VIRGINIA WAY

The philosophy that produced this corruption spread beyond these lists, which were important but represented a relatively small percentage of admitted students. The extent to which UVA's admissions as a whole were influenced by wealth was highly unusual for a public university, as documented by Nick Anderson of the *Washington Post*.[53] In 2015, the graduating year of the students who were admitted in the spreadsheet that opened this chapter, UVA had a lower percentage of students receiving low- and middle-income Pell Grants than any school in the Ivy League. The 12 percent of UVA students receiving Pell Grants was far below UNC's 21 percent. Admissions director Roberts claimed to Anderson that one reason for UVA's low percentage of middle-class students was that Virginia was a wealthy state. This defense was not accurate. For example, the closest state to Virginia in its median yearly household income was California (14th- and 13th-highest in America in 2016, respectively, separated by less than $200 out of about $66,500); however, of California's flagship universities, Berkeley had 23 percent of its students receive Pell Grants, and UCLA had 30 percent.[54] California's other public universities had even higher percentages, including 41 percent at UC-Irvine, the highest of any of the top 150 schools in the nation that were included in the study. California's system was characterized as "an upward mobility machine," and many of its state schools were at the top of national rankings on helping low-income students. UVA fell outside of the top 100 national universities in these rankings (UNC was no. 16).[55] It was telling that Roberts knew very well exactly the sort of wealth-based affirmative action he was engaging in, but he offered a specious defense that did not reveal what he was doing.

The few hundred qualified students who were unfairly penalized and did not receive admission were just the tip of the iceberg. The Virginia Way at the state's flagship university was manifested in the interrelationship of the school with the state's political system via the UVA Board of Visitors.[56] In the period from 1994 to 2010, just 3 percent of members of the board held PhDs, but 91 percent had made political contributions of over $1,000.[57] The board reflected the values of people who were not merely wealthy but also chose to trade that wealth in the pursuit of transactional political power, and their ethos was transmitted throughout the highest levels of the university. In essence, UVA Board members were the governor's largest campaign contributors.

There was a significant proportion of the alumni base and people with power who evidently knew how to work the system, manipulated it to their own families' benefit, and hid it from the rest of the community. Then-chairman (rector) of the board Bill Goodwin admitted in response to the scandal that "he personally has tried to recommend applicants for admission."[58] Goodwin was one of the most prolific donors to Republican politicians in Virginia.[59] In another case, censors overlooked redacting the name "Dubby," which appeared on the line above a candidate he recommended. John "Dubby" Wynne was the former chairman of

UVA Board Member	Gov. Appointed	Donations to Gov. Who Appointed	Total Va. Political Donations	Notes
Bob Blue	McAuliffe	$2,500	$51,535	E.V.P. of Dominion Energy, largest corporate donor
Mark Bowles	McAuliffe	$1,725	$18,971	Finance Co-Chair of McAuliffe Inaugural Committee
Whitt Clement	McAuliffe	$1,500	$31,523	
Frank Conner (chair)	McAuliffe	$52,338	$311,683	
Elizabeth Cranwell	McAuliffe	none	$8,995	Cranwell's husband, Richard, donated $12,294 to McAuliffe and $120,353 total
Thomas DePasquale	McAuliffe	$79,399	$685,035	
Barbara Fried	McAuliffe	$130,000	$1,328,100	
John Griffin	McDonnell; McAuliffe	$50,000; none	$106,000	Donated to McDonnell's leadership PAC
Robert Hardie	Kaine; McAuliffe	$133,850; $205,010	$572,506	Including donations to leadership PACs; son-in-law of Bill Goodwin, one of state's largest donors

UVA Board Member	Gov. Appointed	Donations to Gov. Who Appointed	Total Va. Political Donations	Notes
Maurice Jones	McAuliffe	none	$2,000	Served as McAuliffe's Secretary of Commerce
Babur Lateef	McAuliffe	$22,250	$164,140	
Tammy Murphy	McAuliffe	$25,000	$83,000	
James Murray (vice chair)	McAuliffe	$96,000	$681,625	
C. Evans Poston	McAuliffe, Northam	none; $10,073	$15,070	
James Reyes	McAuliffe	none	$1,829	
Jeffrey Walker	McAuliffe	$70,000	$271,500	
L.D. Britt (medical)	McAuliffe	$1,000	$32,500	Slot reserved for academic medical expert under Va. § 23.1-2201
Margaret Riley (faculty)	n/a	none	$3,500	Non-voting slot reserved for faculty under Va. § 23.1-1300
Brendan Nigro (student)	n/a	none	none	Non-voting slot reserved for student under Va. § 23.1-1300

UVA Board Members' political donations, October 1, 2018. Contribution data from Virginia Public Access Project includes donations to leadership PACs.

Censors overlooked former board chair John O. "Dubby" Wynne's name during their redactions.

Landmark Communications, another one of the largest donors to Virginia politicians, and served as UVA's rector from 2009 to 2011.[60]

Professionals who had earned their place meritocratically well understood how dysfunctional leadership hampered the school's potential. "There is a corporate governance problem!" wrote Commerce Dean Carl Zeithaml. Board of Visitors members "have little or no idea what goes on in the schools. On top of it, there is essentially no oversight of the BOV and little accountability except for what the public can muster."[61]

By law, one member of the board had to be an expert in academic medicine; appointing people who were qualified to lead universities was a start toward good governance, but that Board slot was an outlier. Dr. Edward Miller, former dean of the Johns Hopkins Medical School, was appointed to the slot and released the following after his resignation from the board in 2015:

> I do not believe I have been able to bring any of my expertise in academia, health care, or research to the University....And year after year, I have implored the administration to put an end to tuition increases that mire Virginia's students and families in a mountain of unnecessary debt. And no matter what anyone says, the latest decision to increase tuition by 23 percent over two years was not done in a transparent manner. To have such a colossal tuition hike and the plan behind it presented at the very last moment to the entire Board and the public was totally unacceptable. I don't understand why the faculty isn't protesting this time. Looking at tuition alone without addressing other issues is simply poor business management. A long-range plan is vital in order to understand the true financial status of the University, but the administration has failed to provide a viable one. With a nearly $6 billion dollar endowment and a faculty that can

and should bring in more research dollars, we could have kept tuition and student aid at responsible levels. Sadly, that did not happen, and the only thing the administration has done during my time on the Board of Visitors is mortgage a significant part of the Commonwealth's academic future.[62]

The modus operandi of the board was to repeatedly declare financial crises in order to justify its unpopular actions, including the board's disastrous "coup" that briefly removed President Sullivan from office in 2012 and elicited the largest protests in the history of the university.[63] To name one example of the impunity with which board members operated, over the past twenty-five years, during a time of continued budget cuts and tuition increases, they had secretly amassed a $2.2 billion extra-legislative, extra-endowment "Strategic Investment Fund" that they would now spend in their sole discretion.[64] How and why it was kept hidden for twenty-five years of tuition increases have still never been explained.

To the extent that it intersected with the Virginia Way, the University of Virginia was corrupted by ideologues who ran the university in their own image and for their own benefit. One result was that parental wealth substituted for academic achievement and created a double standard for the rich and the rest.

There were victims when children were rejected or accepted because of wealth. To give one example of the injustice UVA had caused over the years, a mother of an ordinary citizen emailed me to share her story:

> *My daughter applied to UVA last year and was not accepted for the fact that the slots were being held for donors. My daughter was an African American honor graduate involved at every level in high school and not even considered to be waitlisted. It's time that someone look into the politics of the admissions department. After multiple calls and no concrete answers, I was threatened not to call anymore by the Dean of Admissions to question her denial for acceptance.*[65]

The story of hundreds of other innocent families mirrored hers. It was a fitting irony that this happened at Mr. Jefferson's university, whose founder had written the most sublime words while denigrating them with his daily actions.

RICHMOND GOVERNMENT

PUBLIC SCHOOLS AND PRIVATE SPECTACLES

Our lesson is, that there are two Richmonds.
—Charles Dickens

In Richmond's oligopolistic media landscape, the *Richmond Times-Dispatch* set the agenda for other local news organizations, and what was printed there became common knowledge among residents who kept up with the daily news. On June 19, 2017, K. Burnell Evans published a horrifying exposé on a city elementary school just one and a half miles from the state capitol. She reported that "teachers begin their days by wiping rodent droppings from students' desks, said Ingrid DeRoo, the George Mason [Elementary School] site coordinator for Communities in Schools of Richmond. 'Some teachers wear breathing masks all day in order to teach,' DeRoo said of the air quality in what is widely acknowledged to be the district's worst school building among dozens in need of major repairs."[1] Mason had opened ninety-five years earlier and was last renovated when Jimmy Carter was president.[2] The story fomented a passionate response across the city: parents and teachers donned surgical masks in public meetings; politicians pledged to do better; a petition to fix the problem collected 14,000 signatures in a city of 230,000; and reporters wrote dozens of follow-up pieces in the city's other news outlets.[3]

The Richmond School Board called a public meeting to hear citizens' concerns.[4] They responded with a litany of severe problems: "extreme hot and cold conditions, leaking bathrooms, falling tiles and infestations of bugs and rodents in their classrooms. A teacher said she regularly has to rescue children trapped in bathrooms, due to the failure of old doorknobs."[5] "My son has been sick 10 times in a row, and I can't afford to miss work," a parent of two children at Mason said. Fourth-grade teacher Hope Talley told the board: "Our parents want what's best for their kids, just like any other parent. They speak [their fears] to us, we hear them, and we have to explain why their child had to do without heat today."[6] "From 2006 to 2017, I've cleaned up rat poop every morning before my kids come in," she told a reporter. "Every. Day."[7] "I cannot stress to you enough that the building of George Mason is in a state of emergency," DeRoo said. "It is unsafe, unsanitary and harmful to our students and staff."[8]

Interim Superintendent Tommy Kranz noted that the "building leaks like a sieve."[9] He acknowledged to Evans that every couple of months, the smell of natural gas became so overwhelming that "the fire department and city officials respond."[10] On the other hand, he maintained the school was safe and stated that "if I wouldn't send my grandchildren into a building, I'm sure not going to send anyone else's child."[11] (Two years earlier, Kranz had sung a different tune, saying that the slightly better but still inferior Overby-Sheppard Elementary School "isn't one we should have our children in."[12]) He proposed options for Mason with costs ranging from $105,000 to $10 million; building a new school would cost "between $22 million and $35 million" and would take years to complete.[13] The school board meeting adjourned without action, guaranteeing that the elementary would remain "a place where children will still confront the acrid smell of urine."[14]

It was no surprise when the board voted two weeks later to fund the absolute lowest option presented, for $105,000.[15] To some extent, the board's hands were tied, as overall tax and budget levels were set by the mayor and city council.[16] Chairwoman Dawn Page noted that they had "facilities plans for all schools dating back 20 years, but with no funding, the plans cannot be executed."[17] In the most recent example, after the board experienced a 100 percent turnover after the 2016 elections—not a single member was reelected, though two successfully ran for city council—the new members requested $207.4 million for "school buildings needs" and received less than 4 percent of their request from city council.[18]

Many residents felt that Richmond government had plenty of money to address these issues. "We're not lacking in money, y'all, we're lacking in moral commitment," said former councilman Marty Jewell.[19] Richmond protected its bond rating by assiduously maintaining a "self-imposed," arbitrary debt level. Even within this constriction, the city had "about $8.5 million in [bond] capacity through 2021, and about $321 million combined between 2022 and 2026."[20] Many Richmonders pointed out that city government had built the Washington Redskins a $10 million training camp and paid them a $500,000 annual subsidy based on lofty promises that never materialized, just as experts predicted.[21] The *Richmond Times-Dispatch* published "a photograph of a decrepit boys' bathroom at the city's George Mason Elementary school, last renovated 37 years ago, showing two of four urinals in working order and only one operational sink."[22]

The editorial board angrily wrote:

> *Whatever publicity Richmond might be getting out of the* [Redskins] *deal can't begin to stack up against the need to improve Richmond's schools. Fixing them would do more for the city than any sports or entertainment offering possibly could. As any real estate agent will tell you, schools are the top concern for most people who are looking to relocate. They're the main reason young families move out of Richmond to the counties, and a major reason families from the counties don't move into the city. Nobody from outside the area is ever going to look at the city and say: "I'm going to move to Richmond. My kid will have to sweep rat droppings off his desk*

George Mason Elementary School bathroom, Richmond, 2018. *From the* Richmond Times-Dispatch.

at school and his teachers will have to wear surgical masks because the air is so bad, but at least I won't have to drive far to watch [quarterback] *Kirk Cousins run drills.*"[23]

This was just the most egregious example: the city had somehow shelled out more than $20 million—about the price of a new school—to Stone Brewery to build a restaurant and small brewery in the city.[24] Nor was it all the fault of city council and the mayor. Jason Kamras, who came in as a new superintendent in late 2017, would make $250,000 per year, and his top five staffers would make roughly $180,000 each, about $30,000–$50,000 more than each had made the previous year in top positions in Washington, D.C.'s public schools.[25] For comparison, the Virginia secretary of education made about $160,000, and the U.S. secretary of education made around $200,000 per year.[26] Richmond was only the twelfth-largest school district in Virginia.[27]

Doug Wilder, who made history as America's first elected African American governor, had attended Mason when it was segregated. "Recently an advertisement appeared requesting volunteers to help paint George Mason Elementary School, so that it might be opened in September," he lamented. "Imagine how that made parents and students feel about their status in the community—about their grasp of the American Dream."[28] Wilder and other commentators noted the remarkable disconnect between the impassioned public debate over the Parisian Confederate statues on Monument Avenue and the resistance to improving toxic city schools that were living monuments to white supremacy.[29]

While the recriminations continued, another school year started with little to distinguish it from the prior one. A group of about one hundred people, including teenagers from Henrico High School, volunteered to apply some fresh paint to the hallways before Mason opened its doors for the fall. On the day of volunteer action, "hot water would not turn on and the bathroom door would not lock on the bathroom at the school's main entrance." "The rest of these fixes are nothing but expensive Band-Aids for problems that we shouldn't be continuing to have," said teacher Hope Talley. "I hate the expression, 'Lipstick on a pig,' but that's all I can think of," said another teacher.[30] Three weeks after the school reopened for the fall, water there tested high for lead, and the school had to begin "providing bottled water to students, faculty and staff."[31]

SYSTEM FAILURE

No Richmonder would claim that these problems were unique to George Mason Elementary. Something deeper was happening: Richmond was one of the wealthiest areas of the state, but its public school system had the worst high school graduation rate in Virginia.[32] Evans's original piece acknowledged the inertia of decades of inaction: "The issues that arise at every public meeting—from childhood trauma to challenges with special education—are so chronic and entrenched that they have become enshrined in a gallows humor–style bingo sheet passed around at Monday's meeting. On the list are the school's outdated facilities, which have been the subject of years of successive plans and little action."[33]

Heartbreaking stories about the city's dilapidated school buildings had become their own beat among reporters, commentators, broadcasters, and anyone else who cared to notice. The tales did not become less wrenching for their frequency; so widespread and indisputable were the facts and pain caused to innocent children that each story could fairly present a new and different problem. The prior analogue to Evans's 2017 article was a 2014 cover story in *Style Weekly*, Richmond's venerable newsmagazine.[34] The indelible images there were from Fairfield Court Elementary, where "watery, foul-smelling drops of diluted tar fell into classrooms and hallways" and "a ceiling tile fell on a student." The superintendent said that "the buildings are the worst he's seen in a career that includes Washington's notorious public schools." Two school board members (the two who would be elected to city council in 2016) looked through past reports and came to the same conclusion as Evans: "There's the report from 2002 calling for the closures and renovations and new buildings. A 2007 report calling for the same. They outline critical building issues that remain unaddressed [*sic*]." George Mason Elementary School was on both the 2002 and 2007 lists of schools to replace.[35] Other plans from 2012 and 2015 had "collected dust on office shelves."[36] "We've had plan after plan after plan to fix things," said the school board chair, "and what has changed?"[37]

The reason nothing changed was clear. "We have resegregated schools that are underfunded and get blamed for the deliberate segregation that has been imposed on them," said Ben Campbell, Rhodes Scholar and author of *Richmond's Unhealed History*. "The General Assembly isolated the City of Richmond and made it economically nonviable in the middle of three affluent suburban counties that were created for the purposes of racial segregation."[38] Many of Virginia's "great men" had dedicated the bulk of their careers in the mid-twentieth century to supporting one of the country's greatest crimes, racial segregation, by shuttering public schools rather than having black and white children attend school with their neighbors. This state policy violated the *Brown* decisions, and federal district court Judge Robert Merhidge nearly compelled Richmond to annex much of the adjoining suburban counties, as many comparable cities from Charlotte to Chattanooga to Louisville had done voluntarily.[39] Richmond could have avoided so many of its problems if this ruling was not enjoined by the Fourth Circuit Court of Appeals and then upheld by a 4–4 U.S. Supreme Court decision that Justice Lewis Powell, who had served on the Richmond School Board, recused himself from.[40] Richmond really had, in a grotesque sense, "a perfect school system," said a local nonprofit leader, "because it was designed to give children of color an inferior education and put them in inferior buildings and teach them as little as possible, and that's exactly what we do every day."[41]

History does not present controlled experiments, but it is important to consider what happened with Lost Cause iconography in Richmond and elsewhere in the South in recent years. After a Confederacy-glorifying lunatic murdered black churchgoers in 2015, South Carolina—the birthplace of the Civil War—immediately removed the Confederate flag from its capitol grounds.[42] New Orleans—hardly a bastion of racial tolerance—similarly removed its Confederate statues from 2015 to 2017. When its ninety-foot-tall Lee monument was taken down in Lee Circle in May 2017, journalists outnumbered the protesters, there was no violence, and people returned to their daily lives.[43] When a Lee statue faced relocation in Charlottesville in August 2017, thousands of neo-Nazis and other psychopaths—the leaders of which were UVA alumni but most of whom were not from Charlottesville—rioted in its streets and murdered a peaceful counter-protester. In 2019, the statues on Monument Avenue in Richmond—Lee, Davis, Jackson, Maury, Stuart, easily the most prominent Confederate memorials in the world—remained untouchable except by an occasional activist who may douse one with red paint. Moreover, the position of the Richmond Democratic establishment in its July 2018 final report was to call for the removal of the Jefferson Davis monument and contextualization of the others.[44] Meanwhile, Richmond's slave-trading center in Shockoe Bottom—after New Orleans, the second-largest slave market in America; the site of Solomon Northup's imprisonment and Gabriel Prosser's martyrdom—was "memorialized" as a cordoned-off vacant lot with a plaque.[45] These events are complex and multifactorial, but Richmonders should at least contemplate, as many Charlottesvillians are, how this came to be and remains.[16]

"A reader of the textbook would not be aware that any controversy existed over integration if this were his only source of information," Fred Eichelman wrote of the Orwellian Virginia history textbook discussed in the introduction.[17] After years of massive resistance, up to and including closing public schools rather than integrating them, "the whole thing blew up in 1959 when both the state and federal courts ruled that the obstructionist legislation enacted by Virginia was unconstitutional."[18] The city "supposedly began integrating its schools" in 1960, but the following year, just "37 of 23,000 black students attended white schools."[19] The denial of history continued for many Richmonders. As one example, according to the 2019 school history on the website of Collegiate School, perhaps the premier private school in Richmond:

> *The Town School and Country Day School merge*[d in 1960], *operating on the campus off River and Mooreland Roads. In a "coordinate" configuration, a Girls School* [was] *formed for grades 5–12, led by former Town School Headmistress Catharine Flippen. The Boys School, also grades 5–12,* [was] *led by new Headmaster Malcolm U. Pitt, Jr. Elizabeth Burke head*[ed] *up the coed Lower School. Our first capital campaign raise*[d] *$1 million to build two classroom buildings, a gym, science building and music building. Included in the funds raised* [was] *a donation by Mr.* [Louis] *Reynolds of an additional 30 acres.*

In 1963, the website continued, "the first boys graduate[d] from Collegiate."[50] I visited the school's archives and asked to see the board minutes from the 1950s and 1960s. The archivist told me that he had asked the same question and looked through those minutes. He said there was no mention of race or any reason whatsoever for why a small girls' school on Monument Avenue was suddenly the beneficiary of a massive capital campaign to build a much larger country school that started to enroll boys. Racism was the driving force, of course, but it was all implied, even in private internal documents. There was an unwritten code that the plainest and most salient fact—Collegiate was and is a segregation academy—was and continues to be repressed.[51]

It was not written in stone that events from two or three generations ago should maintain omnipotence over the present; conditions in the twenty-first century persisted with the acquiescence and support of modern

Richmond. It was not for lack of knowledge or a measure of empathy about the plight of the city's public schools. Collegiate's alumni magazine reported on its 2010 Winter Party and Auction at the Westin Hotel:

> *In keeping with fundraising for our new library and Academic Commons, this year's adopted community cause was children's literacy. Whitney Cardozo, a current parent and Vice President of Education for the Children's Museum of Richmond, chaired a book drive. Through her efforts and the generosity of the Collegiate community, we collected 10,000 books that have been donated to four schools with whom we have established community service relationships: Oak Grove–Bellmeade Elementary School, William Byrd Community House, St. Andrews School and George Mason Elementary School.*[52]

Certainly, these were not evil people; few in Richmond were. It would be unjust to accuse those who were clearly acting out of genuine kindness to try to soften the edges of a harsh inequity. Yet at some point between the hand-me-down book drive and codified segregation, there was a system that built some children a "new library and Academic Commons" while routinely evacuating an elementary full of equally innocent children rather than fix its dangerous gas leak, and that was evil. The dichotomy of Collegiate's annual Westin Winter Party and Auction and George Mason Elementary's "leaking bathrooms, falling tiles and infestations of bugs and rodents" was not something foreign and unchangeable that came down from Mount Sinai. It was a local problem in which real people could make a noticeable difference. It was, in many ways, a symbiosis, created and continued by people who bore varying degrees of moral responsibility for its maintenance.[53]

Campbell "could not figure out why this place seemed so stuck, or why the values people kept stating seemed to have very little impact on what actually happened. The place seemed immobile," he stated.

> *My current answer to the paralysis of the Virginia temperament that is so exhibited here is that we had a half-revolution in 1783: half the population went into freedom, and half the population went into a totalitarian state.... To proclaim the highest values that had ever been stated in any nation in the world, and to simultaneously practice a horrible level of human oppression is paralyzing to the human spirit. It means you cannot function because you are living with guilt and shame at every moment: moreover, you constructed*

your society in that way. That paralysis is unadmitted and has continued to paralyze us for almost 250 years.[54]

There were two Richmonds, wrote Michael Paul Williams, "one ascendant, the other mired in violence and decay.…George Mason and much of the [public] housing stock are remnants of an era we never truly left behind. Even as [other] neighborhoods gentrify and industrial areas such as Scott's Addition and Manchester morph into eclectic residential communities, Richmond's public housing and school buildings remain largely frozen in time."[55] The best definition of the two Richmonds was provided by Joe Morrissey:

- One is public and visible, the other is private and hidden;
- One is largely white, the other is predominantly black;
- One is successful, thriving, and hopeful, while the other is characterized by poverty, despair, and hopelessness;
- One is safe at night while the other suffers from gunfire and violence;
- One sends its children to dynamic, secure private schools, while parents from the housing projects send their children to crumbling, unaccredited, 50-year-old schools.[56]

Joe Morrissey, like many of the people who said they wanted to fix the schools, was running for mayor.

NEW MAYOR, SAME PROMISES

In Richmond's elections, mayors had to win the majorities in five of nine city council districts.[57] It was one of many unfortunate consequences of Virginia's legacy that race mattered in elections, but it did, and five districts were majority black, three were majority white, and one was plurality black.[58]

The fifty-seven-year-old Morrissey had spent a career bouncing from personal to professional scandal and back again. He was easy to caricature, but observers were wise not to underestimate his tenacity: he won a state wrestling championship, purportedly two weeks after he tore his ACL; graduated from UVA and Georgetown Law School; and had won election to the state legislature in 2015 when nearly every Democratic official in the state turned out to oppose him.[59] He parlayed a courthouse fistfight into the slogan "Fightin' Joe" and adorned his campaign literature with boxing gloves, in case anyone missed the point.[60] It was unusual in any American city, much less Richmond, to see a white lawyer whose substantial base of political support was in the working-class black community.[61] His political acumen was illustrated when he was the sole primary challenger to win against an incumbent state senator in 2019 despite the opposition of seemingly every Democratic official in the state. His detractors had plenty of ammunition but should have conceded that he was a good politician, like a local Trump who turned scorn from the media and establishment opponents into electoral pay dirt.

Morrissey was the frontrunner for mayor and had seemed to overcome a 2014 sex scandal involving a then-seventeen-year-old receptionist at his office.[62] In one of the most surreal scenes in American politics, Delegate Morrissey had served time in 2015 with work release, so that he would write laws in the legislature during the day and drive his Jaguar back to jail each night.[63] He had since married the young woman and claimed he had repented, until it was reported on October 28, 2016, that he had texted a client on Valentine's Day asking her in Trumpian terms to shave herself.[64] This scandal was a bridge too far for some supporters who may have believed in his redemption story, but he still won 21 percent of the vote and a majority in the city's two poorest African American districts, good enough for a third-place finish.[65] He surely would have forced a runoff if he could have controlled the Valentine's Day story (or, better yet, if he had elected not to sext his legal client while his fiancée was taking care of their three-month-old infant).

The leading fundraiser was Jack Berry, the head of a city public-private booster organization.[66] In a city that gave Hillary Clinton 81,259 votes to Donald Trump's 15,581, a white businessman with Republican ties had little chance of winning.[67] He ended up finishing second with 34 percent of the vote and majorities in the two mostly white districts. Five other minor candidates would garner less than 10 percent of the vote combined.[68]

Morrissey's scandal was superbly timed for Levar Stoney, the putative runner-up Democratic candidate. The thirty-five-year-old's "humble beginnings [stood] out among the frontrunners in the race. The child of two teenage parents, he was raised by his grandmother throughout his adolescence and went to public school on free and reduced lunch. He was the first of his family to complete high school, and in 2004 he graduated" from James Madison University after serving as student body president.[69] Stoney was a newcomer to city politics who had worked his way up through the state Democratic Party to serve as Governor McAuliffe's Secretary of the Commonwealth. Stoney benefited from being the closest protégé of McAuliffe, who himself was the closest friend of the Democratic couple that many people assumed would move into the White House in January 2017. Stoney raised more than $900,000, just $200,000 less than Berry, and he adroitly used that money to run a professional campaign.[70]

Stoney's campaign reflected public opinion by trumpeting education as his top issue. He said he would be "the education mayor" and sent out literature stating that "Jack Berry voted for a plan to cut $23.8 million from our public schools," a claim PolitiFact rated "mostly false."[71] It may have seemed that the stars aligned for the young challenger who had trailed in every poll prior to election day, but he won 36 percent of the vote while eking out victories in five of the city's districts. The day after the election, Stoney reiterated: "The number one priority is going to be schools."[72]

THE VIRGINIA WAY MACHINE

Stoney's predecessor, Dwight Jones, had also promised reform and investments in schools, but left office with an abysmal 26 percent approval rating after a string of ill-conceived economic development projects had siphoned public funds into private coffers.[73] Compared to other governments, there was not a great deal of money for lavish handouts from city government: Richmond's annual budget was around $700 million (Virginia's state budget was roughly $50 billion), and about $170 million was earmarked for Richmond Public Schools.[74] Among Jones's expenditures were $9.5 million on an international bike race, $14 million to renovate the Altria Theater, about $15 million to the Redskins camp, more than $20 million to Stone Brewery and a proposed $200 million baseball stadium-hotel-apartment development that never got off the ground.[75] In the most salacious example, the FBI came calling when it was revealed that Jones had potentially used city resources to help with construction at a church where he served as pastor.[76] Jones was cleared of wrongdoing after being represented by Richard Cullen, who would go on to represent Vice President Mike Pence a few years later.[77]

The criticism of "Stepping Stoney" was that he was unconnected to Richmond and had higher office in mind.[78] During the campaign, he released a glossy commercial showing him running through the city and gazing over it into the sunset.[79] Time had since borne out that Stoney's election victory had less to do with luck than many assumed, and the young Stoney possessed significant political skills. He spoke the language of someone who would clean up a corrupt Democratic machine. While Jones had negotiated the Redskins deal, Stoney said that "I do believe a city as cash-strapped as we are should not be in the business of writing a check to a multibillion-dollar franchise."[80] Stoney was also not as beholden to Richmond's stultified Democratic machine—no church construction patronage from him—yet he seemed to feel that his political ambitions demanded a certain fealty to the monied Richmond establishment that had served as a launching point for many politicians' statewide political careers.

On June 27, 2017, eight days after Evans released her bombshell story on George Mason Elementary School, "the leader of the superintendent search committee, Dominion executive Tom Farrell, had come out in favor of a $130 million new" local sports arena, a figure that would soon balloon to $300 million and then an astonishing $620 million in public funds.[81] The money that would be necessary to fund emergency repairs at decaying and dangerous elementary schools was suddenly very much at risk of being siphoned off to private interests in a way that would make the Redskins look like amateurs.

CRUSADER WITH A CONSCIENCE

Into the fray stepped Paul Goldman, who had teamed a decade earlier with Republican political rival George Allen to push historic tax credits—a popular way that President Reagan and a Democratic Congress had conceived to revitalize dilapidated structures without raising taxes—as a tool for rehabilitating old schools.[82] They had a model: "Maggie Walker High School, built for African-American students during the Depression, was renovated with help from private investors and now houses an acclaimed magnet high school."[83] Richmond government understood very well how to teach children: the city boasted one of the best public high schools in the country, which was fully integrated and drew children from all over the surrounding counties.[84] Maggie Walker enjoyed widespread support, not least because educating gifted children was probably one of the best investments society could make and private investors made plenty of money from the tax credits. Prior to that, Goldman had worked as Doug Wilder's top adviser during his stint as mayor of Richmond and had tried and failed to earmark a real estate tax windfall for schools. "If you leave it to the normal vagaries of the politicians, they're going to spend it on anything but schools, because that's what they've always done," he noted presciently.[85]

Anybody who had worked in Virginia politics over the previous forty years knew three things about Paul Goldman. As a brilliant young New York transplant, he had masterminded Wilder's statewide wins for lieutenant governor and governor in the 1980s and cemented Virginia as the first state ever to elect an African American governor. As late as 2019, there had only been one other: Deval Patrick of Massachusetts, elected in 2006.[86] Second, Goldman looked like he lived under a bridge; he resembled the shark hunter from *Jaws*. And third, Goldman had the rarest of gifts in politics: a sincere, relentless idealism.

Furthermore, Paul Goldman had no ego. "Goldman never wanted office," Dwayne Yancey wrote in *When Hell Froze Over*, which remains one of the two best books ever written on Virginia campaigns. "If he did, maybe the establishment could understand him better, and maybe it could have bought him off long ago, dispatching him to some far-flung do-gooder office where he'd be out of the way. Nor was Goldman interested in money. If so, he could have cashed in long ago as a political consultant. In a jungle full of mercenaries, Goldman is more of a missionary, a crusading zealot in the game for a higher purpose. He only signs on with candidates he believes in, then pushes their cause with a single-minded fanaticism as unnerving as his ragtag personal style."[87] He was simultaneously full of intrigue and guileless.

He had been beating a drum for years about the shameful state of Richmond's public schools. In 2017, Goldman had an unused ace up his sleeve in the power of public opinion. Where top-down reform had not worked, perhaps the will of the voters could in the form of a citizen referendum. Goldman had the wherewithal to do it, having led a successful 2003 petition drive to allow Richmond citizens to popularly elect their mayor. (Critics noted that Wilder was the first beneficiary of this legislative change.) He would launch a petition drive to put the issue before the voters and ask simply that the mayor either come up with a plan to fully fund school modernization within six months without tax increases or else say it could not be done. The first coverage of Goldman's plan in the *Times-Dispatch* was in an article by K. Burnell Evans on June 5, 2017—two weeks before her exposé of the rat feces and surgical masks of George Mason Elementary School, and three weeks before Farrell's Coliseum pitch.

"This is not aimed at anybody," Goldman said. "This is about the needs of children who attend inadequate schools."[88]

Richmond's political structure did not feel that way. It was no exaggeration to say that its members responded with uniform antagonism to try to stop the initiative from passing and even from appearing on the ballot. If Richmond was a society where politicians reflected the will of their voters, then Paul Goldman would have received a key to the city. Instead, he was targeted with dismissal, whispering, ridicule, and personal and political attacks of every sort—until, ultimately, the politicians acknowledged the wisdom and morality of his ideas and provided desperately needed funds to Richmond's public schools so the city's children could have brighter futures.

Mayor Stoney's actions were mostly behind the scenes, and the public heard their echoes as various surrogates popped up to spout his talking points. In the first response to the petition drive, his press secretary stated that the mayor's "Education Compact" was sufficient to deal with schools' challenges.[89] Former Virginia secretary of education Anne Holton quickly came to the defense of the Compact in a *Richmond Times-Dispatch* op-ed twelve days later.[90] The Compact itself, which had not yet passed city council, was largely a list of platitudes whose substantive mandate was that the mayor, city council, and the school board would hold joint quarterly meetings.[91] One of the mayor's top advisors acknowledged that the Compact "doesn't bind [Richmond's public schools] to anything."[92] On June 26, facing pushback from different quarters who saw it as a Trojan horse for privatization, Stoney himself admitted, "There's no metrics here. No measurements here. All it is is a framework."[93] "Well, that should fix everything," retorted the *Times-Dispatch* editorial board.[94] "I think people want to see some action on this issue," Goldman noted.[95]

Goldman needed to collect about 10,400 petition signatures from city voters, a daunting figure in a city of just 143,675 registered voters.[96] The 10,400 represented the threshold of 10 percent of the voters who turned out for the previous election, which was a high-turnout presidential year. Considering unavoidable mistakes like duplication, illegibility, and signatures coming from Greater Richmond but not the city of Richmond, the Virginia Board of Elections recommended that signature gatherers collect 50 percent more than the required number.[97] Goldman had his work cut out for him. To give a comparison, presidential candidates could appear on a statewide ballot in Virginia by submitting 5,000 signatures, criticized as one of the strictest requirements in the nation.[98] And he had to get these 15,600 signatures by August 18. Stoney told people that it could not be done.[99]

When Goldman set out to get signatures, he was relentless, as he was when he set out to do anything. Goldman looked like he lived under a bridge because he truly did not have any hobbies outside of political work on behalf of the downtrodden. "Paul Goldman is the most single-minded political operative I have ever seen," said politico Darrel Miles. "He lives, breathes and sleeps politics seven days a week." "His metabolism is always teetering on the brink of him falling asleep," said Ira Lechner, a close friend of Goldman. "He has no visible means of support. He drives a car jammed with stuff. He sacks out at people's houses. He's almost like a vagabond. Nobody knows where Paul came from. He just always shows up in different campaigns."[100] "A lot of other places don't have the type of person like me who's crazy and just won't take no for an answer," Goldman said. "Thank God I don't love mountain climbing, or I'd be dead."[101]

He and volunteers collected 6,619 signatures when registered voters were easiest to find, on primary day, June 13, 2017. This was far and away the most signatures ever collected in a single day in the history of Richmond. One volunteer, a sixty-one-year-old retiree, herself signed up an additional twenty volunteers to work the polls throughout the city. "I did it for the children," she said.[102]

To complete the task would require a more targeted effort, but the Virginia Department of Elections refused to provide Goldman with a registered voters list. A range of people and organizations, from candidates, to parties, to committees, to voter nonprofits, could access this public document for a nominal $300 fee, yet Goldman and his petition drive group were barred from doing so. Not to be outdone, Goldman filed a twenty-five-page suit on June 30 asking the court for a preliminary injunction against the department, its commissioner, and its board members.[103] "I was right, and they knew I was right," he said. "What they were doing was unconstitutional. But I settled since I couldn't get legal fees for representing myself, and I couldn't spend all my time writing briefs, I had to get those signatures. They gave me the list, and they were supposed to give me my costs back, but they haven't even done that yet."[104]

By early August, Goldman had created a citywide campaign for collecting and submitting signatures to the Board of Elections for review. On August 14, four days before the deadline, a Richmond judge certified that Goldman had passed the threshold to appear on the ballot in November. He had collected more than fifteen thousand signatures. "You don't get a lot of people to sign a petition like this unless there's a strong public feeling that this is something they want their city to do," he said modestly.

School Board chairwoman Dawn Page, who had not even responded to an interview request for the first article about the referendum in June, told the press that Goldman's victory was "good news." More than that, she was now on board: "Hopefully, it gets the votes necessary in November." The mayor's press secretary again released a statement trumpeting the Education Compact as the right path for the city.[105]

With the mountain climbed, the Mayor's Office was just beginning. The first thing the successful drive did was to prod the mayor into action: the heralded Education Compact passed city council precisely one week after a judge certified the referendum.[106] Three days later, a new gambit was tried. City Attorney Allen Jackson could usually be spotted lounging at city council meetings and occasionally telling the politicians his opinion of what was permitted under the city charter. On August 23, he emailed the Mayor's Office and city council advising that the referendum violated the charter. Worse news than that, for signatories of the petition, was that Jackson advised the council and mayor to challenge the referendum in court. The timing of this was striking, to say the least, but Jackson was playing on Goldman's turf. Richmond City Council members Kristen Larson and Kim Gray—the same two who had sorrowfully looked over dusty school facilities reports in front of reporters—immediately took the bait and publicly advocated for suing.[107] The *Times-Dispatch* editorial board, which four days earlier had called passage of the referendum "an important symbolic step" quickly piled on, uncritically adopting Jackson's reasoning that the measure was supposedly illegal.[108] But Goldman, wearing two hats as attorney and operative, was unperturbed. "If the mayor wants to sue, I'll be happy to beat him. Let's focus on what matters: fixing up the schools for these kids who have been long denied. It's time to stop talking and take action."[109]

The reality of the situation had begun to dawn on observers and opinion leaders throughout Richmond. "This petition gambit is well-played," wrote Michael Paul Williams. "Richmond residents are eager to vent their frustration over the state of the city's schools, which are viewed as hindering the Great RVA Comeback. Any elected official who opposes the referendum—or questions whether this charter amendment goes beyond 'the structure or administration of city government' as opined by City Attorney Allen Jackson—risks being labeled as anti-voter and anti-democratic." Councilwoman Larson, who five days earlier had wanted to sue Goldman, explained exactly the box that Richmond politicians were in: "The way it's being sold is, 'Do you want to improve Richmond Public Schools with no new taxes?' Of course you do." Stoney announced that he would refuse the city attorney's advice to sue, and no lawsuit came from anyone else.[110] Whereas once the mayor had said that Goldman could never collect all the signatures, he now told people that the measure could not pass in November.[111]

But Goldman had crafted the measure so that it was essentially guaranteed victory if it were to appear on the ballot. Notwithstanding Stoney's obstinacy, its passage was a fait accompli. Never one to rest on his laurels, Goldman began lining up political sponsors who would shepherd the bill through the state legislature once it passed. Goldman was the former chairman of the Democratic Party of Virginia, yet he could not find a single Democratic sponsor. "The people Goldman really infuriated were those in the Democratic establishment—staid, cautious types who thought they had things under control and wanted to keep them that way," Yancey wrote. "They don't just hate him," said a former colleague. "He's like an itch they can't reach. They can't get rid of him."[112] Two Republicans understood the politics and would not be so stubborn. Delegate Manoli Loupassi signed on during his tough reelection battle.[113] So did Senator Glen Sturtevant, who faced reelection in a swing district in 2019.[114]

Richmond's Democratic politicians, and particularly Mayor Stoney, haplessly tried to spike the measure. In early September, Stoney penned the first opinion column that he would write as Richmond's mayor; he again praised his Education Compact but did not address the referendum.[115] In late October, Stoney and Governor McAuliffe announced a philanthropic initiative to provide vision screening and eyeglasses to all of Richmond's public schoolchildren.[116] Four days before the election, he blasted a "scathing" letter to the school board criticizing members for not coming up with a plan to fix the schools.[117] In fact, the board had years of plans: lack of funding from the mayor and city council was the problem. The day before the election, Stoney, who was usually a careful and disciplined politician, petulantly tweeted that he would not vote for the referendum "on principle."[118] It was as if Richmond politicians could not comprehend a political operative who just believed in equality; there must have been another angle to it. When Goldman was asked why politicians would oppose a popular measure certain to pass, he replied, "It's a good idea, it's good politics, and it works. The only reason I can think of that these politicians oppose it is personal: they convince themselves I'm trying to make them look bad so they go full 'kill-the-messenger' mode."[119]

On November 7, 2017, Richmond voters thwarted the will of their mayor and nearly every other person of power in the city to deliver 85.4

percent support to the referendum, with landslides in every council district and precinct—black, white, rich, poor, young, old, everywhere.[120] "Eighty-five percent is about as close as you can get to unanimity in the political system," said Goldman. "The people have spoken and sent a message to city leadership."[121] Yet not a single Democratic politician supported it in an overwhelmingly Democratic city. "Nothing," said Goldman. "Baffling, really, since I was trying to get them money for their constituents and they still wouldn't do anything."[122] That would change.

THE WILL OF THE VOTERS

With public opinion at their backs, others felt free to oppose the mayor and come forward in support of the schools. Delegate Loupassi lost his reelection bid in that year's backlash to President Trump, and the referendum was briefly left without a lead sponsor in the state legislature.[123] Sturtevant agreed to take the mantle. A week after the landslide vote, Stoney's spokesperson shifted his claim to a new straw man that the mayor "does not think that we need the General Assembly to tell us how to" fix the schools.[124] Stoney's intransigence notwithstanding, in mid-November, Democratic Delegate Jeffrey Bourne, a Stoney ally and former Richmond School Board chairman, signed on to lead the bill through the House of Delegates. His explanation was simple enough: "Eighty-five percent of the people said they want the charter changed, and it's our duty to do what the people want."[125] The Richmond NAACP had sat out the signature-gathering and did not activate its political operation to turn out the vote for the referendum. So, too, had school board members, who had their own bases of support as well as a public platform to call supporters to action. They had been in office for nearly a year and had failed to present a facilities plan, until they presented one two weeks after the referendum and passed it two weeks after that.[126] A month after the landslide election, the head of the Richmond NAACP and five school board members held a press conference outside of George Mason Elementary School to call on the mayor and city council to find $158 million to bridge the gap between what the board had asked for and what they received for upgrading Richmond school facilities.[127] "We have a plan on the table and what we also have is the city made a statement in November: we want to make change," said board member Kenya Gibson. "We've had plans again and again, and nothing's happened. Now, we have to fund the plan."[128]

Mayor Stoney sat down with the *Richmond Times-Dispatch* for a reflective interview at the end of his first year in office. His much-touted Education Compact had accomplished nothing except for quarterly meetings between the mayor, city council, and school board. Within six months, those meetings would devolve into internecine squabbling and become sparsely attended.[129] Stoney proudly noted that he had visited all forty-four district schools and had launched the eyeglasses initiative. These were helpful palliatives, but after an entire year, Stoney had little else to show.[130] The gap between the image the mayor wanted to project and the reality of his administration was growing. With the inescapable 85 percent vote, the political system in Richmond had shifted underneath the mayor's feet.

No politician can resist the will of the voters forever. After their voices sounded loudly at the polls, the recriminations of 2017 would rapidly give way to meaningful change. "When things move in Richmond, they really move," said Ben Campbell. "You can do something in Los Angeles that only affects the block next to you, but when something moves in Richmond, everybody feels it."[131] The first sign of change was when Delegate Bourne submitted a different bill to the House, one that would modify the referendum language to permit a tax increase to fund schools. "The mayor believes Delegate Bourne's version is an improvement," said Stoney's spokesman. Sturtevant's Senate version of the bill remained identical to that passed by Richmond voters.[132] Bourne's bill died a quick death in a House subcommittee, where the chairman coolly "told Bourne after the bill was killed to 'take a good look' at the Senate version."[133] The next day, Sturtevant's bill passed unanimously through the full Senate, and less than three weeks later, Sturtevant's bill passed through that same House subcommittee unanimously.[134] On its way to passage, the bill would not receive a single vote against it from any politician in the state.[135] Governor Northam signed the bill into law on April 4, 2018. "Stoney repeated his objection," a reporter wrote, "saying that putting the referendum on the ballot is easy, but finding funding is the hard part." "After 62 years of being denied, the children of Richmond will finally get a plan," Goldman said.[136] Levar Stoney had been checkmated.

IN ACTION

The inaction on schools that had distinguished Stoney's first year would not characterize his second. Delegate Bourne's legislative ploy in mid-January augured a more public effort by the mayor to actually use his substantial political capital. On January 23, 2018, Stoney announced a proposal to increase the city's meal tax by 1.5 percent to fund school facility needs. The revenue would be earmarked for a $150 million bond issue for schools that would fulfill the school board's request.[137] That same day, he gave his first State of the City address and made the meals tax its hallmark proposal. He telegenically held up two pennies. "One and half cents—for our children," he said to applause. "Less than these two pennies I have in my hands."[138] It was an unexpected play. During his 2016 campaign, Stoney had offered a milquetoast sentiment that cigarette taxes should be raised in order to lower businesses taxes and protect the city's bond rating but had not offered anything concrete.[139]

Regardless of where the public stood on schools, there was at least a case to be made that the meals tax was not the best way to pay for them. Some restaurant owners would naturally be opposed; on the other hand, some people claimed that they would dine out even more in order to support schools.[140] Some restaurant owners publicly supported the tax.[141] Others noted that, given city hall's history of corporate welfare and cronyism, there was unused money to be found in the budget.[142] City council was initially uncertain, and the first vote count stood at two to two, with five undecided.[143]

Political power in the restaurant community was diffuse. A vote count a week later showed that three members of city council now supported the proposal, with four undecided.[144] Stoney praised and cultivated restaurateurs in press releases and photo ops.[145] It was a difficult position for them to be in, and they could not come up with a winning argument. "We know that there is a problem with the schools, we know they need to be fixed, and we know restaurants should not be the one bearing the full cost of that burden," said Frank Brunetto of the Virginia Restaurant, Lodging and Travel Association.[146] The meals tax was approved by a 7–2 vote of the city council on February 12, just twenty-two days after Stoney's State of the City speech. "By city government standards, Stoney's proposal has moved at warp speed," a reporter marveled.[147] The $150 million would pay for replacing George Mason and another elementary and middle school that were among the worst in Richmond's portfolio.[148] The alacrity of his successful meals tax push demonstrated what Stoney was capable of accomplishing when he wanted. It was an important start, but as a result of decades of neglect, there was another $650 million to go until all city schools were modernized.[149]

The case for meals taxes could be made much more strongly for cigarette taxes, but that ignored the Virginia Way. The same day that the

Richmond Mayor Levar Stoney pitched a 1.5 percent meals tax increase for schools as "less than these two pennies I have in my hands." *From the* Richmond Times-Dispatch.

majority of city council voted to pass the meals tax, Councilman Parker Agelasto introduced an $0.80-per-pack cigarette tax proposal that would raise $5.4 million per year for school maintenance, a significant amount in a city that had only budgeted $1.5 million for it that year. Unlike the disorganized power of the restaurant community, cigarette giant Altria was headquartered in adjacent Henrico County, had a significant Richmond presence in a cigarette factory and research center, and, most importantly, was the most lavish campaign donor in Virginia, other than Dominion. Altria was Stoney's fifth-largest donor and had given money to seven out of nine city council members.[150] The Stoney administration echoed the unusual objection voiced by Altria lobbyists that this would be a declining revenue source over time.[151] This was patently untrue, but even Agelasto uncritically accepted it.[152] The percent of Americans smoking was not declining but had leveled off in recent years; Richmond's population and, therefore, the total number of smokers, continued to grow.[153] Nobody could accuse Virginia of harboring anti-tobacco bias; Virginia's cigarette taxes were the second-lowest in the nation, and Richmond was "the only major city in the state without" a cigarette tax.[154] The council delayed a vote on the issue.[155] The rationale was particularly galling considering Richmond actually paid $1.25 million per year to the company, as it had every year since 2008, for the "Philip Morris Real Estate Grant" that was supposedly necessary to get the company to build a research center in its hometown.[156] The next month, Stoney's administration offered the more specific rationale that he would not support a cigarette tax to back bonds, but might for the general fund.[157] "We thought we could borrow against it. The administration said they don't want to do that. OK. That's fine. Let's use it on a cash basis," Agelasto said. "That's even better."[158]

The final vote in April was not without fireworks. "I know some of you questioned about Philip Morris giving some of us council members a donation—yes, I got a donation," said Councilwoman Reva Trammell, whose service on the council was most distinguished by being found "talking about crime" with a police officer in a parked car at 4:15 a.m. while she was dating another one. The scandal blew up when the "talking" cop described details of her anatomy to the boyfriend cop.[159] Regardless, she represented the district with the cigarette factory in it. "I was proud to get the donation, and let me say this: the mayor…got $25,000…damn, that's a lot of money." As with the meals tax, the mayor had ultimately called the shots, and the reason why he felt dining should be taxed while smoking should not was crystal clear. Council voted down the cigarette tax 6–3, with just one member who had taken money from Altria voting for the tax.[160]

Stoney's obstinacy never permitted him or many on city council to acknowledge the referendum as a driving force, but money began to turn up for schools where there had supposedly been none before. Readers of the *Richmond Free Press* were presented with a striking juxtaposition between the May 4, 2018 headline, "No More Money for School Maintenance" and the August 16, "More Money Found for School Maintenance."[161] The source of the money was never fully explained, but apparently, an additional $9.5 million turned up when "city and RPS departments reconciled their school capital maintenance and construction accounts."[162]

FIELD OF SCHEMES

It was as if a parallel universe existed in the other Richmond, where "a shadow government of big business chieftains, lawyers, bankers and planners relentlessly tries to push things its way."[163] At the same time that school emergencies were banner news, the other Richmond sought to hamstring the city's ability to finance school construction for future generations by earmarking public money for private pockets. June 2017 saw the triumvirate of Goldman's referendum, Evans's seminal article, and Dominion CEO Tom Farrell's $1.4 billion urban renewal proposal. As news of the latter emerged, its inconsistencies quickly began to pile up into a shaky house of cards that revealed the true intent.

The details of the proposal were vague and kept out of public view. They were negotiated behind closed doors between Stoney's office and what was often euphemistically referred to as "the business community," essentially a handful of establishment Republican CEOs of Richmond companies. The same people were always behind ostensibly civic projects that had been pushed for decades, usually to the detriment of the public coffers. The Coliseum proposal reconstituted the business-political alliance that had led to boondoggles such as the despised Redskins deal. In the most recent iteration, the business community shifted the location of a proposed public-private megaproject from the Boulevard and Shockoe Bottom areas to the Richmond Coliseum and replaced Mayor Jones with Mayor Stoney. Dominion's other lead on the project besides Farrell was Jones's former chief of staff, Grant Neely.[164] The lynchpin was replacing the Coliseum, built in 1971, with a larger arena, which would be financially successful for some unstated reason.[165] The project would be funded by tax increment financing, whereby any tax revenue collected from an area above current revenue levels would support thirty-year construction bonds. Real estate appreciation would naturally increase the value of the project zone by three or more times over thirty years; inflation alone would double it. Those taxes would flow to the city anyways, but they would now be dedicated by law to private investors. The arena would be joined with a new hotel and apartment building that would replace a federal building, the city courts, a few parking lots, and two buildings hosting a variety of city functions such as social service and job agencies.

Jeremy Lazarus of the *Richmond Free Press* pointed out that these city facilities would have to move somewhere, but during the first year and a half the proposal was under discussion, it was not mentioned by a single

The proposed urban renewal project area. *City of Richmond*.

person where those federal and city offices would move.[166] Only in late 2018 did it begin to come out that the social services building would move to an out-of-the-way former Altria operations center with sporadic bus service six miles down I-95.[167]

This precise area had been the focus of at least four big-ticket urban renewal projects over the past sixty years, about once every fifteen years, as if on schedule. Richmond had a relatively small budget and strict debt limits that were lavishly tapped four times for these projects—and failed four times in a row. The original sin was to bulldoze the prosperous area of town known as "Black Wall Street" to build the I-95/64 highway. That destroyed and hollowed out the neighborhood.[168] Secondly, the unsightly Richmond Coliseum was built in 1971 with $16 million in taxpayer funds; it had since received millions more in public subsidies, including $7.1 million in renovations in 2003.[169] In the 1980s, the Sixth Street Marketplace at Sixth and Broad cost more than $30 million in city bonds and opened to much fanfare; retail tenants in the Blues Armory slowly left when customers failed to materialize. The frontispiece was a pedestrian bridge crossing Broad; the bridge and much that remained of the project was razed at the cost of an additional $800,000 in 2003.[170] The Convention Center cost more than $170 million in city and county funds in the early 2000s. Its backers, too, had promised that construction would develop what was now suddenly in need of redevelopment.[171] "Time after time the city commissions some consultant, many of whom I know and respect, to provide gaudy numbers on how one project or another will pay back the taxpayers, but none of these publicly funded land deals ever end up working the way they were sold," concluded School Board member Jonathan Young.[172]

The area slated for renewal was adjacent to the expanding VCU Medical Center, and it was striking to see what could only be described as willful amnesia among the business community about what had taken place within the last few years. The cornerstone of Mayor Jones's Boulevard redevelopment project was building a children's hospital with the help of a generous $150 million pledge from local philanthropist Bill Goodwin. One of VCU's main objections was that the Boulevard was five miles away from the medical campus that hosted hospitals, clinics, offices, and dental, medical, nursing, and allied health schools and would thus warrant inefficient duplication of many facilities and services.[173] None of this happened in a minor footnote somewhere: an entire forest probably gave its life for all the press coverage of that unsuccessful idea, and Goodwin himself was a member of the Coliseum group.[174] Now, the very parcels not available to VCU to build a pediatric hospital because they housed critical government services were free for the taking if Hyatt would build a hotel there with the help of public funds.

The neighborhood was not some ghost town that nobody visited, and it was astonishing to hear it repeated again and again that the area was some variation of an "urban wasteland," as the *Richmond Times-Dispatch* editorial board opined.[175] The board had seemingly forgotten its prior take on sports venues versus schools, when its members had written that "fixing [schools] would do more for the city than any sports or entertainment offering possibly could."[176] "In a city that claimed to worship history," the most important truths were unmentioned because of Richmond's cognitive dissonance about plain facts: the area north of Broad Street had been historically black and south historically white.[177] There was still some of that segregation today, especially in housing, but the VCU Medical Center and surrounding government areas were probably the most integrated and accessible places in the entire city: everyone got sick or had to go to court or city hall at some point. There were plenty of people in the area slated for "redevelopment": Richmond was a majority black city, and maybe two-thirds of the people in this area at any time happened to be African

American residents just living their lives. Yet Richmond's chamber of commerce leaders penned their feelings about it in Richmond's inimitable coded language:

> *Do we want the space between the VCU Medical Center and the convention center to become a walkable, attractive area filled with residents and visitors or do we prefer blocks of unattractive old office buildings that encourage folks to stay away?*[178]

"Folks" did not "stay away." Even in the earlier map that the city submitted in its request for proposals, one can see hundreds of cars in mostly full parking lots. Thousands of people worked and conducted business there every day, despite the chamber leaders' evident fear to even walk in the area.

Ben Campbell noted the conspicuous factor in the psychology of many Richmonders:

> *We had a study about twenty years ago where the Chamber of Commerce went to Richmond's peer cities in the mid-Atlantic—Memphis, Charlotte, Greensboro, High Point—and found that of the cities they studied, Richmond had the lowest crime rate and the highest fear of crime. This is just me, growing up in Virginia, but I think that if you are busy keeping other people down and making a lie of the values that you state, that basically you are afraid of them, because you know that the people you are harming want to get you, or you think you know they might want to get you. If you read the stories of Richmond, there is constant fear of black people.*[179]

There were two projects in recent years showing perhaps the most important motive for the project. Kanawha Plaza in downtown Richmond was closed for much of 2015 and 2016. The supposed impetus was sprucing up the city like a Potemkin Village for the September 2015 UCI Bike Championships, but the Plaza was a longtime encampment for the homeless, and it was closed during the race. In August 2015, a representative from Enrichmond, another group representing the same business community, pledged to city council that an unnamed group of private backers would provide $6 million to bulldoze and rebuild Kanawha Plaza. He asserted, falsely, in response to a question from Councilman Agelasto, that the names of these backers had to be revealed in the nonprofit's annual 990 tax forms.[180] That never happened and never would happen because that money was never there, and that information was not and could not be publicly disclosed in 990 forms.[181]

As of this writing, the financial backers of the Coliseum project had also not been revealed, if they even existed.[182] After the Plaza was bulldozed, the phantom backers withdrew their commitment and left city taxpayers on the hook for reconstruction. It was re-engineered as an anti-homeless park: it looked mostly the same, but structures like a pedestrian bridge and trees were destroyed. Areas where poor people would congregate were redesigned to prohibit sitting, and embankments were studded with metal plates so that people could not lie down. From 2016 to 2018, the target of urban renewal was Monroe Park, where homeless people also gathered, and its makeover bore the same hallmarks. It was closed for a couple years, and the city threw a lot of money at it to make some cosmetic changes. Monroe Park had been imperfect but functional, and $6.8 million in renovations, with about half coming from the city, was a great deal of money. The budget for Richmond's homeless services in 2018 was roughly $500,000. The renovations also removed most of the park's benches and added a police substation.[183] When the park reopened, the homeless had disappeared.

There were a handful of homeless people who also lived in the Coliseum area, and the city's cold-weather homeless shelter was in the Public Safety Building. The city began looking for a new cold-weather shelter away from downtown in late 2018. "Regardless of the benefits of having a centralized downtown facility to serve the homeless, Dominion's Tom Farrell and the City want it out of the way," wrote developer Michael Hild. "It is a poor solution at best," he continued. "The City is attempting to turn its back on the issue and push the downtrodden across the river, and hoping no one will notice. Leader's [sic] of other cities have been excoriated for giving the homeless bus tickets and moving them out of town before sporting events such as the Super Bowl or World Cup. This sure feels awfully similar."[184] It was not like spending all this money actually solved the problem; it merely displaced one or two dozen people so businessmen would not have to look out their windows at them. Rather than inventing urban renewal projects to wipe out the problem, it would have been cheaper to invest in decent services and schools to prevent the perpetuation of desperate poverty.

It was not clear if there was a good reason for the Coliseum even to exist, argued Lazarus and *Style Weekly*'s Jackie Kruszewski.[185] There was a problem with the outdated Coliseum and its $1.75 million annual subsidy from the city that could be solved by selling it on the free market. During this time, Richmond was going through a commercial real estate boom and had no problem attracting hundreds of millions of dollars in private investment.[186] The city valued the Coliseum parcel at $12.3 million and could have easily opened the area for competitive bidding; this would undoubtedly be the path that would generate the most revenue to fund city services and schools.

Instead, the captains of industry who usually trumpeted capitalism wanted to distort it with cronyism, just as they and their forebears had mismanaged development of the area for decades. It was difficult to understand how the four-block Coliseum parcel would suddenly become filled with more people during the day if it were replaced with a larger arena that would also necessarily hold events only at night or on weekends. But some of the business community's motives were highly questionable, at best. In 2007, many had banded together as a "gang of 26" led by Farrell to try to abolish Richmond's elected school board.[187] Farrell had also used $1 million in public funds in 2014 to make what one reviewer called a "contemptuous" Confederate movie, *Field of Lost Shoes*, that depicts Abraham Lincoln and Ulysses Grant conspiring to murder children. His film company was called Tredegar Filmworks, named after Tredegar Ironworks, the slave factory adjacent to Dominion headquarters that was the "Ironmaker to the Confederacy."[188] Farrell was a member of the Gray family, whose patriarch had sat on the Dominion board and who bore as much responsibility as any Virginian other than Harry Byrd for massive resistance.[189] None of this was to stop the group from race-baiting, for example, by trumpeting that the proposal included "$300 million in contracts for minority-owned businesses," a patently illegal racial quota under the U.S. Supreme Court's *Richmond v. Croson*.[190] "It comes up in every meeting: this can take Beyoncé," said the investment group's spokesperson, Jeff Kelley.[191] The indelible image for the schools crisis was teachers wearing surgical masks to teach in Richmond's true "urban wastelands"; here, the indelible image was a group of men stoking each other's egos and repeating, "if we build it, she will come."

Stoney kept mum about his thoughts on the proposal while he openly opposed the school referendum. An October 2017 poll showed that 64 percent of Richmonders supported paying more in taxes for schools, while 65 percent were opposed to using public money on the Coliseum project.[192] Amazingly, just two days after the November 2017 elections and referendum, Stoney held a press conference to announce "his" request for proposal (RFP) on a development project that was nearly identical to the one proposed by the business community. "I am well aware of their ideas," Stoney said, "but this is a city of Richmond project." The RFP differed little from Farrell's proposal except to call for a rebuilt bus transfer station and affordable housing as part of the new apartment complex.[193] "I prefer competition," Stoney said. The extent of the competition was clear when the RFP closed in February 2018

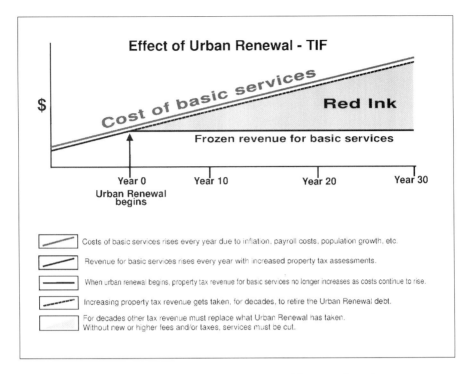

Effect of Urban Renewal - TIF

$

Cost of basic services

Red Ink

Frozen revenue for basic services

Year 0 | Year 10 | Year 20 | Year 30
Urban Renewal
begins

Costs of basic services rises every year due to inflation, payroll costs, population growth, etc.

Revenue for basic services rises every year with increased property tax assessments.

When urban renewal begins, property tax revenue for basic services no longer increases as costs continue to rise.

Increasing property tax revenue gets taken, for decades, to retire the Urban Renewal debt.

For decades other tax revenue must replace what Urban Renewal has taken.
Without new or higher fees and/or taxes, services must be cut.

Tax increment financing (TIF) was sold as revenue neutral but actually took money away from city coffers. *Wikimedia Commons.*

and only one group submitted a proposal: the same group that had initiated the RFP.[191] "Our city made it clear that our priority should be our schools, and I agree," school board member Kenya Gibson said wistfully.[195]

The financial numbers behind the proposal were impossible to believe. Tax increment financing was itself a disingenuous ploy. As noted, any real estate in downtown Richmond would appreciate over the course of thirty years; earmarking this revenue toward a bond proposal would starve the city of resources and was no different than raising taxes by any other means. A new arena would cost around $220 million and "over 30 years would require an annual payment of $11 million to $22 million a year, depending on the interest rate"; the taxes on such an arena would amount to just $2.4 million yearly. "Several developers the [*Richmond Free Press*] consulted and who spoke on condition of anonymity could not fathom how a private coliseum could generate enough income to cover debt, let alone generate a return on the investment," Lazarus wrote.[196] The bottom line for the new project began at $1 billion in total investment, but, as time went on, that grew to $1.4

billion, and the money that the public would put up went to $300 million, or $620 million with interest, nearly the cost of completely modernizing all of the city's schools.[197] The proposal took time and money from such efforts: by September 2018, the city was canceling scheduled events at the Coliseum and had spent about $500,000 just reviewing the single proposal. "I can't wrap my mind around half a million dollars for studying a Coliseum deal that we haven't even had a public conversation about as council," Councilwoman Gray said.[198]

Richmond City Council and the public continued to be kept in the dark about any details, but the public got the best look at the cronyism and unstable financing of the proposal in documents uncovered by reporter Mark Robinson.[199] The project would now be funded by tax increment financing as well as the taxes from Dominion's downtown office buildings, which were so far away from the project that they do not even appear on the map included in this chapter. Unbelievably, Farrell "said it's just a coincidence that Dominion's new tower is part of the proposal." He must not have checked with his public relations team, because Grant Neely claimed in another article that "it's the closest taxable property to this area." This was patently false: there were dozens of taxable properties from small and large businesses to apartment buildings to hotels that were closer. "If that is the proposal, that would not be palatable for me," said City Council President Chris Hilbert, who deemed it "troubling."

As tenuous as those numbers were, they seemed almost reasonable compared to other aspects of the deal. The purported projections for arena revenue seemed to be invented out of whole cloth. The group claimed that it would "generate $3.7 million in revenue to help cover debt service payments in its first year in operation, and $5.8 million by its third year." However, the "nine comparable arenas" that the group cited "made an average of $953,000 annually. The highest grossing venue brought in $2.9 million." The group also claimed that meals tax revenue from new restaurants in the area would not displace meals tax revenue from other restaurants because, they claimed, the only people who would eat in the area would be new tourists and new residents. Staid and independent experts looked through the details and raised a number of serious red flags. Esson Miller, the former staff director of the Virginia Senate Finance Committee, wrote that the businessmen were "rummaging through the city's fiscal well-being, putting it at severe risk that could have long-term detrimental impact."[200] Analyst Justin Griffin found that the modeling assumed that every attendee at a Coliseum event would spend an average of $458.48 on popcorn, candy, and so forth.[201] The capstone of the deal called for transferring these properties to the investment group for ninety-nine years, a giveaway usually seen only in kleptocracies and which would long outlive every person reading these words. Farrell had pledged that he would not see any money from the project; the electricity for the new businesses and residents would be provided by Dominion. Stoney, who well knew about the damning details that demonstrated the project was not on solid financial footing, was left in a bind and discarded his usual careful rhetoric. "This is our project," he said. "This is not Dominion's project. It's not any other entity's project. This is our project. This is my vision....I don't care if it's Tom Farrell or Johnny on the street, if it does not benefit my city, this project will not move forward."[202]

The fantastic veered into propaganda at the headline claim Stoney repeated like a chorus that this would somehow create nine thousand permanent jobs.[203] A $1.4 billion investment spread over thirty years worked out to about $47 million per year, or about $5,100 per year for every "permanent job." In any event, most of the cost of the project would be spent on materials, not labor. To give an example that backers should have been familiar with, Dominion employed about sixteen thousand people and had about $12.6 billion in revenue annually.[204] It was a 100 percent certainty that this project would not possibly create nine thousand permanent jobs and might actually increase unemployment through hiring fewer teachers, firefighters, and cops.

RICHMOND TO RURAL

School problems were not exclusive to Richmond, and the 2008–9 recession had decimated education funding throughout the state. One city was not enough for the politico that left master politicos awed at how he pursued his "cause with a single-minded fanaticism."[205] Goldman had given Richmond politicians every opportunity to sign on to and even take full credit for an idea that could win elections and help a lot of people. He had no ownership: he wanted them to take credit and offered it up fully formed on a silver platter. When they refused, he took his idea elsewhere, to members of a party that had actually been listening to him, and to voters. Kids in rural Virginia needed good schools, too. "Education is a conservative value: if you work hard, you can make something of yourself," Goldman said.[206]

State Senator Bill Stanley represented parts of southern Virginia like Galax that had historically supported agriculture and textiles but had

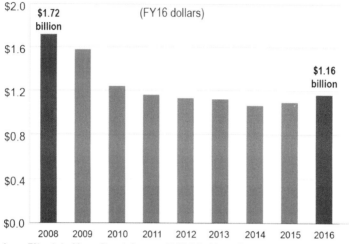

Cuts in Capital Spending

State and local spending on school construction, renovations, and upgrades

$1.72 billion (FY16 dollars)

$1.16 billion

2008 2009 2010 2011 2012 2013 2014 2015 2016

Source: TCI analysis of Census Bureau's Summary of Public School System Finances for Elementary-Secondary Education by State: 2008-2016

THE COMMONWEALTH INSTITUTE

Virginia's spending on school facilities was decimated after the 2008–9 recession. *The Commonwealth Institute.*

suffered deindustrialization and were economically depressed compared to more populous areas of Virginia.[207] The schools there were often just as dilapidated as in Richmond. When the *Roanoke Times* editorial board described the local situation, the place names were different, but the conditions were indistinguishable from what was happening in the capital:

> *At Flatwoods Elementary in Lee County, students and teachers last year had to set out buckets to catch the rain dripping through the roof (the roof has since been repaired). At Jonesville Middle School just up the road, there's another leaking roof plus walls that have separated from the foundation. Flatwoods was built in 1950; Jonesville in 1957. Lee County was a prime beneficiary of that school construction binge in the 1950s. Of its 11 schools, three pre-date World War II; an astonishing seven others were built in the 1950s; only one since then. Unfortunately, that also means Lee County is today often cited as the poster child for those "crumbling schools."[208]*

Unlike Richmond, Stanley's jurisdictions could not reasonably raise enough taxes to pay for much of its school modernization needs. "How can localities afford to upgrade these schools?" the *Roanoke Times* asked in another editorial. "Many simply can't. In Bristol, Highland View Elementary (built in 1935) was declared 'functionally obsolete' in 2011. The city also has been declared 'fiscally distressed' by state auditors. The city can barely pay its bills, much less pay for a new school. And raising taxes to generate more revenue? Forget it: More than 42 percent of the city's residents qualify for some sort of government assistance."[209]

In April 2018, Stanley announced that he would form a bipartisan Senate subcommittee on school modernization and appointed Goldman as policy advisor.[210] Stanley "credited Richmond for 'being the catalyst' in raising an issue plaguing poor school districts."[211] "Stanley said the passage—and subsequent signing by Gov. Ralph Northam—of the Richmond charter change is what inspired the formation of the subcommittee. 'It was a much more serious issue, not just for the city of Richmond, but for the commonwealth of Virginia,' he said."[212] It was a welcome sight for people to see a Democrat and Republican join forces to build good schools, and journalists and editorialists were eager to report and comment on it.[213]

The mind that was always at work had found an untapped source of funds that could be earmarked for school modernization, and he and Stanley penned a joint op-ed to describe their plan. "In his inaugural address, Gov. Northam singled out the growing crisis of educational inequality caused by the increasing number of 'crumbling,' decrepit, dysfunctional school buildings across our state," they wrote. The U.S. Supreme Court had just found that states were owed sales taxes from online shopping. This amounted to maybe $250–$300 million a year in Virginia, just half of which would pay for a $2–$3 billion bond issue. "This still leaves half for other state needs. Moreover, we can achieve this record proposal without raising taxes," they enthused.[214]

The haughty dismissiveness that greeted Goldman in Richmond was counterposed with the hearty enthusiasm that welcomed him in other areas of the state. The political pull of this solution was palpable once Goldman and Stanley started pitching it outside the Richmond bubble. "Norfolk Mayor and former state senator [Kenny] Alexander has asked Stanley's committee to hold hearings there. Alexander sees the politics—and doesn't care. He just wants to help."[215] "Goldman is right," declared the *Roanoke Times* editorial board.

There's the potential for a grand coalition here—rural areas, central cities, even some suburbs. The problem is these are not parts of the state that normally work together, so that grand coalition is not going to just magically happen. It needs somebody to make it happen. We need to have the mayors of Richmond and Norfolk (both African-American Democrats) standing side-by-side with board of supervisor chairmen from Southside and Southwest Virginia (generally white Republicans) to demand action.[216]

IMITATION AND FLATTERY

Stoney was a Clintonian public figure, in the best and worst senses of the word, though his personal life was far less tarnished. The conclusion of this story so often in Richmond's history was that the people who owned the city's private resources also controlled its government. Smart money was on "the business community" co-opting yet another politician, but Stoney was seemingly not as malleable as his predecessor. In August 2018, Stoney called a reporter to tell him that Farrell's proposal was not yet living up to his goals on affordable housing and briefly stalled the negotiations.[217] The trepidation that his designs on higher office would cause him to ignore the city may have been misplaced; the fact that he would need a base of voters for the future could instead serve as a corrective. Stoney was barely elected; Mayor Jones had pursued the same policies Stoney was pursuing and left office with the popularity level of Richard Nixon.[218] There was one reality that proved more indelible than schoolteachers' surgical masks, grandees' Beyoncé fantasies, or any opinion poll or political theory, and that was that 85 percent of Richmond voters wanted him to fix the schools.

In mid-October 2018, Goldman announced that he would pursue a second ballot initiative, "Choosing Children over Costly Coliseums," that would require that 51 percent of money from any tax incremental financing in the city go toward modernizing schools.[219] He had nine months to collect signatures—nine months to let the inevitable landslide vote sit like a sword of Damocles over the mayor's political future.[220] "Levar Stoney should have known better than to play political chess with a grandmaster like Paul Goldman," *Style Weekly* concluded.[221]

Stoney penned an opinion piece in late October 2018, not for his city, but for his hometown *Virginian-Pilot*:

Many of our school buildings are well beyond their lifespan and are literally crumbling. They are no longer the safe, healthy environments our students need to thrive. But these facilities are just one part of the education crisis facing us today—our entire K-12 education system is woefully underfunded....Failing to provide for the most vulnerable among us today is not just unacceptable, it is immoral.[222]

He called on Virginians to join him in marching on the state capitol on December 8.

On November 1, 2018, Stoney unveiled the program that he had kept under wraps during months of secret negotiations. It made a lie of all the financial promises about how "additional" revenue would pay for the construction in the eight-block zone. The TIF district would be expanded from eight to eighty blocks, encompassing essentially all of downtown Richmond and all of its office buildings between First and Tenth Streets and I-95/64 and I-195. The area east of this zone was largely VCU and government-owned, and thus untaxable. Under this program, the additional money that would be needed to pay for citizens' schools, police, firefighters, snow removal, trash pickup, and all the other vital services that cities needed to function would for at least the next thirty years be earmarked to paying back private investors.[223] Goldman's referendum would mandate that 51 percent of any TIF revenue go to schools; under Stoney's plan, only 50 percent of "surplus" revenue after bondholders had been paid back would go toward schools and public services.[224] Sixty years ago, Richmond's power brokers had bulldozed neighborhoods and endowed schools like Collegiate to prevent integration, but they had never dreamed of effectively annexing the city's financial district. The Stoney-Farrell project consummated the final dream of massive resistance by taking the most lucrative and stable revenue source for the city and turning it over to wealthy businessmen for the remainder of this century and beyond.

So far as can be determined, no city in the history of the United States had ever done such a thing. There was no precedent in Virginia since long before the Revolutionary War; one had to go back to the Virginia Company of London, when King James would simply decree that common land belonged to whomever he wanted.[225] In this case, the role of King James was played by the largest campaign donor in the state. It was indescribable.

On December 8, 2018, Stoney led a march of more than a thousand people on the state capitol to call for more funding for education. He said to the crowd:

Mayor Stoney proposed that additional tax revenue from most of Richmond's downtown would be earmarked for a $1.4 billion construction project for thirty years. (Dark area = original area proposal). *Google Earth*.

Each and every day, there is a young man or a young woman who wakes up with a dream, and it is our job—as elected officials, as teachers, all working together—to give them the legs to stand on to achieve that dream.[226]

Whereas Stoney had flashed a smile and easily gotten city council to raise taxes for schools earlier that year, city council bucked the mayor for the first time in an 8–1 vote in mid-December 2018 to establish a commission to review financial details of the increasingly dubious proposal.[227] In January 2019, the majority of council members rejected Dominion money or any donations from Tom Farrell.[228] Days later, Stoney made what could only be described as a deliberate insult to his own voters by submitting a two-page non-binding "plan" that he claimed met his obligations under the referendum.[229] There was just as much construction money to be made from building schools as there was from building an arena; the choice to pick one over the other was a moral judgment.

Robert Caro wrote:

> *Although the cliché says that power always corrupts, what is seldom said, but what is equally true, is that power always* reveals. *When a man is climbing, trying to persuade others to give him power, concealment is necessary: to hide traits that might make others reluctant to give him power, to hide also what he wants to do with that power; if men recognized the traits or realized the aims, they might refuse to give him what he wants. But as a man obtains more power, camouflage is less necessary. The curtain begins to rise. The revealing begins.*[230]

Though the public was clear on its priorities, it seemed sometimes as if Mayor Stoney, the humble kid and ambitious pol, was torn between the two Richmonds. It seemed that way, that is, until one saw that Stoney just did whatever his donors wanted. "Choosing children over costly coliseums" required the tripartite realization that it was good politics, it was the right thing to do, and that blind fealty to the Virginia Way was a lost cause.

4

LAWMAKING

HEALTHCARE AND MEDICAID EXPANSION

Are you unaware that vast numbers of your fellow men suffer or perish from need
of the things that you have to excess?
—*Jean-Jacques Rousseau*

The most consequential partisan battle in Virginia state government during these years was the debate over whether to accept federal funds to expand Medicaid health insurance to nearly half a million working Virginians. There were myriad economic and ideological considerations, but in hindsight, the basic contours of the political battle were that the Republican legislature would only agree to this if there was a Democratic governor in office whom legislators happened to like personally. Governor Terry McAuliffe, a brash New York politico, made it the centerpiece of his legislative agenda for four years, but he failed; Governor Ralph Northam, a reserved Virginia aristocrat, succeeded him, and the legislature passed Medicaid expansion by May of his first year in office. In McAuliffe's term, he enjoyed a split Senate that was functionally Democratic because Lieutenant Governor Northam could break ties; when Northam took the reins in 2018, he faced a Senate in Republican control. A number of Republican legislators who had remained implacably opposed to Medicaid expansion for years flipped within weeks of Northam's inauguration. This chapter explores why.

MEDICAID POLITICS IN STATE AND NATION

The ability of states to voluntarily expand Medicaid coverage with the federal government picking up most of the cost was a consequence of the contentious politics of the Obama presidency. Prior to the passage of the Affordable Care Act/Obamacare, states would receive matching federal funds for Medicaid insurance ranging from 50 to about 73 percent based on a sliding scale related to a state's wealth.[1] The states had different eligibility requirements for receiving Medicaid, and some set the income levels very low. Virginia "had one of the most restrictive Medicaid programs in the nation, ranking 46th among states in per-capita spending." Disabled people's yearly incomes were capped at $9,700, a family of three could have only up to $6,900 annual income, and adults without children were not eligible, no matter how poor. The ACA/Obamacare mandated that states would provide Medicaid to citizens earning up to 138 percent of the federal poverty level, or $28,677 for a family of three and $16,754 per year for individuals.[2] In a controversial 5–4 opinion that many viewed as a political compromise, the U.S. Supreme Court in 2012 upheld the constitutionality of most of Obamacare while voting 7–2 to make expansion of Medicaid optional rather than mandatory for each state.[3]

A large majority of states chose to expand Medicaid, and as the decade progressed, their number continued to grow. Adoption had begun in liberal states, and by 2019, a number of conservative states had joined them, including legislatively in Louisiana, West Virginia, and Indiana when Vice President Mike Pence had served as governor there, and through ballot referendums in Idaho, Nebraska, and Utah. The Medicaid reimbursement rates under Obamacare were much higher, and unlike the states, the federal government could run continual deficits if it did so sustainably and modestly. The federal reimbursements for state expenditures on Medicaid expansion was 100 percent through 2016, "95 percent in 2017, 94 percent in 2018, 93 percent in 2019, and then 90 percent in 2020 and beyond."[4] Most state and local government programs received matching funds (as an example, about half of all Virginia state revenues came from the federal government in the 2018–20 biennial budget), but few offered such a high level of reimbursement.[5]

Stories of the sick and destitute Virginians who would benefit from Medicaid expansion revealed tragedies that citizens suffered through no fault of their own. For example:

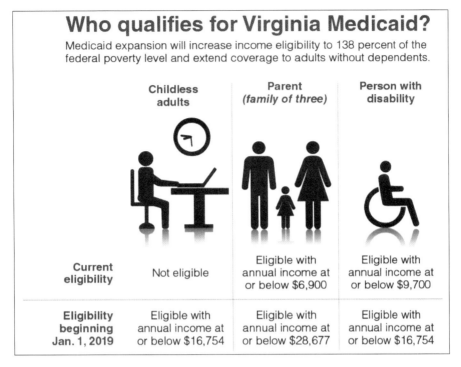

Who qualifies for Virginia Medicaid?

Medicaid expansion will increase income eligibility to 138 percent of the federal poverty level and extend coverage to adults without dependents.

	Childless adults	Parent *(family of three)*	Person with disability
Current eligibility	Not eligible	Eligible with annual income at or below $6,900	Eligible with annual income at or below $9,700
Eligibility beginning Jan. 1, 2019	Eligible with annual income at or below $16,754	Eligible with annual income at or below $28,677	Eligible with annual income at or below $16,754

Virginia Medicaid eligibility with and without expansion. *CoverVA.org*.

Eunice Haigler of Fredericksburg is blind in one eye and lacks peripheral vision in the other as a result of a brain tumor that pressed too long on her optic nerve. She needs eyeglasses and has nearly exhausted the medication required to keep the part of the tumor that couldn't be surgically removed from growing. She's also about to run out of the prescription medicines that regulate her thyroid and blood pressure and provide the cortisone her body no longer produces on its own. Haigler, 63, lost her Medicaid coverage in December after taking on a one-day-a-week job at a day care center needed to supplement her disability income and put food on her table, she said.[6]

Virginians lived under a system that discouraged a poor woman with a brain tumor from working for fear that she would lose health insurance, and the Supreme Court's ruling kept this perverse incentive in place. It was even more galling that part-time legislators had voted to bestow upon themselves full-time insurance, which "paid for the weight-reduction surgery of at least one senator."[7] As if to reinforce the point, Speaker of the House William Howell took time off from his mission of blocking coverage expansion to

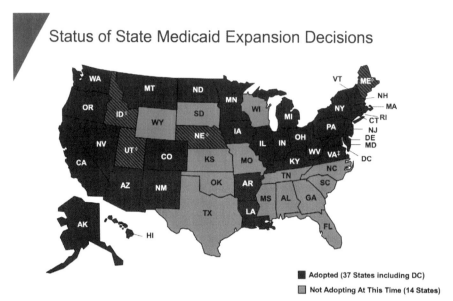

Status of State Medicaid Expansion Decisions

■ Adopted (37 States including DC)

■ Not Adopting At This Time (14 States)

NOTES: Current status for each state is based on KFF tracking and analysis of state activity. °Expansion is adopted but not yet implemented in ID, ME, NE, and UT. ‡VA began enrollment on November 1, 2018 for Medicaid expansion coverage that will take effect on January 1, 2019. (See link below for additional state-specific notes).
SOURCE: "Status of State Action on the Medicaid Expansion Decision," KFF State Health Facts, updated November 26, 2018.
https://www.kff.org/health-reform/state-indicator/state-activity-around-expanding-medicaid-under-the-affordable-care-act/

KFF
HENRY J. KAISER
FAMILY FOUNDATION

Map of Medicaid expansion by state, November 2018. *Kaiser Family Foundation.*

undergo hip replacement surgery at VCU Medical Center, courtesy of Virginia taxpayers.[8]

The human suffering was real, and the financial numbers behind expanding Medicaid in Virginia showed just how consequential the issue was. In addition to providing health insurance to an estimated 400,000 people, the program would create 23,000 jobs.[9] In addition, the money was needed in rural and urban health centers. The healthcare industry benefited immensely from Obamacare by receiving additional millions of customers and trillions of dollars in spending, but the windfall was attenuated through decreasing Medicare subsidies to insurers. Obamacare offered an overall increase in funding for hospitals and clinics through decreasing Medicare and increasing Medicaid eligibility and payments. The Supreme Court's decision disrupted that, and what resulted was an unintended version of Obamacare that cost hospitals and other healthcare providers money. The nonprofit Bon Secours Virginia Health System faced "$55.6 million in cuts in federal Medicare payments in the next two years" in its system of seven hospitals, but it "could more than offset those losses with an estimated

$134.7 million in revenues if Virginia expand[ed] its Medicaid program." The ten hospitals of the for-profit HCA Virginia Health System stood to lose a total of more than $25 million each year under the law, but that decreased to about $6.5 million if Virginia accepted the more generous Medicaid reimbursements.

Money to expand Medicaid was enticing from a state legislator's perspective. Actuaries in Virginia's Medicaid office estimated in 2014 that the state budget would save an estimated $1 billion through 2022.[10] Even when federal reimbursement rates decreased to 90 percent, the net cost to Virginia would be $3 million per year in a state of 8 million residents.[11] The Virginia Hospital and Healthcare Association was on board with expansion, and it was by far Virginia's largest healthcare industry donor, contributing about $5 million to candidates over twenty years, compared with $11.3 million from Dominion and $6.5 million from Altria/Philip Morris.[12] The state's academic medical centers functioned in their own right as economic engines, political players, and regional hospitals of last resort for people who did not have health insurance. The University of Virginia and Virginia Commonwealth University and their phalanxes of lobbyists could not be entirely ignored in Richmond.[13] There was no limit to how Virginia legislators could spend such savings, whether for schools, roads, tax cuts, patronage, or all of the above. Most critical to the anticipated cost savings was that Virginia was already bearing much of the expense of healthcare for low-income people through uncompensated charity and safety net care at emergency rooms and state institutions.[14] For example, Virginia spent $6,500 per prisoner per year on healthcare. Other than Kansas, Virginia had the most austere medical clemency policy in the United States; terminally ill patients could only be granted release if they had less than three months to live, long after most had become too infirm to commit any more crimes.[15]

Observers judging Virginia's fight over Obamacare through a conventional liberal versus conservative lens would have concluded that the issue was stalemated. All the biggest names in the Democratic grassroots, including "Virginia New Majority, Virginia Interfaith Center for Public Policy, Virginia Coalition of Latino Americans, Virginia AFL-CIO, SEIU Virginia 512, ProgressVA, Planned Parenthood Advocates of Virginia and AARP Virginia," were on board with expanding Medicaid.[16] On the other hand, repealing Obamacare had been a veritable raison d'être of the Republican Party since 2010 and was the province of conservative organizations like Americans for Prosperity.[17] But observers viewing the

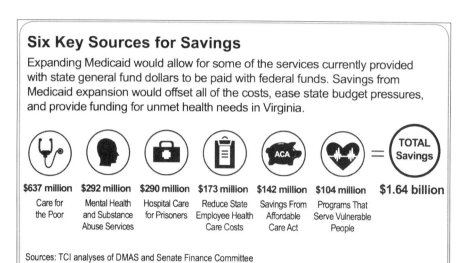

Virginia was already paying for much of the charity and safety net care that the federal government would largely cover if the state legislature accepted Medicaid expansion. The Commonwealth Institute.

machinations through the Virginia Way theory of government could predict that the gravitational pull of donors' money would eventually tip Republicans into supporting that which they claimed to abhor. That is precisely what happened.

2014: TOEING THE PARTY LINE

Terry McAuliffe understood as much and made expanding Medicaid the top policy issue of his 2013 gubernatorial campaign. He won a narrow victory against an adversary who made opposition to Obamacare his own principal policy point, and who had even sued the federal government to stop it, so McAuliffe was able to state with some justification that this was the issue on which he was elected.[18] He did everything that he could to achieve it while in office. The Virginia Senate was split 20–20, but moderate Republicans would go along with the measure.[19] Republicans controlled the Virginia House by 67–33, in what was and may forever remain the high-water mark for the greatest number of Republicans serving in that chamber in Virginia history.[20]

Like many statewide politicians in Virginia's recent history, McAuliffe was a transplant. Unlike Tim Kaine, who was born in Minnesota but married a Virginia governor's daughter, McAuliffe had shallow Virginia roots and tenuous Richmond connections. Fundamentally, McAuliffe was a national Democratic political operative who happened to have Virginia residency by virtue of the fact that he lived in the Virginia suburbs of the D.C. metro area.[21]

Yet it was a mistake to dismiss McAuliffe as a dilettante. Just after Christmas 2014, the governor was thrown off a horse while vacationing in Tanzania with his family. He "could not move or talk for five or six minutes but…he eventually managed to get up," and, evidently, either assumed he was fine or did not care. Though he kept his full schedule and had to sleep sitting up because of the pain, he neglected to tell anyone on his staff about the accident for more than two weeks. When he walked across the street from the Governor's Mansion to VCU Medical Center, doctors took an x-ray and told him that he had broken seven ribs and punctured his lung in several places; blood pooling in his lung was causing shortness of breath. McAuliffe's reaction was, "I've got a State of the Commonwealth in two days. I can't be coming in here." The doctors replied that "there's a chance that the blood could assimilate naturally into your system," and the governor declared, "Great, let's try that." He gave the speech, continued his duties, and never drew any attention to the matter until he had to be hospitalized for it five days later after the pulse oximeter he was self-monitoring showed the blood was still pooling and that he had dangerously low oxygen levels. During his hospital stay, he kept up his daily routine of rising at 4:45 in the morning and going nonstop until around 11:00 p.m. "My father would never go to the expense of paying for Novocaine, when we were children, to have our cavities filled," McAuliffe said. "It was just not in the nature—Irish, you tough it up. Yeah, if you had four cavities [and] you went in and they drilled on the raw nerve, that's just life."[22]

McAuliffe utilized an intriguing tack in calling for Medicaid expansion and a number of other liberal priorities. He knew, as any poll-reader could, that jobs were voters' number one priority; his predecessor, Bob McDonnell, had campaigned on the catchphrase, "Bob's for Jobs."[23] McAuliffe's strategy was to subsume the social issues that distinguished Virginia's two political parties into an economic platform in which Democratic social issues were good for business. For example, when Governor Pence drew national condemnation for a 2015 law that would have permitted businesses to discriminate against gay people under a dubiously constitutional religious freedom doctrine, McAuliffe penned an open letter to the *Indianapolis Star* inviting businesses to come to Virginia for its low taxes because "we do not discriminate against our friends and neighbors, particularly those who are supporting local businesses and generating economic activity."[24] McAuliffe vetoed a bill similar to Indiana's in 2016 and issued a statement that "this legislation is also bad for business and creates roadblocks as we try to build the new Virginia economy. Businesses and job creators do not want to locate or do business in states that appear more concerned with demonizing people than with creating a strong business climate."[25] He asserted in his 2017 State of the Commonwealth address that Virginia should support gay and abortion rights because "attacks on equality and women's healthcare rights don't just embarrass the states that engage in them—they kill jobs."[26]

McAuliffe made the pro-business case for Medicaid coverage expansion in his inaugural address.

> *Like the majority of other states, we need to act on the consensus of the business community and health care industry to accept funding that will expand health care coverage, save rural hospitals, and spur job creation. With a stronger health care system in Virginia as our objective, I will work with the legislature to build on the Medicaid reforms that the General Assembly has already achieved, and to put Virginians' own tax dollars to work keeping families healthy and creating jobs here in the Commonwealth.*[27]

He repeatedly signaled he was willing to cut a deal on healthcare in exchange for using budget savings on Republican priorities such as small business tax cuts.[28]

McAuliffe put his "sleep when you're dead" maxim to the test in trying to work with a House of Delegates firmly in the hands of another party.[29] "McAuliffe devoted the nine weeks between Election Day and his inauguration to ardently wooing Republicans with moderate Cabinet picks, face-to-face meetings and lavish praise for" outgoing Governor McDonnell, who would soon be indicted.[30] He made the pro-business case as best he could and re-appointed both McDonnell's secretary of health and his secretary of finance.[31] McAuliffe also reached out to the capital crowd socially. The Governor's Mansion shared grounds with the state legislature and was well situated for hosting. McAuliffe announced that he would throw "sixty parties in sixty days!" during the legislative session. He replaced the rotgut and swill that customarily greeted revelers with "top-shelf liquors and microbrews at his own expense," in case anyone had forgotten McDonnell's troubles with spending other people's money on luxuries for himself. "Everybody's more charming after a few drinks," enthused Senator Tom Garrett, who would resign from Congress in 2018 to seek treatment for alcoholism. McAuliffe also picked up the tab for daily catered breakfasts. Then again, newspaper articles about how the governor was trying to use food and alcohol to ingratiate himself with Republicans did not come across well. "Clearly he's trying to be friendly, but I'll watch my wallet over there," concluded Delegate Bob Marshall.[32]

At the same time McAuliffe was affably entertaining Republican legislators, he was pushing hard publicly and privately for them to expand Medicaid. The decision to do so rested with Virginia's Medicaid Innovation and Reform Commission (MIRC), which had been set up under McDonnell as part of a legislative compromise. Essentially, Democrats agreed to increase taxes by nearly $1 billion per year to pay for McDonnell's transportation package in exchange for giving MIRC the power to expand Medicaid after an open-ended review process.[33] Granting this authority to another body meant that the policy could be enacted with only a handful of Republicans on the commission taking a politically difficult vote on the issue. While this compromise was billed as historic, Republicans were soon backtracking, and McDonnell subsequently labeled the commission a "firewall against expansion."[34] The commission would have to secure the support of three out of five delegates on the panel; the four Republicans on it were opposed, as was the lone Democrat, who was, not coincidentally, the most conservative Democrat in the legislature.[35] McDonnell's final budget proposal (which outgoing governors always introduced but never enacted themselves because of Virginia's unique, four-year gubernatorial term limits) mandated that any expansion would end by mid-2016, pending another MIRC-like review.[36]

It was a tough nut to crack. McAuliffe wanted this provision stripped and an amendment inserted that would compel MIRC to finish its work in a few months, but this was a non-starter for Republicans.[37] McAuliffe then sought to give himself the authority to expand Medicaid if MIRC did not finish its work, but this was substantially the same as what he had been requesting, and Republicans rejected that, too. "We have been very clear we're not going to expand Medicaid this session," said House Majority Leader Kirk Cox. "The governor seems to find a new way every day to expand Medicaid."[38]

It was clear that Virginia Republicans would follow the Washington trend of refusing to work with chief executives of the opposite party for the entirety of their terms. Scorched-earth opposition was facilitated by Virginia's constitutional prohibition on governors serving more than one consecutive term: it was easier to wait out a governor for four years than it was for Congress to wait out a president for eight. Though there were exceptions, Virginia's Republican politicians largely did not like McAuliffe, did not trust him, and had no intention of working with him on healthcare. To them, McAuliffe was an interloper who was friends with the Clintons and had the audacity to not be born in Virginia. "The honeymoon is over," declared Jeff Schapiro, the Bob Woodward doppelgänger and dean of Virginia's political columnists, less than one month after McAuliffe's inauguration. "But there never really was one to begin with."[39]

Democrats received some help when Lynwood Lewis was certified as the victor by just eleven votes out of more than twenty thousand cast in a special election held for the Senate seat that Ralph Northam vacated when he won election as lieutenant governor.[40] Lewis's win split the chamber 20–20, but Democrats were able to seize power because Northam could cast tie-breaking votes on almost all issues except the budget.[41] Democrats quickly reorganized the Senate to place themselves in charge of committees that were vital to the passage of legislation.[42] The victory did not so much change the underlying dynamics of Medicaid expansion in that chamber (three Republicans still supported expanding coverage) so much as it gave Democrats political momentum.[43]

Within a week, moderate Senate Republicans unveiled "Marketplace Virginia," which was billed as a compromise in which the state would use Medicaid expansion dollars to pay for private insurance coverage.[44] "The idea is we're not going to expand Medicaid, but we're going to cover the people it would be responsible for covering," said Senator John Watkins. "This proposal is simply Obamacare's Medicaid expansion by a different name," Speaker of the House Howell retorted—and though the proposal also called for work requirements and income-adjusted copays, he was more or less correct.[45] Democratic Senators strengthened their hand by attaching Marketplace Virginia to their budget bill, which absolutely had to pass both chambers by July 1, unless legislators wanted to play Russian roulette with their careers by shutting down the government.[46]

Marketplace Virginia was an important development in a duel that was becoming less about policy options and more about political optics. It had the imprimatur of a private business plan that would allow recalcitrant Republicans to claim victory while voting for a Democratic priority. The Virginia Chamber of Commerce illustrated this well when a poll of its members found a majority both opposed Medicaid expansion and supported Marketplace Virginia.[47] The announcement broke a floodwall of support that, it seemed, had been awaiting just such political cover. Notwithstanding McAuliffe's suspect pedigree and salesmanship, a party and state that claimed to revere business was faced with a growing chorus of business supporters that nobody could fairly dismiss as liberal agitators. Joining the Virginia Hospital and Healthcare Association, UVA, and VCU were other industry forces like insurance companies and independent hospitals across the state.[48] Republicans whose party loyalty could not be questioned—like former lieutenant governor Bill Bolling, three other McDonnell cabinet officials, and Bill Goodwin, the party's most prolific donor—championed the issue in public and private.[49] McDonnell's former transportation secretary had shepherded the historic transportation deal through the legislature the previous year; in early 2014, he took a job as head of the Virginia Hospital and Healthcare Association.[50] Proponents of expanding Medicaid secured the ultimate pro-business bonafides when they garnered the support of the Virginia Chamber of Commerce.[51] "Normally, business interests like chambers of commerce and hospitals can count on pretty cooperative Republicans and legislatures. But that traditional alliance has really broken down," remarked Professor Stephen Farnsworth of the University of Mary Washington. The National Federation of Independent Business and Americans for Prosperity still opposed expansion, but those groups had become relative outliers: the main opposition came from the conservative grassroots.[52]

With both sides dug in, each day of inaction moved the state government closer toward a shutdown for the first time in Virginia history.[53] The Senate and the House passed their respective budgets, but only the former included Marketplace Virginia.[54] The conference committee where senior legislators from both parties and chambers typically forged compromise by cutting deals behind closed doors also found itself at an impasse.[55] McAuliffe left no stone unturned. He abandoned his velvet glove strategy and began twisting arms by threatening House Republicans with loss of funds for the patronage projects they needed for their districts; naturally, they went to the press.[56] He launched a campaign-style tour in which he held press conferences at hospitals across the state that stood to benefit from Marketplace Virginia and pointedly included a hospital in Speaker Howell's district.[57] The yearly legislative session ended in March without compromise on the budget.[58] When the legislature met to consider vetoes later that month, McAuliffe called Republicans' bluff and offered to begin the program as a two-year pilot, just as McDonnell had purportedly wanted; the proposal was voted down in the House Appropriations Committee that day.[59] Even Speaker

Howell acknowledged that a shutdown would be "disastrous for the state....I sure wouldn't want to be governor when we lost our AAA bond rating for the first time in state history."[60] Chris Jones, chairman of the House Appropriations Committee, predicted that "our teachers would not get paid...law enforcement wouldn't get paid. [The Virginia Department of Transportation] would probably have to shut down, and we'd have to lay state employees off"—and concluded by blaming Democrats.[61] The battle was becoming a self-fulfilling prophecy. A poll taken in April showed that in just two months, support for expansion had plummeted from 55 percent to 11 percent of Republicans and climbed from 58 percent to 77 percent of Democrats.[62] As if to reinforce their disingenuousness, in their budget, Republican delegates were offering to increase Medicaid funding by a substantial $118.6 million over two years, so long as it was paid for by the state and did not come with a match from the dreaded Obamacare.[63] The fight was no longer about numbers, or business, or healthcare; it had even come to transcend the normal give-and-take of politics. Medicaid expansion had become fundamental to both sides' identities. Both parties were driving toward a cliff, and neither one would be the first to tap the brakes.[64]

Virginia's politicians clung to their immutable and irreconcilable visions as they hurtled toward the July 1 shutdown deadline, until, in early June, a political earthquake moved the ground beneath their feet. On June 8, Senator Phil Puckett (D) announced that he would resign his seat, thus giving Republicans 20–19 control of that chamber.[65] Though the three moderate Republicans would remain, the Republican Senate leader could block votes and organize committee representation to ensure that Marketplace Virginia was killed.[66] Most importantly, Republicans now possessed the political momentum to do so: it had become the governor against a unified legislature, and no governor could win that fight.[67] Four days after the resignation was announced, both the Senate and House passed the same budget, without Medicaid expansion, and almost entirely on party lines.[68] In a last-ditch effort, McAuliffe signed the budget, but line-item vetoed a provision that prevented him from accepting Medicaid funds via an arcane executive order mechanism. The Speaker put a stop to any such attempt when he cleverly ruled that this veto was procedurally out of order and not subject to any further legislative vote.[69]

The circumstances of Puckett's resignation quickly came under scrutiny. His daughter, Martha Ketron, served as an interim family district court judge, but a full appointment had been delayed by the legislature "in part due to a tradition against awarding bench appointments to family members of sitting legislators," according to a report.[70] This stance was odd, to say the least, given that the Virginia Way was built upon cozy conflicts of interest and the House had already voted to support her nomination. (In 2019, the House and Senate would install Senator Ben Chafin's sister and former law partner Teresa to a judgeship on the Virginia Supreme Court in a unanimous vote after Senator Chafin lobbied on her behalf.[71]) At the same time, Republican Delegate Terry Kilgore chaired the Virginia Tobacco Commission that distributed hundreds of millions of dollars from Virginia's share of the tobacco company Master Settlement Agreement that paid governments back for costs incurred due to smoking.[72] Emails uncovered under the Freedom of Information Act showed "that the GOP-controlled commission appeared to create a position solely for Puckett and even solicited his input in crafting the job description."[73]

Democratic cries of foul play came across as especially sanctimonious when it came out that McAuliffe had enlisted every Democratic leader in the state to try to convince Puckett to stay and, when he failed, told people that Puckett could "rot in hell."[74] McAuliffe's chief of staff had left a voicemail on Puckett's phone imploring him: "If there's something that we can do for [your daughter], I mean, you know, we have a couple of big agencies here that still need agency heads. We could potentially, potentially, subject to approval of the governor and so forth, you know, the Department of Mines, Minerals and Energy could be available. So we would be very eager to accommodate her, if, if that would be helpful in keeping you in the Senate. We, we would basically do anything." U.S. Senator Mark Warner also mentioned various opportunities for Ketron in a call to Puckett's son that Warner later claimed was just "brainstorming."[75] The day after Puckett announced his resignation, he also announced he was withdrawing his name from consideration for the tobacco commission job.[76] McAuliffe left a voicemail of his own for Puckett, saying "Medicaid is done. I hope you sleep easy tonight, buddy."[77] Democrats were complaining because they got outmaneuvered.[78]

This may have seemed business-as-usual for the Virginia Way, but the FBI and Department of Justice did not share that sentiment. Within ten days, the U.S. Attorney's Office for the Western District of Virginia had empaneled a grand jury and subpoenaed documents from the tobacco commission.[79] The parties were cleared of any illegality, and Kilgore's attorney, Thomas Cullen, would be appointed the U.S. Attorney for that same Western District of Virginia in 2018.[80] Republicans appointed Puckett's daughter to her coveted judgeship when the legislature reconvened the following January.[81] By the midpoint of McAuliffe's term, Virginia would be the only state in the nation led by a Democratic governor that had not expanded Medicaid.[82] There was nothing more to be done: as McAuliffe said, "Medicaid is done," and it would be for as long as he remained in office.[83]

2018: SAME STORY, DIFFERENT RESULT

Elected politicians have to be charming and likeable almost by definition, and Ralph Northam was no more or less likeable than Terry McAuliffe. But Northam was an army doctor who had chaired the Honor Court at Virginia Military Institute, whereas McAuliffe had been a political operative who had chaired Hillary Clinton's 2008 presidential campaign.[84] As a pediatric neurologist in the state's best children's hospital, Northam harbored a softer persona and was more than smart enough to play his Eastern Shore drawl to his advantage.[85] He also knew the arguments, counterarguments, and counter-counterarguments for a dozen healthcare debates as well as or better than any legislator in the state.

Most importantly, Northam and McAuliffe's policies were all but indistinguishable, the most notable difference being that Northam campaigned on increasing the minimum wage to fifteen dollars an hour, which had become a tenet of the national Democratic Party over the last four years.[86] McAuliffe may not have been well-liked among Republican legislators, but his administration was relatively scandal-free, the economy was doing well, and his approval rating during his term hovered in the low to mid-50s, while President Trump garnered approval ratings in the mid-30s in Virginia.[87] It was easy to understand that Northam would run his 2017 campaign promising to build on McAuliffe's legacy.[88] Just before the transfer of power, McAuliffe and Northam held a joint press conference in which they pledged unity and continuity. Northam would reappoint many of McAuliffe's top officials, and those who left could merely hand over the briefing books to their successors. "This has been the smoothest, easiest transition in Virginia history," McAuliffe purred, for once perhaps not speaking with hyperbole.[89] McAuliffe's final budget submission included Medicaid expansion, as had all his previous budgets, though this time it was paid for by increasing taxes on hospitals that would benefit from the program.[90]

Northam faced a legislature even more firmly in Republican hands in 2018 than McAuliffe had faced in 2014. The 2017 blue wave had lopped fifteen seats off the Republican majority in the House, but, as in 2014, there was not a single defector among the bunch. The fact that the majority had slimmed from sixty-six to fifty-one would not change the predicted outcome. Moreover, the Senate was firmly in Republican hands: of the three moderates who had supported coverage expansion in 2014, only one remained in 2018.[91] There were twenty firm *no* votes on Medicaid expansion in the Senate, and the newly elected lieutenant governor, Democrat Justin Fairfax, could not constitutionally vote on the budget even in the event of a tie.

Yet Northam did not make the same pro-business pitches that McAuliffe did. In his inaugural address, Northam said:

> *We all have a moral compass deep in our hearts. And it is time to summon it again, because we have a lot of work to do. We're going in the wrong direction on health care in Virginia and America. More people need coverage, not less. It is past time for us to step forward together and expand Medicaid to nearly 400,000 Virginians who need access to care.*[92]

He repeated this theme in his first speech to the legislature. "That was the worst partisan speech I've ever heard!" said House Appropriations Vice Chairman Steve Landes.[93] Jeff Schapiro had marked the end of McAuliffe's honeymoon by February 2014; in 2018, a similar Schapiro column landed just a week into Northam's term.[94] Republicans and Democrats dug into their soundbites, offered various versions of the same proposals, and sniped at one another in the press. The Senate health committee killed expansion bills along party lines at the end of January.[95] History was repeating itself.

Until it suddenly stopped repeating. Speaker Howell had retired, and Kirk Cox had risen to command the slim Republican House majority. At the end of January, he wrote an open letter to Northam that promised to work with the governor on expanding Medicaid if it included work requirements for non-disabled adults.[96] This might have been dismissed as another delaying tactic, but Cox's own committee voted the next day to impose work requirements on Medicaid beneficiaries as a step toward negotiations with Democrats on coverage expansion. The playing field had shifted dramatically, and the debate was now over what sort of situations would qualify for a work exemption.[97] Speaker Cox wanted to cut a deal.[98]

Delegate Terry Kilgore, whom we have seen both in the bribery investigation of Senator Puckett and pictured with a trophy full of fake cash, announced in mid-February that he had flipped on the issue. Expanding Medicaid was important, he argued, because "the time has come to begin growing our Southwest Virginia economy again—and we must start with ensuring we have a healthy workforce."[99] Whether or not one believed this viewpoint had merit, the man had done everything in his power for the past six years to try to prevent what he now wholeheartedly endorsed. By this logic, Kilgore was admitting that he had harmed the economy and made his constituents sicker for years.

In theory, the personality of the Democrat occupying the Governor's Mansion should make no difference at all in a legislator's vote: one either supports or does not support a proposed law. For all the appeals to immutable principles, House Republicans were on board with expanding Medicaid just as soon as Governor McAuliffe left office. In fact, Republicans were now supporting a Medicaid expansion program that had grown less generous and more costly to the state because of the delay; the window for 100 percent reimbursement by the federal government had passed. The version Republicans ended up supporting in 2018 was much closer to traditional, Great Society Medicaid than the private insurance-based Marketplace Virginia plan that had supposedly been too reckless to pass in 2014. Scholars and journalists pointed to the 2017 elections as giving momentum to Medicaid expansion; perhaps they were correct, but this explanation was not entirely convincing.[100] In 2018, House Republicans served districts so red that they had just survived the largest Democratic wave in thirty years; if anything, House Republicans should have been more ideologically conservative because the swing districts were now occupied by Democrats. The measure was just as toxic among Republican grassroots activists: the Virginia Tea Party signaled the import of the matter by scoring just two bills in the 2018 session—the Dominion corporate welfare bill and Medicaid expansion. Republicans in conservative districts in 2018 had much more to worry about from primary or convention challenges from their base than they did from the Democratic blue wave that they had all survived.[101] In the final House vote on the matter, eighteen Republicans flipped, and the budget with expansion passed 67–31 with two abstentions.[102] Republican Senate Leader Norment was asked to explain why the legislature flipped. He and Northam had both attended VMI, years apart. "I consider him a friend," he said. What about McAuliffe? a reporter asked. Norment wished him well "as he speeds in his little green car down to Alabama," referring to one of McAuliffe's failed business ventures.[103] Years of obstruction followed by support of Medicaid expansion was carried out seemingly for no reason whatsoever other than interpersonal spite.

The Republican-controlled Senate initially proved as resistant to Medicaid expansion at it always had, and there was a lot of gnashing of teeth, but donors ultimately got what they wanted.[104] Senator Frank Wagner was best known for reliably and uncritically carrying bills written by Dominion's lawyers while denying it was tied to the boatloads of money he received from the company; like Terry Kilgore, he was for sale to the highest bidder.[105] He flipped his vote in early April, giving expansion a 21–19 majority in the Senate; there would be some maneuvering around the edges on work requirements and the hospital tax, but passage had become a fait accompli.[106] Perhaps there was some electoral justification for this—Northam won Wagner's district by seven points—but Wagner's votes for the Dominion bills in 2015 and 2018 were deeply unpopular among essentially everyone who was not paid by Dominion, and two other Republicans in swing districts did not flip.[107] Electoral reasons certainly did not and could not explain the votes of three other Republican senators—all of whom were in deeply conservative districts—who ended up voting for expansion.[108] Emmett Hanger had supported expansion throughout the McAuliffe years on principle, so his vote was no surprise. In a wry twist, Republican Ben Chafin replaced Phil Puckett and fought hard against expansion for four years; he flipped on the final vote. So did Jill Holtzman Vogel, who, like McAuliffe, had cut her teeth for the national party in the D.C.–Virginia suburbs.[109] Electoral self-interest could not explain the nineteen Republican delegates who voted for the final budget.[110] It was hard to see how giving Democrats a win on their biggest issue helped Republicans, and harder to imagine Republicans doing something more antagonistic to their grassroots activists than voting to raise taxes on hospitals to pay for expanding Obamacare. It was as if all the ink that had been spilled over nearly a decade as Republicans proclaimed fealty to their highest values evaporated into air and miraculously condensed into the opposite position. Love of money and hatred of McAuliffe were the only explanations that made sense.

As citizens witnessed time and time again, there was a bipartisan consensus that transcended partisanship. "It feels like the right thing, done the right way, by the right people, and that's the Virginia way," said a lobbyist for the Virginia Hospital and Healthcare Association at the bill signing on the capitol steps.[111] In June 2018, the Greene County

Republican Committee unanimously passed a resolution censuring its state senator, Emmett Hanger, for his vote on Medicaid expansion; by the end of that year, healthcare companies and lobbying groups were Hanger's five largest campaign contributors for his 2019 reelection bid; he won his June 2019 primary challenge from a conservative who made his Medicaid vote the top issue.[112] A poll of Virginians in September 2018 showed a deep well of support for Medicaid expansion: 76 percent for, 18 percent against, and the rest undecided.[113] Under the Virginia Way, money was a revolutionary force.

DEMOCRACY

VOTING RIGHTS, GERRYMANDERING, AND ELECTIONS

Our goal is to make the Democratic districts, particularly the marginal ones,
a bit better than they are now.
—*Democratic Senate leader Dick Saslaw*

Never in the remainder of our chronological life is
the House of Delegates going Democratic.
—*Republican Senate leader Tommy Norment*

I n a system of government in which politicians viewed themselves as walking in the mythical footsteps of the Founding Fathers, voters were remarkably removed from making decisions about their own society. Virginia's bipartisan economic consensus dictated that citizens' lives did not change much when this or that Republican or Democrat came into office. One hidebound aspect of the Virginia Way was the extent to which it functioned as an anti-politics machine that discouraged citizen participation: politicians proclaimed the highest ideals of democracy and republicanism even as they instituted some of the most restrictive electoral laws in the country. The sacred right to vote should not have been subject to partisan machinations, but under the Virginia Way, it became a window into the exercise of power that showed both parties and all three branches of government at their worst.

The unusual staggering of Virginia's state and federal elections was one way in which democracy was discouraged, intentionally or not. The origin of Virginia's gubernatorial off-year elections (the year after presidential elections, e.g., 2013, 2017) and off-off-year state senate elections (the year before presidential elections, e.g., 2015, 2019) was not a result of prejudice or political self-interest; it was "pure accident." Virginia's post–Civil War constitution called for gubernatorial elections in the year that it was ratified, which happened to be 1869, the year after a presidential election.[1] This was not designed as a discriminatory matter, as some assumed: in fact, that constitution enfranchised black men and was submitted to voters with a measure that would have disenfranchised many Confederate soldiers who had committed treason, though this measure was ultimately voted down.[2] The odd timing of elections continued in every constitutional revision since then. The practical effect was that voter turnout plummeted in gubernatorial and state senatorial election years.

Year	Turnout	Election Type
2018	58.6%	Congressional midterms
2017	47.6%	Gubernatorial
2016	72.1%	Presidential
2015	29.1%	State senate
2014	41.6%	Congressional midterms
2013	43.0%	Gubernatorial
2012	71.1%	Presidential
2011	28.6%	State senate
2010	44.0%	Congressional midterms
2009	40.4%	Gubernatorial
2008	74.0%	Presidential
2007	30.2%	State senate
2006	52.7%	Congressional midterms
2005	45.0%	Gubernatorial
2004	70.8%	Presidential

Year	Turnout	Election Type
2003	30.8%	State senate
2002	31.6%	Congressional midterms
2001	46.4%	Gubernatorial
2000	67.2%	Presidential

Virginia voter turnout in November general elections, 2000–2018. Virginia Department of Elections.

Virginia's electoral battles shaped how elections were carried out long before citizens entered voting booths. Many other electoral policies were pernicious, their origins were in modern times, and they were not accidental.

VOTING RIGHTS: GUBERNATORIAL PARDONS AND LEGISLATIVE RESTRICTIONS

It was an unfortunate symptom of partisanship that debates over voting rights in Virginia increasingly broke down over partisan divisions. By 2020, both sides could claim the other was engaging in bad faith efforts to influence elections.

Voting rights for convicted felons who had served their time was an issue that became unfairly and rapidly polarized with the ascension of Terry McAuliffe to the governorship in 2014. One can affirm with hindsight what seemed likely all along: the Republican House of Delegates was determined to not grant him a meaningful policy victory on any issue, including voting rights.

Virginia was a relative outlier in the nation in permanently stripping voting rights from ex-convicts who had served their time. In 2014, roughly one in five African Americans in Virginia was disenfranchised.[3] As a matter of justice and morality, it was debatable whether a lifetime ban was the correct stance, whether violent and nonviolent felons deserved the same treatment, and whether criminals were truly deterred by the threat of losing the right to vote. Most states automatically restored the voting rights of citizens who were out of prison or had completed parole; Maine and Vermont never removed felons' voting rights even during incarceration.

Virginia joined twelve other states, mostly in the South, in taking the austere stance of prohibiting felons from voting until their rights had been actively restored by executive clemency or similar processes.[1]

Virginia's governors had exercised their discretion to restore voting rights with increasing frequency in the twenty-first century. During this time, the prison population had grown exponentially due to nonviolent offenses, even as the winds of public opinion and political support for the War on Drugs had shifted considerably. Felony convictions for low-level drug crimes had over the past twenty years been increasingly viewed as draconian, expensive, and socially harmful.[5] Not merely rights restoration but full clemency and lessening of sentences for minor drug users was becoming far more politically acceptable for leading politicians from both parties, up to and including President Trump.[6] The burden of felony disenfranchisement in Virginia fell mostly but not entirely on poor offenders; minors from wealthier families were, in fact, more likely to use alcohol and marijuana and less likely to be incarcerated for it.[7] In the last five years, the opioid crisis had spread into many areas of the country not known for drug overdoses, and treatment was usually seen as the preferred option. From a pragmatic perspective, many law enforcement officers felt there were too many users to arrest.[8] Even reactionary Senate Republican leader Tommy Norment introduced a bill that would have eliminated jail time for first-time marijuana offenders, but "while the state Senate approved the measure 38–2, with two Democrats urging more sweeping decriminalization, a panel of the House Courts of Justice Committee killed it."[9] In a nation of patchwork laws where the majority of people supported legalization of marijuana, and many cities and states had legalized the industry even as it remained illegal at the federal level, it made less and less sense to prosecute and incarcerate people for behavior that in most instances was innocuous.[10]

MCDONNELL'S GROUNDWORK

Before Terry McAuliffe, the greatest champion for felon voting rights restoration in the history of Virginia had been his predecessor, former prosecutor Bob McDonnell. In his January 2013 State of the Commonwealth address, McDonnell called on the legislature to pass a constitutional amendment that would allow automatic restoration of voting rights for nonviolent felons.[11] Attorney General Ken Cuccinelli, who would later that year narrowly lose the governor's race to McAuliffe, spoke in support of the amendment in front of the House Elections committee.[12] It passed by a resounding 30–10 in the Senate but did not even get out of a House Elections subcommittee. "It is disappointing that the General Assembly was not able to enact this common-sense reform to restore the fundamental rights to vote and serve on juries to these citizens who have atoned for their earlier mistakes," McDonnell said. That same day, the same subcommittee also killed bills that would have established nonpartisan redistricting commissions.[13]

Thus stifled by the legislature, McDonnell did what McAuliffe would later do and accelerated the use of his constitutional power to restore felons' rights. Cuccinelli formed a commission on the subject and issued a report in May that outlined ways McDonnell could act alone to expand voting rights within the confines of Virginia law.[14] In a sad commentary on Virginia's partisanship, McAuliffe and Cuccinelli both embraced felon voting restoration in their campaigns, but Cuccinelli was criticized by state Democrats for flip-flopping from his rejection of voting rights years earlier as a state senator.[15] Nevertheless, the day after Cuccinelli released his report, McDonnell was joined by NAACP President Ben Jealous when he announced that he embraced many of the report's ideas about using state resources to reach out proactively to ex-felons and further eliminate barriers to re-enfranchisement. Most importantly, the waiting period and burdensome application would be essentially abolished, and rights restoration for nonviolent offenders would become automatic.[16] No administration had gone through and performed a census of eligible ex-felon voters, but within six weeks, McDonnell had put into place many of the public and internal systems and partnerships that would expedite individual restoration of rights.[17] McDonnell significantly accelerated the rate at which felons received their rights back from roughly one thousand each year in the early years of his administration, including disgraced Republican operative Scooter Libby, to roughly three thousand in his last.[18] In many ways that would not be fairly acknowledged by partisans, McDonnell laid the groundwork for McAuliffe's efforts on voting rights.

It was ironic that McDonnell would soon be convicted of eleven felonies relating to conspiring to sell the powers of his office to a con man and temporarily lose his right to vote.[19] It has frequently been declared since then that McDonnell was innocent, but that has not yet been proven: the convictions were vacated by the U.S. Supreme Court based on faulty jury instructions by the Reagan-appointed judge. The case was sent back to the Fourth Circuit Court of Appeals to determine if there was enough evidence

In **May 2013,** rights restoration gained momentum when then-Gov. McDonnell ended Virginia's policy of permanently disenfranchising all citizens with felony convictions. His action automated rights restoration for people completing sentences (including payment of any fines, fees, and restitution) for convictions classified as non-violent and eliminated their two-year waiting period, though it required that each person receive an individualized rights restoration certificate before registering to vote.

In **April 2014**, Gov. Terry McAuliffe announced that he would further streamline the restoration process. The policy change broadened the category of people who automatically received their right to vote upon the completion of their sentence, and shortened the rights restoration waiting period for rehabilitated violent offenders to apply from five years to three.

In **June 2015**, Gov. McAuliffe removed the requirement that citizens fully pay court costs and fees to have their voting rights restored.

In **April 2016**, Gov. McAuliffe issued an executive order restoring voting rights to Virginians with felony convictions who, as of that date, had completed the terms of their incarceration and any period of supervised release (probation or parole). He issued similar orders in May and June. These orders were challenged in court, and in **July 2016**, the Virginia Supreme Court ruled in *Howell v. McAuliffe* that they violated the state constitution, which required the governor to make clemency determinations on a case-by-case basis.

In **August 2016**, Gov. McAuliffe announced that his office would issue restoration orders on an individual basis to Virginians with completed sentences, starting with the approximately 13,000 citizens who had their voter registrations cancelled in the wake of the *Howell* decision. The governor also announced that, going forward, the Secretary of the Commonwealth would identify individuals with completed sentences, starting with individuals who have been released from supervision the longest. The Secretary would then recommend individuals for rights restoration on a rolling basis to the Governor for his final approval. Individuals may also receive an expedited restoration order by applying directly to the Secretary's Office online or by mail. According to the announcement, the Secretary will announce citizens that received an individualized restoration order on a monthly basis.

Summary of felon voting rights changes in Virginia, 2013–16. *Brennan Center for Justice.*

to retry, but President Obama's Justice Department declined to pursue the matter.[20] In contemporary reporting and especially in the increasingly ideological and revisionist history attending the matter, it was almost never mentioned that grifter Jonnie Williams's motive in ingratiating himself with McDonnell was to get state medical schools to test Williams's pill made from microwaved tobacco on state employees. McDonnell set up a meeting with Secretary of Health Bill Hazel in order to facilitate this, and innocent people were spared from this potentially catastrophic, large-scale medical experiment only by Hazel's judgment.[21] Regardless, McDonnell has his voting rights back, and people who supported such measures should have recognized his contributions.

MCAULIFFE MAKES HISTORY

Governor McAuliffe expanded on McDonnell's efforts. He would shatter his predecessor's record for felon re-enfranchisement while being subjected to hyperbolic and sometimes successful partisan attacks. He would also use his executive pardon authority to bypass the legislature—though, unlike McDonnell, McAuliffe would for a time push the boundaries of his clemency powers beyond constitutional limits.

The legislature met from roughly January to March each year, so it was not a coincidence that McAuliffe's executive actions on voting rights were issued in the summer. Legislative efforts to expand voting rights were all scuttled in the House in his first year in office, as they had been during McDonnell's last.[22] There was an unclear delineation to be made among various felonies, and McDonnell, for example, had not restored rights to people who had committed nonviolent election fraud felonies.[23] In April 2014, after his first legislative session had been concluded, McAuliffe announced that he was expanding the scope of McDonnell's policies on nonviolent felon voting restoration by moving drug dealing from the list of "violent" to "nonviolent" felonies.[24] McAuliffe also further reduced the waiting time for violent offenders to apply to have their rights restored from five years to three and shortened the application for violent felons from thirteen pages to one page, as McDonnell had for nonviolent offenders.[25]

The House of Delegates again killed automatic re-enfranchisement in 2015.[26] That summer, McAuliffe announced that he had restored the civil rights of more than eight thousand people, more than any governor in Virginia's history. He also announced that felons could receive their rights back even if they had not paid their court costs and fees, which garnered almost no media coverage but represented a significant philosophical shift on the issue.[27] There was an argument to be made that was convincing to a broad spectrum of political leaders that felons who had paid their debts to society should be able to participate in it, but McAuliffe expanded that to expressly include those who had not paid their debts, though the counterargument was that these fines were unjust and burdened the poor. "It is a good thing for Commonwealth that many of our citizens have been granted a second chance after serving their debt to society [*sic*]," said Delegate Peter Farrell, son of the Dominion CEO.[28] In the 2016 session, the legislature not only failed to act on voting rights restoration but also removed funding from the budget that would have paid for more staff to help restore those rights.[29]

By far the most momentous event in this rights restoration campaign came when McAuliffe signed an executive order on the steps of the state capitol on April 22, 2016, that re-enfranchised all ex-felons who had completed their sentences, an estimated 206,000 Virginians.[30] A.E. Dick Howard, lead author of the modern Virginia Constitution, "spoke of the historic significance of the occasion in relation to Virginia's 1901–1902 constitutional convention, which set up poll taxes, literacy tests and disenfranchisement for felons as barriers for African-American participation. 'Today, the last ghost of the 1902 convention was buried,' Howard said."[31] "This will be the single most significant action on disenfranchisement that we've ever seen from a governor," said Marc Mauer, executive director of the Sentencing Project.[32] Reverend Ben Campbell would recall:

> *I was on the Capitol steps when Governor McAuliffe announced the voting rights restoration for persons with felony convictions. He asked me to come give a little speech. It was one of the most stunning moments of my life because it was done voluntarily.*[33]

It would have benefited the public to witness and participate in an honest discussion of the merits of justice and reconciliation, but the measured local responses and bipartisan support from those on the ground who knew the issue best sadly and quickly deteriorated as they were subsumed into state politicians' and the national media's Pavlovian reactions. Virginia Republican leadership was partly to blame for this reaction, and the Speaker and Senate Majority Leader all blasted McAuliffe on that day with variations on the line that McAuliffe wanted to help elect Hillary Clinton president. If that was the case, then they themselves were necessarily "guilty" of trying to restrict voting rights to elect Donald Trump; McAuliffe had been trying to elect Republicans for the past three years; and Bob McDonnell was also trying to elect Hillary Clinton. Leading Republican gubernatorial candidate Ed Gillespie said McAuliffe was "benefiting convicted rapists, murderers and child molesters."[34] It was important to reiterate that Virginia was a relative outlier in this category, and the majority of Americans in the majority of states were automatically granted their rights back after they had served their time. If this sentiment was to be believed, then conservative states like Utah were also working very hard to elect Democrats. The *National Review* argued that the order should have logically restored Second Amendment rights as well but misunderstood that the order did indeed make it easier for ex-felons to receive their gun rights back by removing the first hurdle before they were permitted to petition a court for restoration.[35]

The liberal reaction was broadly supportive, but responses ignored what was a crude but partially valid point by Gillespie. There was at least a contention to be made that some crimes were so egregious that people should not be able to vote. This was the de facto stance of all states (except Maine and Vermont) that did not allow prisoners to vote yet sentenced some people to life imprisonment. There were, according to supporters of the death penalty, some crimes so unforgivable that the perpetrator did not justly deserve to live, much less vote or serve on juries. It was also a manifestly fair question to consider that if McAuliffe felt this was an issue of justice, then he should have issued an executive order immediately upon taking office and not waited until the 2016 legislative session had ended and the presidential election was imminent. It was disingenuous not to note that McAuliffe had chaired Clinton's 2008 campaign and Virginia was a swing state. McAuliffe also noted that "if I were to do this for political reasons, I would have done it last year when I had my General Assembly up and if I had picked up 5,000 more votes, I'd have control of the state Senate."[36] Then again, he chose to issue the 2016 executive order precisely two days after the legislature had adjourned for the year.[37] It may have surprised partisans to see that, of the national media, the *New York Times* fairly noted the facts and context, including the political benefits to Democrats and Clinton and the expansion of these rights to "those convicted of violent crimes, including murder and rape."[38] There were not necessarily completely clear answers, and there were ideas that should have been considered on both sides.

HOWELL V. MCAULIFFE

With a partisan legislature unable to override a governor who opposed it, Republicans would have to seek remedy in the courts. The question of whether a governor could restore rights with a blanket order or individually had never been litigated because it had never happened.[39] The Virginia Constitution read, "No person who has been convicted of a felony shall be qualified to vote unless his civil rights have been restored by the Governor or other appropriate authority."[40] The other relevant section reflecting on framer intent was that the governor "shall communicate to the General Assembly, at each regular session, particulars of every case of fine or penalty remitted, of reprieve or pardon granted, and of punishment commuted, with his reasons for remitting, granting, or commuting the same."[11] The reader's opinion on what these sentences meant for McAuliffe's order was probably as sensible as any other.

Expert opinion on the constitutionality of McAuliffe's order was conflicted. Constitutional scholars did not have to reach back to yellow manuscripts to find the original intent of the framers of the Virginia Constitution; it was written in the late 1960s and early 1970s, and its principal author was still teaching at UVA. A.E. Dick Howard said firmly that there was "no question" that McAuliffe's order was constitutional. Virginia Attorney General Mark Herring agreed.[12] Yet Howard had written in his 1974 commentaries on the 1971 Virginia Constitution that rights could only be restored individually.[13] Attorney General Cuccinelli, who supported ex-felon rights, had reported just three years earlier to Governor McDonnell that the legal authority for blanket restoration did not exist.[14] Moreover, "Republicans pointed to a 2010 letter to the ACLU from an attorney for Gov. Timothy M. Kaine, a Democrat, stating that a blanket restoration of rights would amount to a 'troubling' rewrite of state law and the Constitution."[15] Both parties would continue to claim the mantle of justice, but neither side would publicly acknowledge that this fight had become pure politics.

As the partisan soundbites ricocheted in the press, the lives of real people were affected, for better or worse. The McAuliffe administration released a study of the people who had been re-enfranchised. The average age was forty-six; the average time since they had completed probation was eleven years; 52 percent were white, 46 percent black, and 79 percent nonviolent offenders; 93 percent, or about 14 out of 15, would have had their rights restored if they had applied even before the order.[16] More than 1,100 people in their eighties and 367 people over age ninety were included in the restoration.[17] The sort of violent criminals who had fueled Republican talking points and that Democrats did not usually talk about provided some shocking portraits, made all the worse when the Governor's Office was found to have mistakenly restored rights to some felons still serving sentences. Murderer and child sex abuser Ronald Cloud had his rights restored, even as he was serving two life sentences in a West Virginia prison. Former Virginia cop Daniel Harmon-Wright was still on probation in California after shooting "a Sunday school teacher in her Jeep as the vehicle drove away."[18] Another error involved a group of 132 convicted sex offenders who had completed their criminal sentences but were confined to a facility in

Nottoway County under civil proceedings because they were deemed too dangerous to release.[49] McAuliffe's team corrected these errors and forged ahead. At the same time, stories emerged that fueled Democratic talking points of rehabilitated citizens that Republicans did not usually talk about. Marcus Oliver of Lynchburg "was convicted of drug and firearm possession in 2001." "When I really found out that I got my rights restored, all I [could] do was just say, 'Thank you, Jesus,'" he said. "Other people can do the same thing. I just want to make an example." He said he planned to vote for Republican Bob Goodlatte, but he added: "I can't say Hillary, I can't say Donald Trump. I just want to choose the best president I think will help make America great."[50] Forty-five-year-old Democrat Leah Taylor of Richmond had never voted after being incarcerated from 1991 to 1992 for selling crack cocaine. Since then, she had put her life together, performed community service, paid all her fines, and was working two jobs. When she found out about the executive order, she was "so moved she nearly cried" and "promptly signed up."[51]

Speaker of the House Bill Howell and Senate Majority Leader Tommy Norment joined four registered voters in a suit funded by private donors that sought to block the executive order in *Howell v. McAuliffe*.[52] In another moment signifying the strange political alliances forged by the issue, a bipartisan, mostly Republican, group of the state's prosecutors representing jurisdictions with slightly more than half of Virginia's citizens filed an amicus brief in support of Howell and Norment's suit, particularly highlighting their opposition to the Second Amendment consequence that McAuliffe had actually eased the path to restoring gun rights.[53]

The 4–3 Virginia Supreme Court decision, too, was political.[54] The justices found that blanket rights restoration was unconstitutional, but a governor could constitutionally restore the rights of all former felons if he signed their orders individually.[55] "As a textual matter, the Virginia Constitution provides no case-by-case requirement for removing political disabilities," noted an article in the *Harvard Law Review*. However, "rather than cite the Virginia Constitution's plain language as evidence that the power to remove political disabilities is less restricted than other clemency powers, the majority argued that the text is ambiguous enough to impute a case-by-case requirement."[56] Another author argued in the *University of Richmond Law Review* that if the order was constitutional, it would allow a governor to entirely suspend certain laws by granting blanket pardons.[57] There was little about the matter not subject to debate and countervailing evidence.

After the decision, McAuliffe began restoring rights to felons using an autopen under a system originally designed by McDonnell.[38] Within a few weeks, McAuliffe had restored rights to all of the roughly 13,000 people who had registered to vote after his order and had been briefly disenfranchised by the court decision.[39] It later was reported that McAuliffe would "not individually sign the orders or make use of an autopen, but an image of his signature will be printed on each letter." Howell asked the court to hold McAuliffe in contempt, but the court refused, because this was evidently perfectly legal.[60] It was not an exaggeration to state that what had been unconstitutional when it was done with one hand signature became constitutional when it was done with one hand signature repeated 206,000 times by computer, and that the Virginia Supreme Court had somehow discerned this paradox in drafters' intent from the 1960s. It was understandably reported that the Virginia Supreme Court had sided with Republicans in the legislature, but by allowing this interpretation in its ruling, McAuliffe was the actual winner. By the November 2016 elections, McAuliffe had restored the voting rights of about 60,000 Virginians, which affected neither the presidential election outcome in Virginia nor the nation.[61] In April 2017, a year after his original executive order, McAuliffe announced he had restored the rights of more than 156,000 people and broken the American record for voting rights restoration.[62]

REDISTRICTING EQUALED GERRYMANDERING

Other than corruption, gerrymandering was the twenty-first century's most self-serving assault on the will of the citizenry. Redistricting was like a super-election in which the winner secured control of the legislature for the remainder of the decade; consequently, under the Virginia Way, the somber responsibility of drawing federal and state electoral districts was removed from the people and became synonymous with highly partisan and political gerrymandering. The logic of partisan gerrymandering was inexorable. From the 1960s through the present, "not a single decade passed without a Virginia congressional or state legislative redistricting plan being invalidated, whether in federal or state court, and whether based on the federal equal protection clause or Voting Rights Act or the state constitution."[63] If courts declared Virginia's electoral maps unconstitutional, as they had for fifty years and would throughout the 2010s, there would be no penalty to pay except redrawing the maps, and the work of politicians who had served for years in illegal districts would not be undone. During this decade, taxpayers were on the hook for an estimated $5–10 million in legal costs that increased with seemingly endless appeals.[64] Even into 2019, the House of Delegates maps from 2011 were bouncing back and forth between different federal and state courts.

Over the last fifty years, first Democrats, and then Republicans, had drawn the lines that divided Virginia citizens into boxes where they had less and less ability to control their own destinies by freely electing politicians of their choosing. Luckily for Republicans in Virginia and nationwide, the 2009–10 red wave elections resulted in Tea Party–dominated statehouses where redistricting could, for the first time, make use of hyper-targeted software to eke out the most favorable partisan maps in history.[65] It was rare to see ideological opposites entirely in accord on the matter: for example, the *Richmond Times-Dispatch* editorial board called gerrymandering "a sin against democracy," while former Attorney General Eric Holder called it "a threat to our democracy."[66] At the same time, and consistent with the Virginia Way, the people, the press, and civil society were unified and powerless in their opposition, and the clear solution—a nonpartisan, independent redistricting commission—was entirely ignored.

Given the stakes involved and amount of coverage of every facet of national elections, it was curious to see the relatively sparse reporting on gerrymandering as an electoral issue rather than a technical problem, since the public seemed keenly aware of the issue. "Only 16 percent of Virginians wanted the Virginia General Assembly in charge of legislative redistricting after the 2020 census," according to a Virginia Commonwealth University poll.[67] Perhaps citizens perceived how little power they had to affect the outcome. The disconnect between public opinion and voter motivation was in line with another highly technical and politicized event in which power hung in the balance: the Florida presidential election recounts in 2000. Opinion polls then showed that Americans well understood both the stakes and the fact that the process was far removed from their control. Consequently, the public was not incensed over the legal arcana.[68]

The 2017 Democratic elections could have changed things after all signs pointed to an approaching period of Democratic control of state politics for the first time in nearly thirty years.[69] If trends continued, there was only a brief time before the legislature would flip to Democratic control. Democrats had won Virginia's electoral votes in three consecutive presidential elections beginning in 2008. Republicans ran a successful national campaign in 2016, but Virginia was the only southern state that voted for Hillary Clinton and did so with a large 5-point cushion and a Virginian on the ballot.[70] Virginia was becoming a more Democratic state, and President Trump was very unpopular in the populous northern and coastal Virginia areas heavily reliant on federal government spending that Trump and national Republicans regularly attacked.[71] In 2017, Governor Northam was elected with a convincing 9 percent margin, or by about 235,000 votes.[72] His office would have veto power over new maps drawn after the 2020 Census. Democrats controlled the other four statewide offices, and Republicans had lost every single statewide election since 2009. The 2018 elections saw Democrats flip three congressional seats; Senator Kaine secured a 16-point landslide reelection and won majorities in 26 of 40 Senate and 61 of 100 House of Delegates districts.[73] Republican power was whittled down to a tenuous majority of one seat each in both the Senate and the House of Delegates, and the latter was wholly due to gerrymandering: more than 1.3 million Virginians voted for Democratic House of Delegates candidates in 2017, compared with 1.1 million who voted for Republicans.[74] Nothing was ever certain in politics, but the best that Virginia Republicans could reasonably hope for over the next ten years was that there would at some point be an unpopular Democratic president who would fuel backlash turnout. Still, Virginia politicians stonewalled measures that would have instituted nonpartisan redistricting. Because of the perverse incentives, Republicans benefited from delay in the short term, and Democrats seemed likely to do the same within a few years. For the entire decade of the 2010s, governors and legislative leaders of both parties failed to act on this issue out of anything other than purely selfish interests.

FEDERAL ELECTIONS

Under the federal Constitution, drawing congressional district lines was left to the states after each decennial Census. The implications for skullduggery were clear, and Republicans' successful redistricting efforts in Texas after the 2000 Census presaged the modern national effort. George W. Bush was governor, and then president, aided in large part by strategist Karl Rove.[75] The Texas House, however, would not become Republican until 2003, and at that time, the legislature tried to advance a redistricting bill so partisan that Democratic legislators fled the state in a futile effort to deny Republicans a quorum and prevent the bill's passage.[76] The Supreme Court ruled on the case three years later and largely upheld the new districts.[77]

"He who controls redistricting can control Congress," Rove presciently wrote in the *Wall Street Journal* in early 2010.[78] If the expected Tea Party wave materialized, "it could end up costing Democrats congressional seats for a decade to come." The implications were monumental. For example, "the GOP gained somewhere between 25 and 30 seats because of the redistricting that followed the 1990 census. Without those seats, Republicans would not have won the House in 1994." Moreover, "moving, say, 20 districts from competitive to out-of-reach could save a party $100 million or more [in campaign donations] over the course of a decade." The successful plan was to flip control of state legislatures, and "as a result, the GOP oversaw redrawing of lines for four times as many congressional districts as Democrats."[79]

The leader of this national effort was former Republican National Committee chairman Ed Gillespie, who would subsequently win Virginia's Republican nominations in losing efforts for U.S. Senate in 2014 and governor in 2017. "Gillespie is the rainmaker, really," author David Daley summarized. "Goes off on a year-long fundraising tour and shakes the trees and comes up with $30 million at least." His pitch was, "'You will save hundreds of millions if you fund this instead of everything else.'" Gillespie "met with Wall Street donors, oil magnates, hedge-funders, Washington lobbyists and trade associations—anyone open to an audacious, long-term play."[80] Republicans "were able to build themselves a firewall, a full Chamber of Congress for a decade, for less than the price of a losing Senate race in a small state."[81]

The most vexing issue opponents of gerrymandering had to address was the fact that the term itself did not have a well-defined legal standard. Legislatures suffered from inherent conflicts of interest in drawing the districts that could guarantee themselves hyper-partisan control, lifelong jobs, defeat for the opponent of their choice, or all of the above. Courts most often punted on the issue, except in cases of racial discrimination.[82] "Not a single partisan gerrymandering case involving political redistricting has been won by plaintiffs since 1986," a reporter wrote. "That was when the Supreme Court ruled for the first time, in an Indiana case, that complaints about partisan gerrymandering could be settled by the courts. But the justices couldn't put together a majority laying out the standards that had to be met for the disgruntled party to prevail."[83] To solve the national crisis of partisan gerrymandering, it seemed the Supreme Court would have to step into an arbitrary battle, overturn decades of precedent, and come up with a legal standard with conflicting guidance from legislatures in a decision that could flip control of Congress and many state governments. Any court was understandably reluctant to do so.

The game was well known to political insiders but difficult to defend to the broader public. Politicians' verbal jousting approached parody when each side accused the other of partisanship that it had freely engaged in. The earlier quote by former Attorney General Holder was disingenuous but accurately reflected the rhetorical position that Democrats could afford to take. During the 2010s, Democrats called for fairness and balance because more equitable redistricting benefited them, while Republicans appealed to legal ambiguities because delay supported their preferred status quo. If gerrymandering was "a threat to our democracy," then it was equally wrong for either party to do it. Holder's Republican critics like Senator Ryan McDougle were right to note that Holder's National Democratic Redistricting Committee project to tip the scales of gerrymandering in the other direction was hardly just. "Under a Democrat majority in 2011, the redistricting of the Senate of Virginia violated virtually every principle of model redistricting," McDougle wrote. "It ignored communities of interest, violated compactness, and barely complied with contiguity."[81] When asked about Gillespie's history of gerrymandering, Gillespie's campaign spokesman wrote, "In his ten years in office, Lt. Gov. Northam has done nothing to eliminate partisan redistricting maps. In fact, he's voted to gerrymander his own district."[85] That was both true and tragicomic to hear in defense of a candidate who had done more for gerrymandering than anyone in American history. Rightly or wrongly, Republicans had indisputably been much more successful at gerrymandering than Democrats. For example, McDougle and every other Republican state senator voted for the redistricting plan that solidified their party's 8–3 control of Virginia's congressional delegation that would later be declared unconstitutional.

In Virginia, where each party controlled one legislative chamber, redistricting at the congressional level was contentious.[86] Virginia's Third District was racially discriminatory, not compact, and not contiguous except by water. Federal courts repeatedly ruled that the district violated the Equal Protection Clause by racially gerrymandering African American voters to dilute their strength in adjacent districts. The U.S. Supreme Court was almost always the last word on an issue, and advocates who wanted their day in court took a significant risk that the verdict would not be in their favor. The Court spoke with no uncertainty in May 2016 when it considered a challenge

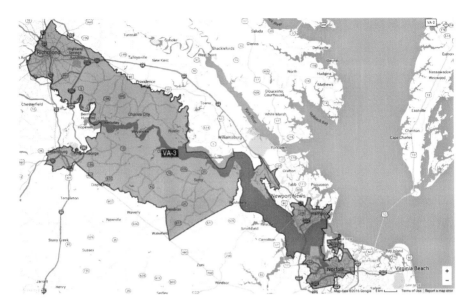

Virginia's Third Congressional District (2011 16) was declared an unconstitutional racial gerrymander by federal courts. *Google Earth.*

by three Virginia members of Congress whose electoral prospects were harmed by earlier court redistricting. Under the plaintiff's logic, there would be "an incumbency protection standing rule," said Justice Sonia Sotomayor. "Every time your district is changed and you believe it hurts you, you have a right to go to court?" she asked, incredulously. The court dismissed the claims unanimously.[87] After two elections with this unconstitutional map, the state's map was redrawn in accordance with the Constitution. However, the solution was relatively conservative: the practical effect was that Virginia's Fourth Congressional District would flip from Republican to Democratic control in the 2016 election and Republicans would hold seven out of the state's eleven House seats.

STATE GERRYMANDERING

State-level redistricting followed a similar pattern. The issue of redistricting was ripe for compromise when the Virginia legislature was split between a Democratic Senate and a Republican House of Delegates in 2011. Both chambers would have to agree on a redistricting plan. They did come to an agreement, but it was one that reflected their own political interests. The Democrats would draw lines to maintain their hold over the Senate, while the Republicans would similarly gerrymander the House. "It's horrific," declared the director of the Virginia Interfaith Center for Public Policy. "Our goal is to make the Democratic districts, particularly the marginal ones, a bit better than they are now," Senate Majority Leader Dick Saslaw stated. "If I lose a few seats in redistricting, and I'm in the majority, I'm not doing a very good job."[88] Fewer than 10 out of 140 state legislators even knew what the lines were before they were introduced, fully formed, in late March 2011.[89] A special session of the legislature was called, and the plans were agreed to on April 7, 2011.[90]

These maps were more powerful than wave elections. Elections oscillated widely throughout the decade, from 2015 elections in which an anemic 29 percent of registered voters participated, to 2017's historic blue wave elections that garnered 47 percent participation. Yet during this time, when Virginia was a swing state equally at play in presidential and statewide races, only one chamber of the state legislature flipped, one time, when Senator Phil Puckett resigned during the Medicaid fight and was replaced by a Republican.

Some voters did not like that politicians were picking them rather than the other way around. In addition to federal laws, the Virginia Constitution mandated that "every electoral district shall be composed of contiguous and compact territory."[91] In 2015, fourteen voters sued to invalidate the districts under the compactness standard. The longer the delay for the party that benefited, the better, and Republicans were masterful in delaying judgment. Each step in the process permitted ample opportunity for motions, answers, defense, countermotions, and all the other measures available to a determined litigant. First, Speaker Howell and House Republicans asked to join the suit as defendants. Circuit Court Judge W. Reilly Marchant ruled they could. The trial would only begin in March 2017, and Marchant understandably declined to invalidate the district lines for the reasons that courts usually do.[92] That was only the first step of the process. The entire production could be repeated at the Virginia Supreme Court, and it was, heralding more motions, another trial, and a ruling in 2018 that again failed to find the compactness standard had been violated.[93]

There was still the matter of federal law. A panel of three judges for the Eastern District of Virginia ruled that the state House gerrymandering was explicable by reasons other than racism, but in June 2016, the U.S. Supreme Court agreed to review Virginia's state House maps. Given the rules of the court, a minimum of four of the justices had to agree to hear a case; this was never a good sign for parties who only had something to lose.[94] But, as Virginians saw time and again, gerrymandering politicians only had to gain by delaying justice for as long as possible. The court may have been the final word, but it was also the slowest and most methodical branch of government: the justices would hear the case six months later and issue a ruling six months after that.[95] At a minimum, an entire year's legislative session would come and go. In March 2017, the Supreme Court overturned the ruling and told the panel to go back to the drawing board.[96]

More than a year went by with the predictably tortured pleas, motions, countermotions, and so forth, until the federal panel found in June 2018 that the districts had indeed been drawn with racial discrimination in mind. The Virginia Way suffered from many internal contradictions and was simply not credible to those who subjected it to scrutiny. Particularly important in this determination were "boundary lines that were 'frequently small residential roads separating predominantly white and predominantly black neighborhoods,' as well as heavily black municipalities that were divided between multiple districts."[97] In a damning critique, the court flatly declared the testimony of the man who led the redistricting effort, Republican Delegate Chris Jones, was "not credible." Between the first and second trial, Jones seemed to have developed an inexplicable case of amnesia. "In light of Jones' very poor memory at the second trial, as well as his inability to account for material inconsistencies in his testimony, we give little weight to Jones' testimony regarding the reasons underlying the many changes made to district boundary lines," the court wrote.[98] The lines for a minimum of eleven House of Delegates districts would have to be redrawn in time for the 2019 elections.[99] Yet in late 2018, the U.S. Supreme Court again agreed to take up a challenge to the districts for which they were only expected to rule in the spring of 2019.[100] Thus, the decade of the 2010s concluded with only a single election in which Virginians voted in constitutional districts not distorted by illegal partisan gamesmanship.

TRUTH AND CONSEQUENCES

Whereas Republicans and Democrats should have worked together to protect the sacred right to vote, neither party had all the facts on its side. While this should have led to honest reassessment, it instead resulted in doubling down on original positions. There were two instances in which a single party engaged in serious electoral wrongdoing.

A provincial election scandal metastasized when Representative Scott Taylor of the Second Congressional District decided that he wanted to split the Democratic vote by helping a Democrat who had lost the primary get on the ballot as an independent. This might not have been ethical, but it was legal, generally speaking. Unfortunately for Taylor, members of his campaign staff illegally forged dozens of signatures on the petitions necessary to get the other candidate's name on the ballot—a felony under Virginia law. It perhaps reflected Darwinism that the dozens of forged signatures included at least four dead people, two Republican delegates, a former employee from Senator Mark Warner's office and the Virginia Beach sheriff.[101] Taylor prolonged the scandal by failing the simple crisis management test of immediately telling the truth and taking full responsibility for one's actions. He thus compounded his staff's errors by making himself the subject of a constant stream of negative news stories with each additional revelation. A special prosecutor was appointed in August 2018, and the Democrat whom Taylor's staff had tried to get on the ballot was taken off by a judge who harshly criticized the petitions for "out-and-out fraud." As if it could not get any worse, four Taylor staffers, a consultant, and a notary all signed affidavits stating they would plead the Fifth if they were called to testify about the matter.[102] Comparing polls taken before and after the scandal broke showed that Taylor had gone from a four-point lead to an eight-point deficit in just four months.[103]

A broader scandal was perpetrated by the McAuliffe administration and only uncovered by an audit of the Virginia Department of Elections (VDOE). The Joint Legislative Audit and Review Committee (JLARC), whose vital work bridged many of the gaps that would ordinarily be filled by a full-time, professional legislature, released a ninety-page audit of VDOE in September 2018. The audit was not all bad news: though the voter registration system worked reasonably well, there were grounds for improvement in IT and state oversight of local election functions. However, the three political appointees who led the agency during the McAuliffe administration were faulted for lacking leadership skills and strategic focus, and JLARC pointed out that much larger agencies in Virginia typically had just one political appointee. Most disturbingly, the audit found that the appointees had acted in a partisan way. "There was a perception among some staff and general registrars of political bias," the audit found. "This bias was reflected in decisions about some policies or aspects of agency operations. According to current and former [VDOE] staff, leadership created an environment in which one party was openly supported over the other."[101] Though it was not mentioned in the report, one of the auditors elaborated "that former agency leaders directed staff to help Democratic groups avoid campaign finance laws and rules that require political groups to put their names on ads. 'We heard of one example where the previous deputy commissioner at the agency very openly stated to a number of people, including to one high-level elections official in Virginia, that one of her key responsibilities was to help Hillary Clinton be elected president,'" according to the auditor. Though the audit noted that it did not find wrongdoing related to this partisanship, this report and the staffer's comments should have been deeply concerning for those who believed in fair elections. "If there's any group that has to have integrity, if there's any group that has to be nonbiased, it's got to be this group," said Speaker Kirk Cox.[105] The report further noted the perception that Governor Northam's appointees did not suffer from the same biases.[106] In the political atmosphere in which many Democrats were incensed over the Russian government's electoral crimes, press reports only quoted one, Governor Northam, who claimed that the problem of political bias in Virginia's elections had been fixed.[107] The ultimate irony was that due to some of the other problems pointed out by the report—namely, mostly but not perfectly accurate voter registration records, faulty IT systems, and poor communication between state and local officials—the VDOE under McAuliffe had assigned twenty-six voters from a Democratic area to the wrong district. The district they should have been assigned to was the infamous Ninety-Fourth House District in which the election ended up in an exact tie and the name of the winner was drawn from a bowl, a Republican won, and his party thereby controlled the House of Delegates 51–49.[108]

It was a measure of Virginia Way karma that Congressman Taylor lost his bid for reelection in a Republican-leaning district, and if McAuliffe's Department of Elections had done its job rather than trying to elect Hillary Clinton, Democrats would have flipped the state House in 2017.

CONCLUSION

LIVING FAITH IN VIRGINIA

I would love to see us do our own work and be proud to be Virginians.
—Ben Campbell

The year this book went to press was the 400th anniversary of the founding of the first legislative body in and the first importation of African slaves to the English colonies that would become America; both happened in Virginia.[1] This was not a representative democracy: in Virginia's original General Assembly, the same people who ran the government also owned the state's resources. The nature of political power over four centuries did not substantively change even as capitalism transformed the seats of economic wealth from dynastic families to immortal corporations.

How did this happen?

The "great men" invented a state religion called the Virginia Way to control the population.

One could discern the echoes into modernity when objective observers assessed Virginia government. This book recounts two events in which Virginia's political establishment reacted very differently from places with worse reputations for racism and corruption. In the first, after Confederate iconography led to violence, Charleston and New Orleans took down their divisive symbols, but the monuments in Charlottesville and Richmond remain untouched. In the second, after pay-to-play admissions scandals, the flagship universities of Illinois and Texas launched independent investigations that quickly led to their presidents' resignations, but the University of Virginia did nothing but dissemble about its wealth-based affirmative action. There were many more examples to show Virginia's true character compared with its deification.

In the national Health of Democracies project, Virginia was ranked fiftieth out of fifty-one states and D.C., earning particularly low marks on voting rights and campaign finance.[2]

> *A 2012 survey by the nonprofit Center for Public Integrity, Public Radio International and Global Integrity on honest government in the states gave Virginia grades of "F" for legislative accountability and campaign financing. A lack of laws and effective regulation to keep legislators from using public funds for themselves, ineffective regulations about the gifts legislators get, their financial disclosures, the work legislators do when they leave office and granting jobs or favors to family or cronies help put Virginia near the bottom when it comes to the risk of corruption, as does the lack of any limits on campaign donations, the survey said.[3]*

An updated survey in 2015, after the McDonnell scandals, ranked Virginia sixteenth out of the fifty states, with F grades for public access to information, campaign financing, and lobbying disclosures.[1] The last several years had also seen some limited electoral progress for women. While Virginia had been dead last in gender equity among elected officials in 2013, in 2018 it had climbed to thirty-seventh out of fifty.[5] Interestingly, while Virginia ranked fourth-, tenth-, and sixteenth-worst on three quantitative corruption measures in an analysis on the website FiveThirtyEight.com, its subjective reputation for corruption among reporters was a respectable sixteenth-best.[6] Workers also were not faring well in Virginia's economy, as "Virginia is now the most unequal state in the country, and is more unequal than at any time on record,"[7] the Commonwealth Institute reported in 2016. The humanitarian aid group Oxfam ranked Virginia dead last of the fifty states and D.C. in its 2018 report on "the best and worst states to work in America."[8]

America made progress to realize the promise of a government of, by, and for the people, but what gains Virginians had achieved had largely come from without. The Union army ended slavery, and federal courts had to step in to integrate schools, to open public universities to women (Virginia Military Institute in 1996; the University of Virginia in 1970), and to permit interracial marriage in 1967 in *Loving v. Virginia*. Virginia did not itself grant women the right to vote and did not ratify the Nineteenth Amendment until

1952; it affected the state only when passage in other states thirty-two years earlier caused it to become part of the federal Constitution.[9]

Attorney and lobbyist Frank Atkinson looked at the state's four hundred years and saw something far different when he wrote his own history of modern Virginia after a career revolving between advising governors and McGuireWoods. Two days after Ralph Northam's odious yearbook photo metastasized around the world, Atkinson published an ode to Virginia in the *Richmond Times-Dispatch*:

> *Four centuries ago, representative government was first planted at Jamestown; Africans first arrived; women were first recruited; entrepreneurship began to flourish; and a Thanksgiving tradition was born.*[10]

James Branch Cabell's passage from 1947 was just as descriptive in 2019:

> *Of beauty and of chivalry and of gray legions they spoke, and of a fallen civilization such as the world will not ever see again, and, for that matter, never did see; of a first permanent settlement, and of a Mother of Presidents, and of a republic's cradle, and of Stars and Bars, and of yet many other bygones, long ago at one with dead Troy and Atlantis, they babbled likewise, for interminable years, without ever, ever ceasing.*[11]

This collective unconscious predated the Civil War, which was merely subsumed into the narrative. When Frederick Law Olmsted visited Richmond in 1854, he had written:

> *What a failure there has been in the promises of the past! That, at last, is what impresses one most in Richmond....* [It] *is plainly the metropolis of Virginia, of a people who have been dragged along in the grand march of the rest of the world, but who have had, for a long time and yet have, a disposition within themselves only to step backwards.*[12]

When the king's rules were being rewritten in 1787, Saint Madison understood the threat that great wealth faced from democracy:

> [I]*f elections were open to all classes of people, the property of the landed proprietors would be insecure. An agrarian law would soon take place. If these observations be just, our government ought to secure the permanent interests of the country against innovation. Landholders ought to have a*

share in the government, to support these invaluable interests and to balance and check the other. They ought to be so constituted as to protect the minority of the opulent against the majority.[13]

The Virginia Way catechism had an economic purpose. The most successful pursuit of Virginia landowners has been to maintain their wealth and power by promulgating an all-encompassing ideology that infuses society with unearned reverence for and unquestioned obedience to them. Throughout its history, Virginia has engaged in "a battle against its own denial."[14] In 2019, a high priest chanted in the face of a racist scandal revealing Virginia to the world that "representative government was first planted at Jamestown; Africans first arrived; women were first recruited; entrepreneurship began to flourish; and a Thanksgiving tradition was born" in Virginia in 1619; his creation myth echoed the government's textbook from the mid-twentieth century, those scribes' revisionist fathers, their defeated grandfathers, their half-revolutionary forefathers, and the ideological justifications dating to colonization. Once one saw the reality behind the myth of the faith, it could not be unseen.

Through the early twenty-first century, Virginia had adopted a bipartisan machine politics in which Republicans and Democrats were two factions of one Money Party. There were individual dissenters, but it was accurate to state that the Virginia legislature had not deviated much from that one-party dominance for four centuries, with one notable exception.

From 1882 to 1884, Virginia was led in the legislature and Governor's Office by a biracial coalition known as the Readjuster Party. The Readjusters' platform was to stop Wall Street from dictating the usurious terms by which Virginia would pay back public debts dating to long before the Civil War. Instead, Virginia would pay the bankers on more reasonable terms that would allow investment in public schools for white and black children. This popular governing coalition achieved many of its goals over just two years before Democrats used a riot to inflame racial tensions a few days before the 1883 elections.[15] Democrats won these elections and instituted their reprehensible segregationist policies that would last nearly one hundred years and continue de facto into the present.

Virginia government was renowned for its gentility because its leaders couched vile policies in soft language, but the truth was that the people with power in Virginia were and always had been reactionary; the power elite in Richmond, where the Virginia Way was and always had been most deeply ingrained, was extreme even within the state. The ascendance of the

Virginia Republican Party after desegregation helped attenuate the worst facets of Pope Byrd's segregationists, but any moderate reformist impulses had long since been purged in service of the state religion.

At the same time, there had always been a hint of Virginia populism, crushed all but once, and in 2019, it had reached an apogee not witnessed by Dominion's corporate papacy in forty years: a crisis in managed democracy, and an old threat to the new mandarins. Dominion lobbyist Bruce McKay put it well as his company launched "a campaign to elect a pipeline" and "compiled a 'supporter database' of more than 23,000 names, generated 150 letters to the editor, sent more than 9,000 cards and letters to federal regulators and local elected officials, and directed more than 11,000 calls to outgoing Gov. Terry McAuliffe and Virginia's U.S. senators." "Nowadays [regulators] are being bombarded by general citizenry, by elected officials who have asked to insert themselves into the process, and this debate swirls around," he said. "Historically non-political processes [are] now political."[16] It may have seemed to him that Dominion's influence-peddling was "non-political," but to be more accurate, its unquestioned monopoly on political power was being challenged by Virginians who had every right to demand answers from their government. In 2015, spokesman David Botkins "could not name a piece of legislation in the past five years in which Dominion did not get what it wanted from the General Assembly."[17] When politicians were no longer beholden to its corrupting money in 2018, the "great men" had to pretend, for the first time, that the people were on their side; rather than changing course, they manufactured a fake congregation to claim the sun revolved around the earth.

The Virginia Way was sold as a formula for growth, but it functioned as a straitjacket holding people back from their God-given potential. The architects had constructed a tenuous artifice of policies and governance that benefited themselves, but there were many more Virginians who lived their faiths by helping others.

Ben Campbell had devoted his life to healing the wounds that were causing so much suffering.

The problem with Virginia that hurts me deeply—and my family has been here since 1760—is that I actually believe in the idealism and values of this state. I believe in the Declaration of Independence. There are some great things that have happened here. And yet, the only times we have been able to live up to those values are when we made the Yankees do it to us. It took the defeat of our people to end slavery, and it took the defeat of our people to make us overcome racial segregation in schools. And as soon as the Yankees left, we did it all over again. I would love to see us do our own work and be proud to be Virginians.[18]

James Ryan, the adopted child and first-generation college student who had ascended to the UVA presidency, loved Virginia and studied its past and present to learn how we as a people could do better. "You're going to feel a lot of pressure to conform, whether in your workplace or in your neighborhood, in raising your kids or in creating your relationships," Ryan said in a speech to students. "Don't be afraid to do what you think is right. Don't be afraid to speak your mind. Don't be afraid to do what you think is fun, to do what you think might work, to do something that hasn't been tried before."[19] In his inaugural address, he announced to a cheering crowd that Virginia undergraduates from families making less than $80,000 a year would no longer pay tuition to attend UVA, and those from families earning less than $30,000 would no longer pay for tuition, room, or board. We want to be "not just great, but good," he said.

[T]he faith I would like to discuss is of the secular variety. It's the faith of the Emily Dickinson poem: "The pierless bridge supporting what we see unto the scene that we do not." The faith that Dr. Martin Luther King, Jr. described as taking the first step, even when you don't see the whole staircase....I have faith that we will be an even stronger university than we are today, and we will have done some good in the world as well. But we will forever remain an unfinished project, just as this nation, whose founding is bound with our own, will also remain unfinished. That fact should not dampen your faith but instead strengthen your resolve. We may never be finished, but we can certainly make progress. The future awaits us, albeit impatiently, and it remains ours to shape.[20]

The tuition changes were effective immediately. "And, like most speeches during Ryan's time so far on Grounds, he ended with an anecdote that balanced humor with heart," a reporter wrote. "Sticking Nike Flyknits out from underneath his black regalia and robes, Ryan asked university presidents, faculty, students and supporters to join him on a mission to make UVA better. 'Friends, my running shoes are laced up.'"[21]

At the end of the second decade of the twenty-first century, we could know with confidence that Virginia government was still for sale to the highest bidder, yet the system in 2019 had the chrysalides within itself to undergo the most significant metamorphosis since desegregation, and perhaps since Reconstruction. It was neither written in our genes nor the stars that the few Virginians who dedicated their lives to wealth accumulation also had to control the people's government.

People who were lucky enough to have freedom faced a moral choice of who they were and who they would become. "Live as free people," Saint Peter wrote, "but do not use your freedom as a cover-up for evil."[22] "If you're not out there trying to solve the problem, you are the problem," Paul Goldman said. "You can't just wish something to happen—you have to actually go out and do it."[23]

What should be done? There were no perfect answers, other than to use precious freedom that so many Virginians had never had to solve problems that nobody else was solving. In this way, ordinary people could win extraordinary victories.

Virginia needed more democracy, not less. Who could be opposed to that?

ARE BALLOT INITIATIVES
A SKELETON KEY?

This book has outlined myriad difficulties in modern Virginia government and politics, all of which beg for solution. Mounting campaigns to reform individual aspects of the Virginia Way may achieve some results but in the long run may prove quixotic: there are too many problems that need solving, and particular legislative solutions alone will not do the trick when other issues will resurface like a multi-headed hydra. The best way to empower ordinary people is to implement a citizen referendum (ballot initiative) process in which citizens may petition to put a proposed law up for a vote, and it will become law if passed. This would not only overturn unpopular laws but also act as a safeguard to check politicians' worst impulses. Richmond has a limited ballot initiative, and we saw how the will of the voters was only heard when education advocates used it to force change on that city's sclerotic political system.

It would be fairly easy to implement direct democracy in Virginia as the groundwork is already in place. Virginia already has statewide ballot initiatives for constitutional amendments and certain bond issues; however, these are only placed on the ballot after they pass the legislature. The legislature also provides many local citizens the ability to put referenda on the ballot through collecting signatures, though, again, the results of these referenda are advisory and still have to pass the legislature.

Twenty-seven states—conservative, moderate, and liberal alike—have implemented this great tool of citizen democracy, and it has been utilized to

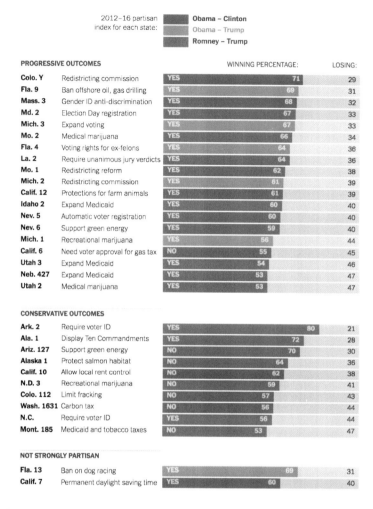

State ballot initiatives in 2018 showed a range of popular outcomes in both conservative and liberal states. *From the* New York Times.

bypass unresponsive government on a wide swath of issues. The 2018 elections saw liberal policies pass by ballot referenda in conservative states and vice versa. Americans in the majority of states are able to govern themselves—why shouldn't Virginians?

METHODOLOGY

Whenever the people are well informed,
they can be trusted with their own government.
—Thomas Jefferson

The above phrase is carved at the entrance to the Virginia Capitol.[1] I agree with it. The purpose of this book is to provide citizens a readable history of modern Virginia politics and government.

Journalism is "the first rough draft of history," as Philip Graham noted.[2] My methodology was to read everything written by Virginia political reporters for the two years covering roughly President Trump's inauguration through early 2019. (I submitted the completed manuscript a few weeks before racist and criminal allegations engulfed the Democratic governor, attorney general and lieutenant governor, and the public is still waiting for the full truth as of this writing.) I summarized what journalists wrote about the areas of Virginia politics and government that had the greatest effect on citizens' everyday lives. Thus, this book is a rough summary of the major issues in Virginia politics and government as they existed in the late 2010s. The real work of this was carried out every day by the diligent Virginia press corps, and I am grateful for all of them.

I selected six comprehensive themes for describing the functioning of Virginia politics and government—the Virginia Way, corporate power, higher education, local government, state policy, and good government—and I chose the most consequential case studies in each category from late 2016 to early 2019:

1) Virginia Way history and mythology in past and present;

2) corporate power, as exercised by Dominion Energy, the author of Virginia's energy policies;

3) higher education, as illustrated by the University of Virginia's affirmative action for the wealthy;

4) local government, as manifested in Richmond's public schools;

5) the most important state policy debate of the last five years, over Medicaid expansion;

6) democracy, as demonstrated in the three branches of government and how they affected the people's interests in good government by elections, gerrymandering, and voting rights.

I feel that chasing partisanship skews objectivity. I have been honored to work with people from the left, right, and everywhere in between in a good faith effort to make our government better serve our people.

I think copyrights generally inhibit the free flow of ideas, and as with my last book, "I grant all permissions for others to quote from and otherwise use this work to the maximum extent permitted by law and by my publisher."[3]

As Daniel Patrick Moynihan said, "Everyone is entitled to his own opinion, but not his own facts."[4] My loyalty is to the facts; I have not seen where anyone has pointed out a single one that I have misstated. Readers are free to form their own conclusions and moral judgments from the material presented here.

It does not and should not matter whether the perpetrators are of a certain party or position: injustice is injustice, whether it is carried out by Republican gerrymandering, a Democratic city machine, or a corrupt corporation. I welcome the company and scrutiny of all who wish to participate in our state's political life.

ACKNOWLEDGEMENTS

The most important people in Virginia politics are its journalists, and without them, this book would not exist. Virginia's reporters are invaluable and consistently excellent. I want to thank Travis Fain and Dave Ress at the *Daily Press*; Derek Quizon and Ruth Serven Smith at the *Daily Progress*; Jeremy Lazarus at the *Richmond Free Press*; Bob Brown, Andrew Cain, K. Burnell Evans, Michael Martz, Justin Mattingly, Olympia Meola, Graham Moomaw, Mark Robinson, Jeff Schapiro, Markus Schmidt, Tammie Smith, Michael Paul Williams, and Patrick Wilson of the *Richmond Times-Dispatch*; Laurence Hammack and Dwayne Yancey of the *Roanoke Times*; Alan Suderman of the Associated Press; Peter Galuszka, Jason Roop, and Edwin Slipek of *Style Weekly*; Nick Anderson, Jenna Portnoy, Gregory Schneider, T. Rees Shapiro, and Laura Vozzella of the *Washington Post*; Mechelle Hankerson, Katie O'Connor, Ned Oliver, and Robert Zullo of the *Virginia Mercury*; Bill Bartel of the *Virginian-Pilot*; and Jim Bacon, Lowell Feld, Norm Leahy, and Jeanine Martin at *Bacon's Rebellion*, *Blue Virginia*, *Bearing Drift*, and the *Bull Elephant*, respectively.

Many thanks to my family and my lifelong friends the Fountains and Tropes for their love and support. And thank you especially to Bumi, Lola, and Scout for being such sweet little evolutionarily optimized serotonin wolves.

NOTES

Introduction

1. Carole Troxler, "That MVP Spur Line? It's All About Gas Exports," *Danville Register & Bee*, August 5, 2018.

2. Duncan Adams, "Pipeline Turnabout: Gas Could Be Sent to India," *Roanoke Times*, June 25, 2015.

3. Virginia Constitution, Article 1, Section 11.

4. Bart Hinkle, "Should Dominion Get to Walk All Over Property Rights?," *Richmond Times-Dispatch*, January 6, 2015.

5. Gregory Schneider, "Perched High on a Platform in a Tree, a 61-Year-Old Woman Fights a Gas Pipeline," *Washington Post*, April 21, 2018.

6. Michael Sainato, "With Treetop Protest, 61-Year-Old Red Terry Is Leading Fight Against Mountain Valley Pipeline," *Common Dreams*, April 22, 2018.

7. Gene Marrano, "'Red' Will Not Go Without Necessities While Tree Sitting to Protest MVP," WFIR, April 13, 2018; Lowell Feld, "Video: 'Red Terry' Takes a Stand—'I Will Come Out of This Tree When These People Get Off My Land,'" *Blue Virginia*, April 17, 2018.

8. Joe Dashiell, "State Lawmakers Call for More Pipeline Oversight," WDBJ, April 18, 2018.

9. Gene Marrano, "'Red' Says Focus Should Be on MVP—Not Her Lack of Food and Water," WFIR, April 19, 2018.

10. David Seidel, "Roanoke County Pipeline Protesters Facing Arrest," Virginia Public Radio, April 19, 2018.

11. Laurence Hammack, "Roanoke County Police Charge 2 Women in Trees Blocking the Mountain Valley Pipeline," *Roanoke Times*, April 19, 2018.

12. Joe Dashiell, "Treatment of Tree Sitters a Continuing Issue, as Pipeline Protest Spreads," WDBJ, April 20, 2018.

13. Schneider, "Perched High."

14. Garrett Epps, *The Shad Treatment: A Novel* (New York: Putnam, 1977).

15. Laurence Hammack, "Roanoke County Police Deliver Pizza, Sandwiches to Pipeline Protesters in Tree Stands," *Roanoke Times*, April 23, 2018.

16. Sarah Jones, "Whose Appalachia Is It, Anyways?," *New Republic*, May 8, 2018.

17. Rhiannon Leebrick, "Environmental Gentrification and Development in a Rural Appalachian Community: Blending Critical Theory and Ethnography" (dissertation, University of Tennessee, 2015), 5.

18. See, for example: Emily Shugerman, "'Frustration, Anger, Helplessness': Virginia Pipeline Protesters on What Drove Them to Live in the Trees," *Independent* (UK), May 5, 2018; Chris Tomlinson, "More Pipelines Needed to Meet Environmental Goals," *Houston Chronicle*, April 25, 2018.

19. Henry Howell III, "A Visit to 'Red,' 'Nutty' and Two NFS Officers: My Name Is Henry Howell, Bar Number 22274, Write That Down!," *Blue Virginia*, April 28, 2018.

20. Henry Howell III, "Why Aren't the Governor and the Attorney General Stepping Up to Help Red and the Other Tree Sitters?," *Blue Virginia*, April 20, 2018, italics in original.

21. Sandy Hausman, "Red Terry Comes Down from Her Tree to Preach Against Pipelines," Virginia Public Radio, May 8, 2018; Jones, "Whose Appalachia."

22. Laurence Hammack, "Mountain Valley Pipeline Cuts Workforce, Delays Project Completion to Late 2019," *Roanoke Times*, August 17, 2018.

23. Laurence Hammack, "Virginia Files Lawsuit Against Mountain Valley Pipeline," *Roanoke Times*, December 7, 2018; "SCC Rejects Dominion Integrated Resource Plan," *Augusta Free Press*, December 7, 2018.

24. Laura Vozzella, "State Attorney General Mark Herring to Run for Virginia Governor in 2021," *Washington Post*, December 7, 2018.

25. Lowell Feld, "Exclusive: Blue Virginia Interview with Virginia AG Mark Herring," *Blue Virginia*, December 18, 2018.

26. Valdimer Orlando Key, *Southern Politics in State and Nation* (New York: Knopf, 1949), 19.

27. Peter Galuszka, *Thunder on the Mountain: Death at Massey and the Dirty Secrets Behind Big Coal* (New York: St. Martin's Press, 2012), 70–72.

28. David Goldfield, "A Place to Come To," in *Charlotte, NC: The Global Evolution of a New South City*, ed. William Graves and Heather Smith (Athens: University of Georgia Press, 2010), 11–23.

29. Robert Caro, *The Passage of Power: The Years of Lyndon Johnson* (New York: Knopf, 2012), 467–68.

30. Brent Tarter, interview with the author, February 3, 2017.

31. John Roemer, *Political Competition: Theory and Applications* (Cambridge, MA: Harvard University Press, 2001), 3.

32. Christopher Newport University Wason Center for Public Policy, "Voters Back Compromise on Medicaid Expansion, Support Marijuana Reform, Minimum Wage Hike," February 7, 2018, https://bloximages.newyork1.vip.townnews.com/pilotonline.com/content/tncms/assets/v3/editorial/c/77/c77f8ee9-47c3-5208-810e-5a45e762a3ee/5a7b20dfb8755.pdf.

33. Susan Davis and Jessica Taylor, "4 Reasons Why Progressives Aren't Thrilled with Clinton's Pick of Kaine," National Public Radio, July 23, 2016.

34. Bernie Niemeier, "Tim Kaine Is Good for Business," *Virginia Business*, October 2018.

35. The federal funding for 2019 would be 93 percent, and 90 percent thereafter. Rudowitz, "Understanding How States Access the ACA Enhanced Medicaid Match Rates," Kaiser Family Foundation, September 29, 2014.

36. Some of this section appeared as the essay: Jeff Thomas, "The Biggest Story in Virginia Politics in 2017 Is Not What You Think," *Blue Virginia*, December 22, 2017.

37. John Chichester, "The Virginia Way," in *Governing Virginia*, ed. Anne Marie Morgan and A.R. Pete Giesen (Boston: Pearson Learning Solutions, 2011), 229, 233.

38. James Madison, *Federalist No. 51*.

39. "Term of the Senate, [26 June] 1787," *Founders Online*, National Archives, last modified June 13, 2018, http://founders.archives.gov/documents/Madison/01-10-02-0044. Original source: Robert Rutland, Charles Hobson, William Rachal and Frederika J. Teute, eds., *The Papers of James Madison*, vol. 10, *27 May 1787–3 March 1788* (Chicago: University of Chicago Press, 1977), 76–78.

40. Alan Suderman, "The Virginia Way: Corporate Money for Personal Niceties," *Daily Press*, Associated Press, February 20, 2016.

41. Madison, *Federalist No. 51*.

42. Jenna Portnoy, "Va. Senate Leaders Spar Over Health Care, Gun Control, Climate Change," *Washington Post*, October 5, 2015.

43. Patrick Wilson, "Records: Norment Admitted to Relationship with Lobbyist," *Virginian-Pilot*, April 3, 2015.

44. Jenna Portnoy, "Federal Investigators Review Top Va. Lawmaker's Relationship with Lobbyist," *Washington Post*, April 23, 2015; Virginia Code §18.2-365, Adultery defined; penalty.

45. Michael Martz, "Richard Cullen to Step Down as McGuireWoods Chairman but Continue Law Practice," *Richmond Times-Dispatch*, September 9, 2017.

46. Wilson, "Records."

47. Patrick Wilson, "Va. Senate Leader Norment to Wed Lobbyist," *Richmond Times-Dispatch*, July 16, 2018.

48. Patrick Wilson, "Watchdog Group Says McGuireWoods Utilized Weak Va. Law by Hiring Former Speaker," *Richmond Times-Dispatch*, July 16, 2018.

49. Jeff Schapiro, "Former Va. Speaker's New Habitat: The Swamp," *Richmond Times-Dispatch*, July 17, 2018.

50. Bill Howell and Tommy Norment, "Rebuilding Trust: Our Pledge to Virginians," *Roanoke Times*, September 11, 2014.

51. Alan Suderman and David Lieb, "Virginia, Missouri, Limit Media Access at State Capitols," *Business Insider*, Associated Press, January 15, 2016.

52. Robert Zullo, "Meet the Mercury: A New Look at the Virginia Way," *Virginia Mercury*, July 17, 2018.

53. Bill Bartel, "Poll: Virginians Want Term Limits, Tougher Ethics Laws," *Virginian-Pilot*, January 28, 2015.

54. William Selway, "Star's Williams Microwaved Tobacco Before McDonnell Probe," *Bloomberg News*, July 1, 2013.

55. *McDonnell v. United States*, U.S. Supreme Court 15-474, 2016.

56. Brett LoGiurato, "Former Virginia Governor Bob McDonnell and Wife Indicted on Federal Corruption Charges," *Business Insider*, January 21, 2014.

57. Corey Hutchins, "Losing the Virginia Way," *Columbia Journalism Review*, July 18, 2013.

58. Kimberley Strassel, "Terry McAuliffe's Solyndra," *Wall Street Journal*, April 11, 2013.

59. Tarter, interview.

60. Michael Martz, "Dominion Rules: After Epic Corporate Feud, Energy Giant Emerges to Dominate Regulators, Legislators," *Richmond Times-Dispatch*, October 13, 2017.

61. Jeff Thomas, *Virginia Politics & Government in a New Century: The Price of Power* (Charleston, SC: The History Press, 2016), 11.

62. Patrick Wilson, "Lobbyists Take Changes to Gift Law in Stride," *Virginian-Pilot*, May 11, 2015.

63. Robert Zullo and Michael Martz, "After Two Years of Defending Rate Freeze, Dominion Says It's Time to 'Transition Away' from Controversial 2015 Law," *Richmond Times-Dispatch*, December 4, 2017.

64. "The High Cost of Compromise: Tobacco Industry Political Influence and Tobacco Control Policy in Virginia, 1977–2009," Center for Tobacco Control Research & Education at the University of California, 2010, 9.

65. Ann Boonn, "State Cigarette Excise Tax Rates & Rankings," Center for Tobacco Free Kids, Virginia Public Access Project, September 18, 2018; "Top Donors—All Years," https://www.vpap.org/money/top-donors/?year=all.

66. Joint Legislative Audit and Review Commission, "Management and Accountability of the Virginia Economic Development Partnership," January 20, 2017.

67. James Southall Wilson, "A Plutarch for Virginia," *Virginia Quarterly Review*, Spring 1930.

68. Lauren Bell, David Meyer, and Ronald Gaddie, *Slingshot: The Defeat of Eric Cantor* (Thousand Oaks, CA: CQ Press, 2016), 1.

69. Editorial Board, "Rainbows," *Richmond Times-Dispatch*, August 2, 2014.

70. Universal Corporation, "Board of Directors: Diana F. Cantor," 2018, http://investor.universalcorp.com/board-directors/diana-cantor.

71. Gordon Morse, "Bill Howell, An Honorable Servant of Virginia," *Virginian-Pilot*, July 29, 2018.

72. Shakespeare, *Hamlet*, act I, scene IV.

73. Shakespeare, *Twelfth Night*, act II, scene V.

74. Ben Campbell, interview with the author, April 2, 2017.

75. Brent Tarter, "Making History in Virginia," *The Virginia Magazine of History and Biography* 115, no. 1 (2007): 2–55.

76. Editorial Board, "How Virginians Came to Be Taught Propaganda," *Roanoke Times*, July 9, 2018.

77. Michael Paul Williams, "For Two Decades, Virginia Textbooks Fed Baby Boomers a Bogus History of Slavery. Why That Matters Today," *Richmond Times-Dispatch*, April 16, 2018.

78. Charles Dew, *The Making of a Racist: A Southerner Reflects on Family, History, and the Slave Trade* (Charlottesville: University of Virginia Press, 2017), 19, 22.

79. James Branch Cabell, *Let Me Lie: Being in the Main an Ethnological Account of the Remarkable Commonwealth of Virginia and the Making of Its History* (Charlottesville: University of Virginia Press, 1947), 281.

80. James Ryan, *Five Miles Away, A World Apart: One City, Two Schools, and the Story of Educational Opportunity in America* (Oxford, UK: Oxford University Press, 2010).

81. Frederick Law Olmsted, *A Journey in the Back Country* (N.p., 1860).

82. Bart Hinkle, "Todd Culbertson Retires," *Richmond Times-Dispatch*, July 21, 2017; see archived screenshot of his byline at Virginia Governmental Employees Association, http://www.vgea.org/files/nov302012RTDOpinionCuccinelliDefyingOdds.pdf.

83. Editorial Board, "Week's End: Wrap-Up," *Richmond Times-Dispatch*, May 14, 2011.

84. Todd Culbertson, "Education Book: Vanishing Act," *Richmond Times-Dispatch*, February 28, 2011.

85. McGregor McCance, "James E. Ryan, Ninth President of the University of Virginia, Takes Office Today," *UVA Today*, August 1, 2018.

86. Editorial Board, "How Virginians Came to Be Taught Propaganda."

87. Campbell, interview.

88. Cabell, *Let Me Lie*, 283, 285.

Chapter 1

1. Federal Election Commission, "Who Can and Can't Contribute," 2019.
2. Jeff Schapiro, "What If Dominion's Money Wasn't Flooding the System?," *Richmond Times-Dispatch*, March 17, 2015.
3. FlightAware aircraft registrations. Search by tail numbers, e.g., https://flightaware.com/resources/registration/N607D, accessed December 17, 2018. See also Fiona Young-Brown, "The Costs to Own and Operate a Gulfstream G450," *Sherpa Report*, May 10, 2016.
4. Mike Colagrossi, "The 5 Highest Paid Execs in the Utility Sector," Investopedia.com, October 9, 2018; Grace Relf, "The Results Are In: Here Are the Most Energy-Efficient Utilities in the US," American Council for an Energy-Efficient Economy, June 13, 2017.
5. Virginia State Corporation Commission, "Status Report: Implementation of the Virginia Electric Utility Regulation Act," September 1, 2016, https://www.scc.virginia.gov/comm/reports/2016_veur.pdf.
6. Michael Martz, "Dominion Retains Controlling Share in Pipeline Company in Restructuring After Piedmont Sale," *Richmond Times-Dispatch*, October 3, 2016.
7. MarketWatch, "Stock Quote: Dominion Energy," June 6, 2019, https://www.marketwatch.com/investing/stock/d.
8. Michael Martz, "Dominion Rules: Attempted Coup," *Richmond Times-Dispatch*, October 13, 2017.
9. Michael Martz, "Dominion Rules: After Epic Corporate Feud, Energy Giant Emerges to Dominate Regulators, Legislators," *Richmond Times-Dispatch*, October 13, 2017.
10. Robert Zullo, "Dominion Fails in Attempt to Bar Testimony on Pipeline's Potential $2.3 Billion Hit for Ratepayers," *Richmond Times-Dispatch*, March 12, 2018.
11. Stephanie Saul and Patricia Cohen, "Profitable Giants Like Amazon Pay $0 in Corporate Taxes. Some Voters Are Sick of It," *New York Times*, April 29, 2019.
12. Peter Galuszka, "No More Hippies in Old Sneakers," *Bacon's Rebellion*, October 30, 2014.
13. GreeneHurlocker, PLC, "Principles of Electric Utility Regulation in Virginia," November 2017, https://www.greenehurlocker.com/Principles.pdf.
14. Manuel Madrid, "Virginia's Power Broker," *American Prospect*, June 22, 2017.
15. Jenna Portnoy, "Va. Bill Would Put a Pause on Dominion Audits Linked to Refunds or Rate Reductions," *Washington Post*, January 28, 2015.
16. Patrick Wilson, "Lobbyists Take Changes to Gift Law in Stride," *Virginian-Pilot*, May 11, 2015.
17. For a more detailed legislative history of the 2015 bill, see Thomas, *Virginia Politics*, 55–78.

18. Dave Ress, "Dominion Surcharges Carve Away at Promised Reform Savings," *Daily Press*, August 5, 2018.

19. Paula Squires, "Electric Utility Reform," *Virginia Business*, March 29, 2018.

20. Glen Besa, interview with the author, January 12, 2017.

21. Michael Martz, "Dominion Rules: They're Not the Problem—It's the General Assembly," *Richmond Times-Dispatch*, October 13, 2017.

22. Jon Sokolow, "Why Is Ralph Northam Allowing a Young Woman to Starve for Protesting a Pipeline?," *Blue Virginia*, May 20, 2018.

23. Alan Suderman, "Facing New Scrutiny in Va., Dominion Energy Turns to Old Friends," WTOP, Associated Press, January 29, 2018; Alan Suderman, "Virginia Lawmakers Need a Raise, Governor's Ethics Panel Says," *Loudoun Times-Mirror*, June 5, 2015.

24. Daniel Marans, "What a Battle Over Virginia's Most Powerful Monopoly Can Teach Democrats Everywhere," *Huffington Post*, February 12, 2018.

25. Will Driscoll, "How Activate Virginia Persuaded 76 Candidates to Sign the 'No Dominion $' Pledge—A Model for Other States," *Blue Virginia*, November 22, 2017.

26. Laura Vozzella, "Perriello Comes Out Against Pipeline and, in a Shift, Says He Is Skeptical of Offshore Drilling," *Washington Post*, February 9, 2017.

27. Madrid, "Virginia's Power Broker."

28. Travis Fain, "Unexpectedly Competitive Democratic Primary Features Two Strong Candidates," *Daily Press*, May 27, 2017.

29. Fenit Nirappil, "What Virginia's Governor-Elect Ralph Northam (D) Promised During His Campaign," *Washington Post*, November 23, 2017.

30. Steven Thomas, "Virginia Republicans Are Literally Choosing to Lose," *The Bull Elephant*, November 7, 2018; Jordan Pascale, "Virginia Dems Are on a Decade-Long Statewide Win Streak, but Tim Kaine Won't Call the State Blue Just Yet," WAMU, November 7, 2018.

31. Editorial Board, "Corey Stewart Rides Again," *Richmond Times-Dispatch*, August 9, 2017.

32. Gregory Schneider, "'They Would Work Their Hearts Out for Him' If Only Northam Opposed Pipelines, Protesters Say," *Washington Post*, July 30, 2017.

33. Madrid, "Virginia's Power Broker."

34. Stephen Nash and Mary Peyton Baskin, "After the Deal Goes Down: Stacked Decks and Virginia Democracy," *Bristol Herald-Courier*, September 25, 2017.

35. Editorial Board, "The 2015 Election Is Really About 2017—and Beyond," *Roanoke Times*, October 9, 2015.

36. Mark Moore, "Virginia Decides Tied Election by Drawing Name from Bowl," *New York Post*, January 4, 2018.

37. Robert Zullo, "Thirteen Candidates Who Refused Dominion Money Win Seats in General Assembly," *Richmond Times-Dispatch*, November 9, 2017.

38. Patrick Wilson, "After Pledging an Aggressive Race Against GOP Del. Jackson Miller, State Democratic Party Abandons Populist Challenger," *Richmond Times-Dispatch*, October 22, 2017.

39. James Bacon, "Follow the Dark Money," *Bearing Drift*, December 1, 2017; James Bacon, "New Chapter for Bacon's Rebellion," *Bacon's Rebellion*, June 15, 2018; Peter Galuszka, "Dubious Oil Lobby Bankrolls Dubious Poll," *Bacon's Rebellion*, June 17, 2015. Partially redacted payment agreement posted at https://www.baconsrebellion.com/archive/pdfs/2015/06/Dominion_BR_sponsorship_2015.pdf.

40. Gabe Cavallaro, "Following the Money: How Dominion's State Political Spending Rates vs. Top Environmental Groups," *Staunton News Leader*, June 19, 2017; Ferit Nirappil, "Democratic Megadonor Tom Steyer to Spend $2 Million in Virginia Governor's Race," *Washington Post*, August 22, 2017.

41. Jeff Schapiro, "Feeling Sorry for Big Power, but Not Too Sorry," *Richmond Times-Dispatch*, February 3, 2018.

42. Graham Moomaw, "Major Democratic Donor in Virginia Aims to Counter Dominion Donations with His Own Money," *Richmond Times-Dispatch*, February 8, 2018.

43. "Clean Virginia Project Takes Aim at Dominion Energy Influence," *Augusta Free Press*, February 9, 2018.

44. Madrid, "Virginia's Power Broker."

45. Alan Suderman, "Facing New Scrutiny in Va., Dominion Energy Turns to Old Friends," WTOP, Associated Press, January 29, 2018.

46. Avery Wilks, "Dominion Energy, Hoping for SCANA Deal, Expands Footprint into Columbia Area," *The State* (Columbia, SC), October 1, 2018.

47. Tony Bartelme, "Dominion Energy: South Carolina's White Knight or a Deceptive Corporate Raider?," *Charleston Post & Courier*, January 6, 2018.

48. Colin Demarest, "Dominion Energy to Pause Advertising Campaign in South Carolina," *Aiken Standard*, February 15, 2018.

49. Virginia General Assembly, 2015, SJ323 Commending Dominion Resources, Inc.

50. Andrew Brown, "Dominion CEO Tells S.C. Senators There Is No 'Silver Bullet' for V.C. Summer Fiasco," *Charleston Post & Courier*, January 16, 2018.

51. Brian Garner, "This Is What the Ratepayers in S.C. Are Up Against," *Chester News & Reporter*, January 19, 2018.

52. Energy and Policy Institute, video of South Carolina legislative hearing, January 16, 2018, https://twitter.com/EnergyandPolicy/status/953425716779061249/video/1.

53. Brown, "Dominion CEO."

54. Avery Wilks, "Dominion to Cancel SCANA Deal, Senators Ready to Slash SCE&G Bills by 13%," *The State* (Columbia, SC), March 29, 2018.

55. Brown, "Dominion CEO."

56. Avery Wilks, "S.C. Senators Upset by Dominion's Plans to Profit from Failed Nuclear Project," *The State* (Columbia, SC), February 14, 2018.

57. Brown, "Dominion CEO."

58. Peter Maloney, "Dominion-SCANA Proposal Shows Shareholder Gains, Few Ratepayer Benefits, Analysts Say," *Utility Dive*, January 11, 2018.

59. Peter Maloney, "South Carolina Cuts SCE&G Rate 15%, Imperils Proposed Dominion-SCANA Merger," *Utility Dive*, June 28, 2018.

60. Avery Wilks, "SC Legislature Overrides McMaster's Veto of 15-percent SCE&G Cut," *The State* (Columbia, SC), June 28, 2018.

61. Dominion Energy, "Statement by Thomas F. Farrell, II, Dominion Energy Chairman, President & CEO in Response to South Carolina Conference Committee Action June 27, 2018," PR Newswire, June 27, 2018.

62. Robert Walton, "Report: SCANA, Dominion Offered $1,500 Refunds to Escape Summer Rate Cut," Utility Dive, July 24, 2018.

63. Maloney, "South Carolina Cuts SCE&G Rate."

64. Andrew Brown and Thad Moore, "Q&A: What Does SC&G Decision Mean for Ratepayers, Investors and Dominion?," *Charleston Post & Courier*, December 14, 2018.

65. Gregory Schneider, "Virginia Power Broker in the Hot Seat in Governor's Race," *Washington Post*, May 4, 2017.

66. "Dominion Gets a Name Change, New Logo," *Marcellus Drilling News*, May 11, 2017.

67. Ryan Grim, "Virginia Power Company Pushing Employees to Protect Pipeline in Democratic Governor Primary," *The Intercept*, June 12, 2017.

68. Bart Hinkle, "Goodbye, and Thank You for Everything," *Richmond Times-Dispatch*, June 12, 2018; Bart Hinkle, "Warnings About Monopoly Power Are Right," *Richmond Times-Dispatch*, December 9, 2017; Bart Hinkle, "Should Dominion Get to Walk All Over Property Rights?," *Richmond Times-Dispatch*, January 6, 2015.

69. Robert Zullo and Michael Martz, "After Two Years of Defending Rate Freeze, Dominion Says It's Time to 'Transition Away' from Controversial 2015 Law," *Richmond Times-Dispatch*, December 4, 2017.

70. Jenna Portnoy, "Va. Senate Leaders Spar Over Health Care, Gun Control, Climate Change," *Washington Post*, October 5, 2015.

71. Dave Ress, "The Virginia Way, Part 6: Giving Gifts, and Gaining Influence?," *Daily Press*, November 20, 2014.

72. Editorial Board, "More 'Cronyism' or Just Politics as Usual?," *Fredericksburg Free Lance-Star*, April 12, 2016.

73. Virginia Public Access Project, "Dominion Energy: Candidates Who Own Stock in Dominion Energy: 2017," https://www.vpap.org/seis/stockholders/120206-dominion-energy/?sei_period=22.

74. Patrick Wilson, "Ralph Northam's Ancestors Owned Slaves. He Found Out Only Recently," *Richmond Times-Dispatch*, June 2, 2017.

75. Beth Reinhard, "Northam Owns Stock in Dominion, Other Companies with Extensive Interests in Virginia," *Washington Post*, October 18, 2017.

76. Stephen Nash, "Gov. Northam's First Chance to Do Something About Money in Politics," *Washington Post*, January 12, 2018; Graham Moomaw, "After Calls for Campaign Finance Reform, Gov.-Elect Ralph Northam Takes Corporate Money for Inauguration," *Richmond Times-Dispatch*, December 22, 2017.

77. Gregory Schneider, "Governor, Attorney General Disagree Over Bill to Regulate Utilities," *Washington Post*, February 5, 2018.

78. Patrick Wilson, "Dominion Executive, Company Law Firm to Help Host Fundraiser for Gov. Northam's PAC," *Richmond Times-Dispatch*, December 21, 2018.

79. Alan Suderman, "Dominion's Donations Partially Subsidized by Its Customers," *Washington Times*, Associated Press, August 22, 2015.

80. Alan Suderman, "Dominion Won't Include Charity Donations in Customers' Bills," *Richmond Times-Dispatch*, September 2, 2015.

81. Patrick Wilson, "Dominion and CEO Tom Farrell Gave Large Charitable Donations to Center Where Key Lawmaker Works," *Richmond Times-Dispatch*, January 23, 2018; Robert Zullo, "Meet the Mercury: A New Look at the Virginia Way," *Virginia Mercury*, July 17, 2018.

82. Michael Martz, "Dominion Offers $5.1 Million in Plan to Aid Buckingham Community Next to Pipeline Compressor Station," *Richmond Times-Dispatch*, November 7, 2018.

83. Zack Colman, "Trump Administration Is Repealing Obama's Clean Power Plan," *Scientific American*, October 10, 2017.

84. Madrid, "Virginia's Power Broker."

85. Robert Zullo, "Bill to Undo Controversial Utility Rate Freeze Faces Unfriendly Panel Monday as Dominion-Favored Plan Is Developed," *Richmond Times-Dispatch*, January 13, 2018.

86. Virginia General Assembly, 2018, SB9 Electric Utility Regulation, Suspension of Reviews of Earnings, Transitional Rate Period.

87. Graham Moomaw, "Virginia Legislator Calls Law that Froze Electricity Rates 'Corrupt'," *Richmond Times-Dispatch*, January 17, 2018.

88. Patrick Wilson, "Senate Committee Kills Bill to Ban Campaign Donations from Public-Service Corporations," *Richmond Times-Dispatch*, January 16, 2018.

89. Virginia General Assembly, 2018, SB966 Electric Utility Regulation, Grid Modernization, Energy Efficiency; Alan Suderman, "Dominion Increased Political Spending While Pushing for Law," *U.S. News & World Report*, Associated Press, July 10, 2018.

90. Jeff Schapiro, "Utility Bill a Riddle Wrapped in a Mystery, Inside an Enigma," *Richmond Times-Dispatch*, February 6, 2018.

91. Dave Ress, "Does Dominion Energy Still Wield as Much Power?," *Daily Press*, January 29, 2018.

92. Schapiro, "Utility Bill a Riddle."

93. Alan Suderman, "Facing New Scrutiny in Va., Dominion Energy Turns to Old Friends," WTOP, Associated Press, January 29, 2018.

94. Gregory Schneider, "Governor, Attorney General Disagree Over Bill to Regulate Utilities," *Washington Post*, February 5, 2018.

95. Robert Zullo, "State Regulators Say Proposed Utility Overhaul Still Limits Ability to Issue Refunds, Lower Rates," *Richmond Times-Dispatch*, February 7, 2018.

96. Gregory Schneider, "Northam Steps into Efforts to Undo Controversial Dominion Rate Freeze," *Washington Post*, January 30, 2018.

97. Dave Ress, "Va. Legislation Calls for Bigger Dominion Energy Refund, but Does It Lock in Higher Rates?," *Daily Press*, February 6, 2018.

98. For adoption of compromise framework, see, e.g., Robert Zullo, "'White Smoke' on Dominion Energy Regulatory Overhaul; Bill Heading to Senate Floor," *Richmond Times-Dispatch*, February 5, 2018; Alan Suderman, "Northam Announces Compromise on Electric Rate Overhaul," WTOP, Associated Press, February 5, 2018; Alex Koma, "Compromise May Restore State Control of Utility Rates," *Inside NoVA*, February 7, 2018.

99. Office of the Governor, "Governor Northam Statement on Rate Freeze Repeal Legislation," February 5, 2018, https://www.governor.virginia.gov/newsroom/all-releases/2018/february/headline-822704-en.html.

100. Gregory Schneider, "The Giant Company that Could: How Dominion Turned Scorn into a Big Payday," *Washington Post*, March 9, 2018.

101. Gregory Schneider, "Governor, Attorney General Disagree Over Bill to Regulate Utilities," *Washington Post*, February 5, 2018.

102. Preston Shannon, "The Evolution of Virginia's State Corporation Commission," *William & Mary Law Review* 13, no. 3 (1973): 533.

103. Virginia General Assembly, 2018, SB966 Electric Utility Regulation, Grid Modernization, Energy Efficiency.

104. Robert Zullo, "State Regulators Say Proposed Utility Overhaul Still Limits Ability to Issue Refunds, Lower Rates," *Richmond Times-Dispatch*, February 7, 2018.

105. Daniel Marans, "What a Battle Over Virginia's Most Powerful Monopoly Can Teach Democrats Everywhere," *Huffington Post*, February 12, 2018.

106. Zullo, "State Regulators Say."

107. Virginia General Assembly, 2018, SB966 Electric Utility Regulation, Grid Modernization, Energy Efficiency.

108. Michael Martz, "SCC Estimates Cost of New Electric Utility Law at Almost $5.6 Billion," *Richmond Times-Dispatch*, August 30, 2018.

109. Julian Walker, "Cuccinelli Opts for More Modest Virginia State Seal," *Virginian-Pilot*, May 1, 2010; Suzy Khimm, "Beyond Breastgate: Jurists Gone

Wild," *Mother Jones*, November/December 2010; Gwendolyn Bradley, "Ongoing Battle over Academic Freedom in Virginia," *Academe*, July/August 2011, 4–5.

110. Robert Zullo, "House Passes Utility Overhaul with Crucial Amendment Aimed at 'Double Dip'," *Richmond Times-Dispatch*, February 13, 2018.

111. Gregory Schneider, "Dominion Bill Passes Va. House with Key Change Aimed at Helping Consumers," *Washington Post*, February 13, 2018.

112. Robert Zullo, "'This Ain't Business': Controversial Utility Overhaul Heads to Governor's Desk," *Richmond Times-Dispatch*, March 1, 2018.

113. Schapiro, "Utility Bill a Riddle."

114. Robert Zullo, "Utility Overhaul Passes House, but with a Big Amendment; Measure, Approved 96-1, Meant to Ensure Power Companies Don't 'Double Dip' in Spending Billions," *Richmond Times-Dispatch*, February 12, 2018.

115. Robert Zullo, "House Passes Utility Overhaul with Crucial Amendment Aimed at 'Double Dip'," *Richmond Times-Dispatch*, February 13, 2018.

116. Daniel Marans, "Virginia Democrats Score a Surprising Win Against Powerful Utility Monopoly," *Huffington Post*, February 13, 2018; Christian Raymond, "Dominion Cronyism: An Attack on Virginia Families," *The Bull Elephant*, February 12, 2018.

117. Jeff Schapiro and Craig Carper, "Political Analysis for Friday, February 23, 2018," WCVE, February 23, 2018.

118. Gregory Schneider, "Dominion Bill Passes Va. House with Key Change Aimed at Helping Consumers," *Washington Post*, February 13, 2018.

119. Brian Reese, "Northam Signs Dominion Energy Backed Legislation," WAVY, March 9, 2018; David Dayen, "Elections Still Matter: Virginia Democrats Stun State Energy Monopoly in Late-Night Rejection," *The Intercept*, February 13, 2018.

120. Daniel Marans, "Virginia Democrats Score a Surprising Win Against Powerful Utility Monopoly," *Huffington Post*, February 13, 2018.

121. Editorial Board, "Northam's Atlantic Coast Pipeline Interference Disappointing, but Not Really Surprising," *Staunton News Leader*, November 30, 2018.

122. Daniel Marans, "What a Battle Over Virginia's Most Powerful Monopoly Can Teach Democrats Everywhere," *Huffington Post*, February 12, 2018.

123. Dave Ress, "Electric Rate Bill Amended to Prevent Double Dip," *Daily Press*, February 16, 2018.

124. Dave Ress, "Business Law-Writers Navigate Conflicting Investments, Interests," *Daily Press*, April 16, 2018.

125. Michael Martz, "Dominion Customers Will Bear the Risks of $300 Million Offshore Wind Pilot; SCC Puts Responsibility on Legislators," *Richmond Times-Dispatch*, November 2, 2018.

126. Graham Moomaw, "Anti-'Double Dip' Provision Added to Senate Bill to Overhaul Electricity Regulation in Virginia," *Roanoke Times*, February 20, 2018.

127. Peter Anderson, "A Watershed Moment in Virginia's Energy Politics," *Appalachian Voices*, March 16, 2018.

128. Zullo, "House Passes Utility Overhaul."

129. Daniel Marans, "Virginia Democrats Score a Surprising Win Against Powerful Utility Monopoly," *Huffington Post*, February 13, 2018.

130. Dave Ress, "Does Dominion Energy Still Wield as Much Power?," *Daily Press*, January 29, 2018.

131. Michael Martz and Robert Zullo, "Virginia Supreme Court Upholds Law Freezing Electric Rate Reviews, but with Strong Dissent," *Richmond Times-Dispatch*, September 14, 2017.

132. Jeff Schapiro, "Toscana and His Muscular Minority," *Richmond Times-Dispatch*, February 20, 2018.

133. Mark Keam, "Why I'm Breaking Up with Dominion Energy," *Washington Post*, March 15, 2018.

134. Alan Suderman, "Dominion Increased Political Spending While Pushing for Law," *U.S. News & World Report*, Associated Press, July 10, 2018.

135. Ken Cuccinelli and Andrew Miller, "Here's Why Your Electric Bill's Too High," *Richmond Times-Dispatch*, September 18, 2017.

136. Patrick Wilson, "Lobbying Firm to Va. Lawmakers: If You Refuse ApCo Money, You Won't Get Any from Us," *Richmond Times-Dispatch*, June 25, 2018. Parenthetical text in original.

137. Ibid.

138. Editorial Board, "Virginia Requires Campaign Finance Reform," *Daily Press*, July 30, 2018.

139. Editorial Board, "'Pay to Play' in the State Legislature," *Lynchburg News & Advance*, July 6, 2018.

140. Sue Sturgis, "Virginia Anti-Corruption Movement Faces Down Corporate Backlash," *Facing South*, July 19, 2018.

141. Robert Zullo, "Dominion to Pay Back Estimated $11 Million to $12 Million to Overcharged Commercial Customers," *Richmond Times-Dispatch*, August 1, 2017; Kevin Green, "Dominion to Refund More than $11 Million in Overcharging," WAVY, Associated Press, August 2, 2017.

142. Martz and Zullo, "Virginia Supreme Court Upholds Law," parentheses in original.

143. Michael Martz, "Dominion Rules: 'They Attacked the Messenger'," *Richmond Times-Dispatch*, October 13, 2017.

144. Samantha Baars, "Dominion's Win: Bills Reduce Refunds, Thwart SCC Regulation," *C-ville Weekly*, March 7, 2018; Tom Cormons, "Tide Is Turning on Dominion Energy," *Daily Progress*, February 18, 2018.

145. Michael Martz, "SCC Rejects Costco Bid to Shop for Electricity to Avoid Rising Dominion Rates," *Richmond Times-Dispatch*, May 30, 2019; Gregory

Schneider, "Costco, Walmart and Other Big Retailers Try to Break Dominion Energy's Grip in Virginia," *Washington Post*, June 2, 2019.

146. Iulia Gheorghiu, "Tech Giants Pressure Dominion for More Storage, Renewables, Less Gas in Virginia," *Utility Dive*, May 14, 2019.

147. Some of this section appeared as an essay: Jeff Thomas, "Dominion's Power Crisis," *Blue Virginia*, June 19, 2018.

148. Tarter, interview with the author.

149. Daniel Marans, "What a Battle Over Virginia's Most Powerful Monopoly Can Teach Democrats Everywhere," *Huffington Post*, February 12, 2018.

150. Robert Zullo, "Dominion Rules: A Changing Landscape for a Power Player," *Richmond Times-Dispatch*, October 13, 2017.

Chapter 2

1. UVA Today, "For Virginians, UVA Offers 'Unmatched Affordability and Value'," August 24, 2016.

2. "Thomas Jefferson and Sally Hemings: A Brief Account," Monticello, 2019, https://www.monticello.org/site/plantation-and-slavery/thomas-jefferson-and-sally-hemings-brief-account.

3. See, e.g., Virginius Dabney, *Mr. Jefferson's University: A History* (Charlottesville: University of Virginia Press, 1988); Ruth Serven Smith, "Sullivan Reflects on Her Tenure at UVa," *Daily Progress*, July 28, 2018.

4. Library of Congress, "Thomas Jefferson: Creating a Virginia Republic," 2019, https://www.loc.gov/exhibits/jefferson/jeffrep.html.

5. Thomas Jefferson et al., *Report of the Board of Commissioners for the University of Virginia to the Virginia General Assembly*, August 4, 1818, https://founders.archives.gov/documents/Madison/04-01-02-0289.

6. Library of Congress, "Jefferson."

7. University of Virginia, "Undergraduate Admissions: Academic Profile of First-Year Class: All Schools: High School Rank," Institutional Assessment & Studies, 2019, http://ias.virginia.edu/university-stats-facts/undergraduate-admissions.

8. The full text of these documents is available at http://www.cavalierdaily.com/article/2017/04/advancement-office-freedom-of-information-act-request-documents.

9. University of Virginia, "Affording UVA," 2019, http://www.virginia.edu/life/affordinguva.

10. University of Virginia, "Financial Aid," 2019, http://financialaid.virginia.edu.

11. T. Rees Shapiro, "At U-Va., a 'Watch List' Flags VIP Applicants for Special Handling," *Washington Post*, April 1, 2017.

12. Derek Quizon, "UVa 'Watch List' Said to Fit the Pattern of Other Universities," *Daily Progress*, April 3, 2017.

13. Watch list, FOIA documents #1, 47, 53.

14. Watch list, FOIA documents #1, 101.

15. Virginia Freedom of Information Act, § 2.2-3705.4.7.

16. Shapiro, "At U-Va."

17. Quizon, "UVa 'Watch List.'"

18. Editorial Board, "U.Va. Admission Should Be Based on Merit, Not Money," *Cavalier Daily*, April 3, 2017.

19. James Bacon, "A Thumb on the Scale for Rich Kids Applying to UVa," *Bacon's Rebellion*, April 2, 2017.

20. Editorial Board, "UVa's Affirmative Action for Rich People," *Richmond Times-Dispatch*, April 6, 2017.

21. Liam Flaherty, "In Defense of U.Va. Admissions," *Cavalier Daily*, April 5, 2017.

22. Sandy Hausman, "Documents Raise Doubts on Fairness of Admissions at UVA," Virginia Public Radio, April 3, 2017; Sandy Hausman, "Richmond Journalist Calling for Federal Probe of UVA," Virginia Public Radio, April 11, 2017.

23. College of William & Mary FOIA officer Lillian Stevens, email to author, September 24, 2018.

24. George Mason University FOIA officer Elizabeth Woodley, email to author, September 25, 2018.

25. Christopher Newport University FOIA officer Tom Kramer, email to author, October 11, 2018; Virginia Commonwealth University FOIA officer Michele Howell, email to author, October 3, 2018; Virginia Tech FOIA officer Bobbie Jean Norris, email to author, September 19, 2018.

26. Derek Quizon, "Author Calls on Federal Prosecutors to Investigate UVa Admissions," *Daily Progress*, April 12, 2017.

27. Jodi Cohen, Stacy St. Clair, and Tara Malone, "Clout Goes to College," *Chicago Tribune*, May 29, 2009; Amanda Paulson, "Admissions Scandal Brings Down University of Illinois President," *Christian Science Monitor*, September 23, 2009; Susan Saulny, "U. of Illinois Trustee Quits Over Scandal," *New York Times*, August 3, 2009.

28. Reeve Hamilton, "Powers Will Give Up UT-Austin Presidency in June," *Texas Tribune*, July 9, 2014.

29. Kroll, *University of Texas at Austin—Investigation of Admissions Practices and Allegations of Undue Influence*, February 6, 2015. Available at: https://static.texastribune.org/media/documents/Kroll_report.pdf.

30. Thomas Roades, "Student Council to Investigate Alleged Preferential Treatment in U.Va. Admissions," *Cavalier Daily*, April 3, 2017.

31. Thomas Roades, "Student Council Releases Admissions Investigation Report," *Cavalier Daily*, April 19, 2017.

32. Thomas Roades, "Student Council Members Debate Admissions Investigation Findings," *Cavalier Daily*, May 3, 2017.

33. Sean Jenkins, email to investment manager Hi Ewald, April 12, 2017, FOIA documents #2, 6.

34. Chief of Staff Nancy Rivers, email to President's Executive Cabinet, March 24, 2017, FOIA documents #3, 401–2.

35. FOIA documents #3, 25 (Bruner), 87 (Wright), 329 (Katstra), 335 (Hysell).

36. John Grisham, email to Associate Athletic Director Barry Parkhill, February 2, 2017; FOIA documents #3, 137; John Casteen, email to Sean Jenkins, February 3, 2017, FOIA documents #3, 134; FOIA documents #3, 110 (Caputo), 61 (Kilberg), 71 (Clement).

37. Iam Baucom, email to Paul Kipps, Michael Citro, Gene Schutt, and Sean Jenkins, November 30, 2015, FOIA documents #3, 25.

38. Sean Jenkins, email to and from Nursing School assistant dean for admissions and financial aid Clay Hysell, January 2, 2017, FOIA documents #3, 335–336.

39. Sean Jenkins, email to Associate Director of Virginia Athletics Foundation Lo Davis, February 20, 2013, FOIA documents #3, 308.

40. Sean Jenkins, emails to [redacted person #1], January 21, 2012, FOIA documents #3, 346.

41. Advancement staffer Ryan William Emanual, emails to and from Sean Jenkins, February 22–24, 2016, FOIA documents #3, 475.

42. Real estate investor Tyler Blue, emails to and from Sean Jenkins, April 25, 2017, FOIA documents #3, 1.

43. Sean Jenkins, emails to and from [redacted person #2], February 19 and 21, 2014, FOIA documents #3, 267.

44. Sean Jenkins, emails to and from [redacted person #3], June 23, 2013, FOIA documents #3, p. 287.

45. Sean Jenkins, emails to and from Executive Director of the Darden School Foundation Locke Ogens, January 29, 2013, FOIA documents #3, 321.

46. Emails between Sean Jenkins and/or Vice President for Advancement Mark Luellen, and/or Senior Director for Administration and External Relations Mike Citro, and/or [redacted person #4], January 19, 21, February 11, 13, 2017, FOIA documents #3, 455–57.

47. Sean Jenkins, emails to Nancy Rivers and Mike Citro, February 17, 2017, FOIA documents #3, 446.

48. Watch list, FOIA documents #1, p. 98.

49. Sean Jenkins, email to Virginia Athletics Foundation executive director Dirk Katstra, March 31, 2014, FOIA documents #3, 245.

50. Sean Jenkins, email to Mike Citro, February 8, 2017, FOIA documents #3, 101.

51. Sean Jenkins, email to Dirk Katstra, March 31, 2014, FOIA documents #3, 247.

52. Email from [redacted #5] to President Sullivan, April 3, 2017, FOIA documents #3, 409–10.

53. Nick Anderson, "Pell Grant Shares at Top-Ranked Colleges: A Sortable Chart," *Washington Post*, October 31, 2017.

54. Kaiser Family Foundation, "Median Annual Household Income," 2016, https://www.kff.org/other/state-indicator/median-annual-income/?current Timeframe=0&sortModel=%7B%22colId%22:%22Median%20Annual%20 Household%20Income%22,%22sort%22:%22desc%22%7D.

55. David Leonhardt, "California's Upward-Mobility Machine," *New York Times*, September 16, 2015; see also associated table, "Top Colleges Doing the Most for Low-Income Students."

56. This is examined in greater detail in *Virginia Politics & Government in a New Century: The Price of Power*, chapter 5, "Manufacturing Crises at the University of Virginia." This section uses several of the same sources.

57. Carolyn Chappell, "The Virginia Commission on Higher Education Board Appointments: The Impact of Legislative Reform on Public University Governance" (dissertation, George Mason University, Summer 2013), 148, 151.

58. Derek Quizon, "UVa 'Watch List' Said to Fit the Pattern of Other Universities," *Daily Progress*, April 3, 2017.

59. Virginia Public Access Project, "Donors: William H. Goodwin, Jr.: All Years," 2019, https://www.vpap.org/donors/5595-william-h-goodwin-jr/?start_ year=all&end_year=all.

60. Carol Wood, "Changes at the Top: Wynne, Abramson to Lead Board of Visitors," UVA Today, June 19, 2009; Virginia Public Access Project, "Donors: John O. Wynne: All Years," 2019, https://www.vpap.org/donors/53151-john-o-wynne/?start_year=all&end_year=all.

61. Hawes Spencer, "Dragas on Board: The Rector Who Wouldn't Go," *The Hook*, August 23, 2012.

62. Nick Anderson, "Medical Executive Quits U-Va. Governing Board, Blasts Administration on Way Out," *Washington Post*, April 13, 2015. Errors in original.

63. Andrew Rice, "Anatomy of a Campus Coup," *New York Times Magazine*, September 11, 2012.

64. Nick Anderson, "U-Va. Set Aside $2.2 Billion for 'Strategic Investments.' A Former Board Member Calls It a 'Slush Fund,'" *Washington Post*, July 13, 2016.

65. Email to author, April 15, 2017.

Chapter 3

1. K. Burnell Evans, "Church Hill School's Building Woes Take Spotlight at Richmond School Board Meeting," *Richmond Times-Dispatch*, June 19, 2017. Part of this essay appeared in Jeff Thomas, "The Last Gasp of Massive Resistance: Richmond's 2019 Coliseum Scheme," *Blue Virginia*, December 9, 2018. I have omitted quotations for stylistic reasons.

2. Justin Mattingly, "Water Tests Positive for Lead at 2 Richmond Elementary Schools," *Richmond Times-Dispatch*, September 26, 2017; K. Burnell Evans, "Teachers and Parents Decry Conditions at Mason Elementary, The Worst Facility in Richmond's Portfolio," *Richmond Times-Dispatch*, July 31, 2017.

3. Mark Robinson, "No Easy Solution," *Richmond Magazine*, September 11, 2017.

4. K. Burnell Evans, "'I'll Help Carry Boxes': Richmond School Board Members Debate Closing 'Deplorable' Elementary School," *Richmond Times-Dispatch*, July 17, 2017.

5. Jackie Kruszewski, "Community Reacts to Administration's Plans to Keep Students in George Mason Elementary School," *Style Weekly*, August 1, 2017.

6. Evans, "Teachers and Parents Decry Conditions." Bracketed text in original.

7. Robinson, "No Easy Solution."

8. Saraya Wintersmith, "Poor Conditions at George Mason Elementary Fire Up School Board," *Richmond Free Press*, July 21, 2017.

9. Kruszewski, "Community Reacts."

10. K. Burnell Evans, "With Only $14 Million in Hand, Richmond School Leaders Aren't Sure How to Start Building a Better District," *Richmond Times-Dispatch*, July 23, 2017.

11. Kruszewski, "Community Reacts."

12. K. Burnell Evans, "City School Officials' Priorities Include South Side Facilities, Dove Project," *Richmond Times-Dispatch*, November 5, 2015.

13. Kruszewski, "Community Reacts."

14. Evans, "Teachers and Parents Decry Conditions."

15. Holly Rodriguez, "George Mason Elementary to Stay Open with Repairs," *Richmond Free Press*, August 11, 2017.

16. Shawn Maclauchlan, "Richmond Passes Budget for 2019/2020," WTVR, May 15, 2018.

17. Rodriguez, "George Mason Elementary to Stay Open."

18. K. Burnell Evans, "Richmond School Board Signals Action on Redistricting and Rezoning, Possibly Soon," *Richmond Times-Dispatch*, March 6, 2017.

19. Kruszewski, "Community Reacts."

20. Evans, "Teachers and Parents Decry Conditions."

21. Carol Wolf, "How Redskins Football Pushed Richmond's Schools to the Breaking Point," *Style Weekly*, April 12, 2016.

22. Liz Clarke, "Redskins and Richmond: A Marriage in Need of Counseling?," *Washington Post*, August 12, 2017.

23. Editorial Board, "Richmond Schools Come Before Millionaire Athletes," *Richmond Times-Dispatch*, August 8, 2017.

24. Ned Oliver, "Richmond Panel Agrees to Rebate $111,000 Real Estate Tax Bill After Challenge by Stone Brewing," *Richmond Times-Dispatch*, July 20, 2017.

25. Justin Mattingly, "New Richmond Schools Superintendent to Be Highest Paid in Division History," *Richmond Times-Dispatch*, November 28, 2017; Justin Mattingly, "Here's Who Will Lead Richmond Public Schools Under the New Superintendent," *Richmond Times-Dispatch*, March 20, 2018.

26. Michael Martz, "Budget Bill Seeks to Raise Governor's Cabinet Members' Salaries to $172,000," *Richmond Times-Dispatch*, January 26, 2018; Caitlin Emma, "DeVos to Give Her Salary to Charities—Including One Trump Would Slash," *Politico*, February 14, 2018.

27. Brent Baldwin et al., "2018 Power List: Education," *Style Weekly*, August 28, 2018.

28. Doug Wilder, "Conversation on Monuments Must Delve Deep into America's Racial History—and Prompt Action," *Richmond Times-Dispatch*, August 26, 2017.

29. Editors, "The Injustice at George Mason Elementary School," *Republican Standard*, September 28, 2017; Michael Paul Williams, "Richmond Is Renaming a School Honoring a Confederate General. In Considering Others, It Must Avoid the Slippery Slope," *Richmond Times-Dispatch*, May 24, 2018; Ben Campbell, "Remove the Real Artifacts of the Confederacy," *Richmond Times-Dispatch*, August 26, 2017.

30. K. Burnell Evans, "'Lipstick on a Pig'—Dozens of Volunteers Work to Beautify George Mason Elementary School," *Richmond Times-Dispatch*, August 22, 2017.

31. Justin Mattingly, "Water Tests Positive for Lead at 2 Richmond Elementary Schools," *Richmond Times-Dispatch*, September 26, 2017.

32. Justin Mattingly, "Richmond Public Schools Has the Worst High School Graduation Rate in Virginia," *Richmond Times-Dispatch*, October 1, 2018.

33. K. Burnell Evans, "Church Hill School's Building Woes Take Spotlight at Richmond School Board Meeting," *Richmond Times-Dispatch*, June 19, 2017.

34. Tom Nash, "Caving In," *Style Weekly*, April 8, 2014.

35. Alix Bryan, "Issues Still Evident Despite Work Underway at George Mason Elementary," WTVR, August 22, 2017.

36. K. Burnell Evans, "Richmond School Board Signals Action on Redistricting and Rezoning, Possibly Soon," *Richmond Times-Dispatch*, March 6, 2017.

37. Evans, "With Only $14 Million."

38. Ben Campbell, interview with author, April 2, 2017.

39. Genevieve Siegel-Hawley, *When the Fences Come Down: Twenty-First Century Lessons from Metropolitan School Desegregation* (Chapel Hill: University of North Carolina Press, 2016), 55–72.

40. James Ryan, *Five Miles Away, A World Apart: One City, Two Schools, and the Story of Educational Opportunity in Modern America* (Oxford, UK: Oxford University Press, 2010), 72–90.

41. Kruszewski, "Community Reacts."

42. Nathaniel Cary and Doug Stanglin, "South Carolina Takes Down Confederate Flag," *USA Today*, July 10, 2015.

43. "Confederate Gen. Robert E. Lee Statute Removed in New Orleans," *New Orleans Times-Picayune*, May 19, 2017.

44. Mark Robinson, "Monument Avenue Commission: Remove Jefferson Davis Monument, Reinterpret Others Honoring Confederacy," *Richmond Times-Dispatch*, July 2, 2018.

45. Michael Kranish, "Richmond Split Over How to Remember Confederate History," *Boston Globe*, July 4, 2015.

46. Louis Nelson and Claudrena Harold, *Charlottesville 2017: The Legacy of Race and Inequity* (Charlottesville: University of Virginia Press), 2018.

47. Rex Springston, "Happy Slaves? The Peculiar Story of Three Virginia School Textbooks," *Richmond Times-Dispatch*, April 14, 2018.

48. Virginius Dabney, *Richmond: The Story of a City*, 2nd ed. (Charlottesville: University of Virginia Press, 1990), 350.

49. Zachary Reid, "100 Years Ago, Richmond's Students Faced a Situation Similar to Today's: Crumbling Facilities," *Richmond Times-Dispatch*, April 30, 2016.

50. Collegiate School, "History: Our School," 2019, https://www.collegiate-va.org/page/our-school/all-about-us/history.

51. The section on Collegiate is derived and quoted from a question I asked Ben Campbell. I have omitted quotation marks for stylistic reasons. See Jeff Thomas, "A Short History of Richmond," *Blue Virginia*, August 4, 2018. I graduated from here nearly twenty years ago.

52. Collegiate School, "Winter Party: A Seussical Success!," *Spark Magazine* (Spring 2010): 62.

53. Kruszewski, "Community Reacts."

54. Campbell, interview.

55. Michael Paul Williams, "We Remain Two Richmonds—RVA Blossomed While Richmond Is Being Left Further and Further Behind," *Richmond Times-Dispatch*, July 24, 2017.

56. Jon Baliles et al.,"Why I Want to Be Mayor of Richmond," *Style Weekly*, September 20, 2016.

57. Richmond City Charter, Section 3.01.1, Election of Mayors. Available at http://www.richmondgov.com/CommissionCharter/documents/Charter_booklet.pdf.

58. City of Richmond, "Richmond Voter District Population Demographics," January 29, 2013. Available at http://www.richmondgov.com/CityCouncil/documents/RichmondVoterDistrictsDemographics2013.pdf.

59. Daniel Dale, "Meet the Ex-Convict Leading the Mayor's Race in Richmond, Va.," *Toronto Star*, October 9, 2016; Jeremy Lazarus, "Joe Fights Back," *Richmond Free Press*, December 27, 2014.

60. Petula Dvorak, "Joe Morrissey: An Embarrassment that Virginia Voters Support and Deserve," *Washington Post*, January 14, 2015.

61. Paul Schwartzman, "In Virginia's Capital, a Political 'Bad Boy' Upends Race for Mayor," *Washington Post*, September 27, 2016.

62. Plea agreement, *Commonwealth v. Joseph Dee Morrissey*, December 12, 2014. Available at http://www.spotsylvania.va.us/filestorage/21027/30276/119/32918/32920/28694/PLEA_AGREEMENT__Commonwealth_v_Joseph_Dee_Morrissey.pdf.

63. Ned Oliver, "To Jail and Back," *Style Weekly*, January 20, 2015.

64. Ned Oliver and Frank Green, "Henrico Judge Releases Joe Morrissey Law Client from Jail Amid Allegations of Sexual Impropriety," *Richmond Times-Dispatch*, October 28, 2016.

65. Virginia Department of Elections, "Richmond City: 2016 Mayor General Election," Virginia Elections Database, 2018, http://historical.elections.virginia.gov/elections/view/81086.

66. Emily Dooley, "Venture Richmond's Jack Berry a Quiet Force for the City," *Richmond Times-Dispatch*, September 21, 2009; Virginia Public Access Project, "Elections: Richmond City Mayor: 2016," https://www.vpap.org/offices/richmond-city-mayor/elections/?year_and_type=2016regular.

67. *New York Times*, Virginia Election Results 2016.

68. Virginia Department of Elections, "Richmond City: 2016 Mayor General Election," Virginia Elections Database, 2018, http://historical.elections.virginia.gov/elections/view/81086.

69. Rodrigo Arriaza Morales and Alex Austin, "How Levar Stoney Hopes to Sprint Past Morrissey, Berry," WTVR, November 6, 2016.

70. Virginia Public Access Project, "Elections: Richmond City Mayor: 2016," https://www.vpap.org/offices/richmond-city-mayor/elections/?year_and_type=2016regular; Richard Meagher, "Why Stoney Won," *RVA Politics*, November 14, 2016.

71. Mark Robinson, "The Hard-Earned Optimism of Levar Stoney," *Richmond Magazine*, June 14, 2017; Warren Fiske, "Levar Stoney Weakly Claims Jack Berry Voted to Cut $23.8 Million from Richmond Schools," *PolitiFact Virginia*, October 31, 2016.

72. Matt Chaney, "'I Will Be a Voice for Everyone': Levar Stoney Wins Richmond's Mayoral Election," WRIC, November 9, 2016.

73. Ned Oliver, "After Eight Years in Office, Mayor Dwight Jones Reflects on Accomplishments, Missteps, and Where He'll Head Next," *Richmond Times-Dispatch*, December 17, 2016.

74. City of Richmond, "Adopted Biennial Fiscal Plan: Fiscal Years 2019–2020," 2018, 69. Available at http://www.richmondgov.com/Budget/documents/BiennialPlans/2019-2020_AdoptedBiennialFiscalPlan.pdf.

75. David Larter, "How a Landmark Deal Came Together," *Richmond BizSense*, July 13, 2012; Jeremy Lazarus, "City Finishes with Loss on UCI Bike Race," *Richmond Free Press*, January 1, 2016.

76. Scott Wise, Alix Bryan, and Jake Burns, "Investigation Finds Mayor Jones Conduct Not Criminal, but Questionable," WTVR, November 30, 2016.

77. Kerri O'Brien, "Findings of VSP Investigation of Richmond Mayor Jones Due Wednesday," WRIC, November 29, 2016.

78. Brent Baldwin et al., "2018 Power List: Politics," *Style Weekly*, August 28, 2018.

79. Stoney for RVA, "Every Day," Levar Stoney campaign commercial, 2016. Available at https://www.youtube.com/watch?v=uyWktNTHka0.

80. Liz Clarke, "Redskins and Richmond: A Marriage in Need of Counseling?," *Washington Post*, August 12, 2017.

81. Michael Schwartz, "Sources: New Arena in the Works to Replace Coliseum," *Richmond BizSense*, June 27, 2017; Mark Robinson, "Stoney Administration Paying Chicago Firm to Review Coliseum Proposal," *Richmond Times-Dispatch*, July 12, 2018; Mark Robinson, "An Explainer: Richmond Mayor Levar Stoney's $1.4 Billion Richmond Coliseum Proposal," *Richmond Times-Dispatch*, November 10, 2018.

82. George Allen and Paul Goldman, "Little Restored Schoolhouse," *New York Times*, October 12, 2009.

83. Jonathan Martin, "Odd Couple Join Forces for Schools," *Politico*, October 13, 2009.

84. Ray Daudani, "Maggie Walker Named 14th Best Public High School in US," WWBT, May 6, 2013.

85. Melissa Scott Sinclair, "The Man Behind the Curtain," *Style Weekly*, March 1, 2006.

86. Frank Phillips, "Patrick Makes History," *Boston Globe*, November 7, 2006.

87. Dwayne Yancey, *When Hell Froze Over: The Untold Story of Doug Wilder: A Black Politician's Rise to Power in the South* (Dallas, TX: Taylor Publishing, 1989), 87–88. The other book is Garrett Epps's *The Shad Treatment*.

88. K. Burnell Evans, "Push for Ballot Measure in Richmond Aims to Force School Funding Discussion," *Richmond Times-Dispatch*, June 5, 2017. The *Richmond Free Press* covered the story prior to this.

89. Ibid.

90. Anne Holton, "Roll Up Your Sleeves, Richmond, for Our Kids and Their Schools," *Richmond Times-Dispatch*, June 17, 2017.

91. Levar Stoney, "Education Compact Proposal," City of Richmond, February 16, 2017. Available at http://www.richmondgov.com/Mayor/documents/EducationCompactProposal.pdf.

92. Jackie Kruszewski, "Advocates Say Mayor Stoney's Education Compact Is Code for Privatization in Schools," *Style Weekly*, June 13, 2017.

93. Ned Oliver, "Stoney's Education Compact Drops Academic Goals, but Calls for Quarterly Meetings with Richmond School Board, City Council," *Richmond Times-Dispatch*, June 26, 2017; Michael Paul Williams, "Schools Compact Raises Questions About Control," *Richmond Times-Dispatch*, June 8, 2017.

94. Editorial Board, "Once Again, Efforts to Reform Richmond Schools Leave the Children Behind," *Richmond Times-Dispatch*, June 28, 2017.

95. Jeremy Lazarus, "Initiative to Get Schools on Nov. Ballot Collects 6,619 Signatures in One Day," *Richmond Free Press*, June 24, 2017.

96. K. Burnell Evans, "Goldman Sues State Board of Elections over Registered Voters List," *Richmond Times-Dispatch*, June 30, 2017; Virginia Department of Elections, "Registrant Counts by Locality: Voters Registered as of 7/1/2017: All Localities," 2017, 166. Available at https://www.elections.virginia.gov/Files/Registration-Statistics/2017/06/Registrant_Count_By_Locality.pdf.

97. Virginia Department of Elections, "November 8, 2016 Elections: Candidacy Requirements for Independent Candidates for President of the United States," December 28, 2015. Available at https://www.elections.virginia.gov/Files/BecomingACandidate/CandidateBulletins/2016Nov_Pres.pdf.

98. Ibid.; National Association of Secretaries of State, "Summary: State Laws Regarding Presidential Ballot Access for the General Election," October 2016, https://www.nass.org/sites/default/files/surveys/2017-08/research-ballot-access-president-Oct16.pdf.

99. Brent Baldwin et al., "2018 Power List: Education," *Style Weekly*, August 28, 2018.

100. Yancey, *When Hell Froze Over*, 89–90.

101. Paul Goldman, interview with author, August 13, 2018.

102. Lazarus, "Initiative."

103. Evans, "Goldman Sues State Board"; Virginia Department of Elections, "Registrant Counts by Locality: Voters Registered as of 7/1/2017: All Localities," 2017, 166. Available at https://www.elections.virginia.gov/Files/Registration-Statistics/2017/06/Registrant_Count_By_Locality.pdf.

104. Goldman, interview.

105. Mark Robinson, "Charter Change to Modernize Richmond Schools to Go to Vote," *Richmond Times-Dispatch*, August 15, 2017.

106. Mark Robinson, "Richmond's City Council, School Board Sign off on Mayor Stoney's Education Compact," *Richmond Times-Dispatch*, August 21, 2017.

107. Mark Robinson, "City Attorney: Mayor, Council Should Challenge Referendum Order in Court," *Richmond Times-Dispatch*, August 23, 2017.

108. Editorial Board, "A Problem Surfaces with Richmond's School Modernization Referendum," *Richmond Times-Dispatch*, August 24, 2017;

Editorial Board, "Trouble and Hope for Richmond's Public Schools," *Richmond Times-Dispatch*, August 19, 2017.

109. Robinson, "City Attorney."

110. Michael Paul Williams, "Vote on Richmond School Modernization No Magic Bullet," *Richmond Times-Dispatch*, August 2, 2017.

111. Brent Baldwin et al., "2018 Power List: Education," *Style Weekly*, August 28, 2018.

112. Yancey, *When Hell Froze Over*, 87.

113. Justin Mattingly, "Richmond Leaders Call on McAuliffe to Endorse School Modernization Proposal," *Richmond Times-Dispatch*, September 1, 2017.

114. Glen Sturtevant and Paul Goldman, "Richmond's Students Need You! Bipartisan Nov. 7 Mandate Will Change Their Lives," *Richmond Times-Dispatch*, October 23, 2017.

115. Levar Stoney, "Make This the Year for Real Success at RPS," *Richmond Times-Dispatch*, September 4, 2017.

116. Justin Mattingly, "Richmond Students to Receive Free Glasses Through Partnership," *Richmond Times-Dispatch*, October 26, 2017.

117. Melissa Hipolit, "Mayor Stoney Says Renovations Taking Too Long in Scathing Letter to School Leaders," WTVR, November 4, 2017.

118. Justin Mattingly, "Richmond Voters Pass Referendum to Fix City School Facilities," *Richmond Times-Dispatch*, November 7, 2017.

119. Goldman, interview.

120. Virginia Department of Elections, "Election Results: 2017 November General: Richmond City: Proposition A," December 8, 2017. Available at https://results.elections.virginia.gov/vaelections/2017%20November%20General/Site/Locality/RICHMOND%20CITY/PROPOSITION%20A%20(RICHMOND%20CITY).html. Support ranged from 72.3 percent in precinct 308 to 96.7 percent in precinct 602.

121. Mattingly, "Richmond Voters Pass Referendum."

122. Goldman, interview.

123. Mattingly, "Richmond Voters Pass Referendum."

124. Justin Mattingly, "Richmond State Senator Steps Forward to Help Carry Schools Initiative Through General Assembly," *Richmond Times-Dispatch*, November 15, 2017.

125. Justin Mattingly, "Ex-Richmond School Board Chairman to Carry Facilities Referendum Decision Through House," *Richmond Times-Dispatch*, November 17, 2017.

126. Justin Mattingly, "An Explanation of the Richmond School Board's Facilities Plan," *Richmond Times-Dispatch*, December 16, 2017.

127. Justin Mattingly, "Richmond NAACP, School Board Members Rally for Facilities Plan Funding," *Richmond Times-Dispatch*, December 13, 2017.

128. Justin Mattingly, "Richmond Facilities Referendum Creator Moves to Fund Plan," *Richmond Times-Dispatch*, December 14, 2017.

129. Justin Mattingly, "Bickering, Blaming and Delays: How Stoney's Education Initiative Has Failed to Deliver a School Facilities Upgrades Plan," *Richmond Times-Dispatch*, April 29, 2018; Justin Mattingly, "Richmond Officials Don't Address School System's Facilities Needs as Many Decision-Makers Miss Education Compact Meeting," *Richmond Times-Dispatch*, May 31, 2018.

130. Mark Robinson, "Q&A: Richmond Mayor Levar Stoney Looks Back on First Year in Office, Ahead to 2018," *Richmond Times-Dispatch*, December 23, 2017.

131. Ben Campbell, interview with the author, April 2, 2017.

132. Justin Mattingly, "House Version of Richmond Schools Referendum Measure Would Allow Stoney to Raise Taxes," *Richmond Times-Dispatch*, January 16, 2018.

133. Justin Mattingly, "House Subcommittee Kills Richmond School Facilities Bill," *Richmond Times-Dispatch*, February 7, 2018.

134. Justin Mattingly, "House Subcommittee Approves Richmond School Facilities Bill," *Richmond Times-Dispatch*, February 28, 2018.

135. Virginia General Assembly, 2018, SB750: Richmond, City of; Amending Charter, Equal Educational.

136. Justin Mattingly, "Gov. Northam Signs Richmond School Facilities Bill," *Richmond Times-Dispatch*, April 4, 2018.

137. Justin Mattingly, "Richmond Mayor Levar Stoney Proposes Raising the City's Meals Tax to 7.5% to Fund School Facilities Improvements," *Richmond Times-Dispatch*, January 22, 2018; Brent Baldwin, "Interview: Mayor Levar Stoney Addresses Concerns Over Meals Tax Proposal," *Style Weekly*, February 4, 2018.

138. Mark Robinson, "In State of the City Speech, Stoney Makes Case for Meals Tax Increase for Schools," *Richmond Times-Dispatch*, January 23, 2018.

139. Michael Thompson, "Mayoral Forum Tests Candidates on Local Business Issues," *Richmond BizSense*, September 14, 2016.

140. Justin Mattingly, "Richmond City Leaders Grapple with Schools Facilities, Meals Tax at Education Compact Meeting," *Richmond Times-Dispatch*, January 29, 2018.

141. Mattingly, "Richmond Mayor Levar Stoney."

142. Editorial Board, "Meals Tax Thoughts, Continued," *Richmond Times-Dispatch*, February 8, 2018.

143. Mark Robinson, "Richmond City Council Divided on Stoney's Proposed Meals Tax Hike," *Richmond Times-Dispatch*, January 27, 2018.

144. Justin Mattingly, "An Explanation of the Proposed Meals Tax Increase in Richmond," *Richmond Times-Dispatch*, February 2, 2018.

145. Michael Paul Williams, "Welcome to Richmond, Mr. Superintendent, Where Drama Is Always on the Menu," *Richmond Times-Dispatch*, February 1, 2018.

146. Mattingly, "Explanation of the Proposed Meals Tax."

147. Mark Robinson, "Richmond City Council Approves Stoney's Meals Tax Increase for City Schools," *Richmond Times-Dispatch*, February 12, 2018.

148. Mark Robinson, "Stoney, Richmond Public Schools Leaders Celebrate New School Construction Supported by Meals Tax Hike," *Richmond Times-Dispatch*, December 19, 2018.

149. Justin Mattingly, "An Explanation of the Richmond School Board's Facilities Plan," *Richmond Times-Dispatch*, December 16, 2017.

150. Virginia Public Access Project, "Levar Stoney: Top Donors," https://www.vpap.org/candidates/57421/top_donors; Virginia Public Access Project, "Altria: Donor: All Years," https://www.vpap.org/donors/110931-altria/?start_year=all&end_year=all&contrib_type=all.

151. Mark Robinson, "Richmond Council Panel Punts on Proposed Cigarette Tax Amid Stiff Opposition and Skepticism," *Richmond Times-Dispatch*, February 15, 2018.

152. Parker Agelasto, "RVA Needs a Cigarette Tax to Help Schools," *Richmond Times-Dispatch*, March 12, 2018.

153. Centers for Disease Control and Prevention, "Current Cigarette Smoking Among Adults in the United States," September 24, 2018, https://www.cdc.gov/tobacco/data_statistics/fact_sheets/adult_data/cig_smoking/index.htm.

154. Robinson, "Richmond Council Panel Punts."

155. Mallory Noe-Payne, "Richmond Council Presses Pause on a Cigarette Tax Proposal," Virginia Public Radio, February 16, 2018.

156. Paul Spencer, "Parker Agelasto Makes a Plea for Reconsidering the Cigarette Tax," *Style Weekly*, March 27, 2018.

157. Mark Hipolit, "Councilman: 'Frankly...Richmond Needs to Implement a Cigarette Tax'," WVTR, March 13, 2018.

158. Mark Robinson, "Richmond City Council Panel Delays Action on Plan to Increase Cigarette Tax," *Richmond Times-Dispatch*, March 15, 2018.

159. Richard Foster, "Was Officer Demoted for Cop-Car Council Meeting?," *Style Weekly*, https://www.styleweekly.com/richmond/was-officer-demoted-for-cop-car-council-meeting/Content?oid=1389417; "The Big Smooch: In Which We Bestow Kisses, New-Century-Style, Upon Some of the City's Most Kissable—and on Some Who Aren't So Lovable," *Style Weekly*, https://www.styleweekly.com/richmond/in-which-we-bestow-kisses-new-century-style-upon-some-of-the-citys-most-kissable-and-on-some-who-arent-so-lovable/Content?oid=1387077. Dates unknown.

160. Sarah King, "Cigarette Tax Proposal Falls Short," *Richmond Magazine*, April 24, 2018.

161. Jeremy Lazarus, "No More Money for School Maintenance," *Richmond Free Press*, May 4, 2018; Ronald Carrington, "More Money Found for City School Maintenance," *Richmond Free Press*, August 16, 2018.

162. Carrington, "More Money Found."

163. Peter Galuszka, "The Push to Restore Richmond's Coliseum," *Washington Post*, July 9, 2018.

164. Mark Robinson, "Coliseum Redevelopment Group Led by Dominion Energy CEO Wants City to Use Dominion Property Taxes for Project," *Richmond Times-Dispatch*, July 7, 2018.

165. Michael Schwartz, "Lead Developers in Place for New Downtown Arena Project," *Richmond BizSense*, September 5, 2017.

166. Jeremy Lazarus, "Mayor Pushes Private Development of New Coliseum," *Richmond Free Press*, November 17, 2017.

167. Michael Paul Williams, "Moving the City's Social Services to Industrial South Richmond Is a Bad Idea. Here's Why," *Richmond Times-Dispatch*, November 12, 2018.

168. Ben Campbell, *Richmond's Unhealed History* (Richmond, VA: Brandylane, 2012), 154–57; Alexia Fernandez Campbell, "The Rise and Fall of Black Wall Street," *The Atlantic*, August 31, 2016.

169. "Photos: If These Walls Could Talk: Inside 46 Years of the Richmond Coliseum," *Richmond Times-Dispatch*, June 27, 2017; Michael Martz and Ned Oliver, "Possible Replacement of Richmond Coliseum Seen as Catalyst for Broader Opportunity to Redevelop Downtown Richmond," *Richmond Times-Dispatch*, June 27, 2017.

170. "A Look Back at 6th Street Marketplace," *Richmond Times-Dispatch*, June 26, 2016; Amy Biegelsen, "Requiem for a Dream," *Style Weekly*, June 27, 2007; Scott Bass, "A Big Step," *Style Weekly*, October 29, 2003.

171. Scott Bass, "Empty Promises," *Style Weekly*, February 28, 2007.

172. Justin Mattingly, "As Richmond Reviews Coliseum Proposal, School Officials Want Focus on School Facilities," July 18, 2018.

173. Michael Martz, "Goodwin Says It's 'Misleading' for VCU to Say Children's Hospital Could Cost $1B," *Richmond Times-Dispatch*, August 15, 2015.

174. NH District Corp. "Mission," 2019, https://navyhillrva.com/mission.

175. Editorial Board, "RVA's Big Arena Opportunity," *Richmond Times-Dispatch*, July 9, 2018.

176. Editorial Board, "Richmond Schools Come Before Millionaire Athletes," *Richmond Times-Dispatch*, August 8, 2017.

177. Campbell, interview.

178. Pat Gottschalk and Kim Scheeler, "RVA Arena Will Be Built by Admirable Intentions and Smart Choices," *Richmond Times-Dispatch*, July 21, 2018.

179. Campbell, interview.

180. August 2015 City Council meeting, author observation.

181. In general, information on major donors is reported on 990 Schedule B, which does not have to be disclosed publicly. See Internal Revenue Service, "Public Disclosure and Availability of Exempt Organizations Returns and

Applications: Contributors' Identities Not Subject to Disclosure," April 2, 2018, https://www.irs.gov/charities-non-profits/public-disclosure-and-availability-of-exempt-organizations-returns-and-applications-contributors-identities-not-subject-to-disclosure.

182. Mark Robinson, "An Explainer: Richmond Mayor Levar Stoney's $1.4 Billion Richmond Coliseum Proposal," *Richmond Times-Dispatch*, November 10, 2018.

183. Caitlin Barbieri and Katie Bashista, "Monroe Park Reopens in Richmond with More Security, Less Benches, and Ping Pong," WTVR, September 29, 2018; Mike Platania, "$96M VCU Dorm and Redone Monroe Park Unveiled," *Richmond BizSense*, October 1, 2018.

184. J. Elias O'Neal, "Nonprofit, Developers Weight Proposed Homeless Shelter Move to Manchester," *Richmond BizSense*, August 7, 2018; Michael Hild, "City Proposes Moving Downtown Homeless Shelter to Manchester to Clear the Way for Coliseum Development," *Dogtown Dish*, July 25, 2018.

185. Martz and Oliver, "Possible Replacement of Richmond Coliseum"; Jackie Kruszewski, "Dominion's Chief Executive Wants to Redevelop the Richmond Coliseum," *Style Weekly*, July 3, 2017; Jeremy Lazarus, "City Center Vision," *Richmond Free Press*, July 21, 2018.

186. Tammie Smith, "Commercial Developers Flock to Richmond Hot Spots," *Richmond Times-Dispatch*, December 7, 2018; Tammie Smith, "Development Projects Underway: From Apartments in Scott's Addition to a 14-Story Tower Along the James River," *Richmond Times-Dispatch*, December 7, 2018.

187. Don Harrison, "The Gang of 26," *Style Weekly*, August 15, 2007.

188. Alan Suderman, "Lawmaker, Dad Benefit from Grant, Tax Credits," *Richmond Times-Dispatch*, November 17, 2014; Nick Schager, "Civil War Drama Field of Lost Shoes Argues No Confederates Were Racist," *Village Voice*, September 24, 2014; as of publication time, the Lincoln-Grant scene was available at: https://www.youtube.com/watch?v=Th19ARVJMNQ; National Park Service, "Tredegar Ironworks—Ironmaker to the Confederacy," 2019.

189. Peter Wallenstein, *Cradle of America: A History of Virginia*, 2nd ed. (Lawrence: University of Kansas Press, 2014), 373–75; Jeff Schapiro, "Farrell Takes to the Political Stage," *Richmond Times-Dispatch*, September 25, 2011; Jo Ann Frohman, "The Gray Era Ends," *Daily Press*, July 14, 1991.

190. Michael Rao, "Navy Hill Would Be Transformative for All," *Richmond Times-Dispatch*, January 7, 2019.

191. Richard Foster, "A 'Killer Arena,'" *Virginia Business*, August 30, 2018.

192. Ned Oliver and Mark Robinson, "RTD-CNU Poll: Richmond Voters Say They Support Tax Increase for Schools, Oppose Public Money for Stadium and Coliseum," *Richmond Times-Dispatch*, October 4, 2017.

193. Michael Martz and Mark Robinson, "Richmond Mayor Stoney Announces Major Downtown Redevelopment Plan Centered on New, Larger Coliseum," *Richmond Times-Dispatch*, November 9, 2017.

194. Ned Oliver, "How Mayor Stoney Says His Approach to Richmond Coliseum Redevelopment Is Different," *Richmond Times-Dispatch*, November 18, 2017.

195. Justin Mattingly, "As Richmond Reviews Coliseum Proposal, School Officials Want Focus on School Facilities," *Richmond Times-Dispatch*, July 18, 2018.

196. Jeremy Lazarus, "Mayor Pushes Private Development of New Coliseum," *Richmond Free Press*, November 17, 2017.

197. Mark Robinson, "Stoney Administration Paying Chicago Firm to Review Coliseum Proposal," *Richmond Times-Dispatch*, July 12, 2018; Justin Mattingly, "Here Are the Two Plans to Modernize Richmond's Schools," *Richmond Times-Dispatch*, December 1, 2017.

198. Mark Robinson, "Records: Review of Arena Proposal Has Cost Richmond Close to $500,000 Since January," *Richmond Times-Dispatch*, September 10, 2018; Justin Mattingly, "VCU Will Not Host a University-Wide Commencement Ceremony in 2019; Coliseum 'Unavailable'," *Richmond Times-Dispatch*, October 30, 2018; Jeremy Lazarus, "Signs of 2019 Shutdown for Coliseum," *Richmond Free Press*, August 23, 2018.

199. Mark Robinson, "Richmond City Council Mulling Own Analysis of Arena Redevelopment Proposal," *Richmond Times-Dispatch*, July 18, 2018; Neely quote from Jason Roop, "Tom Farrell's $1 Billion Idea," *Style Weekly*, October 16, 2018.

200. Esson Miller, "The Proposed Coliseum Replacement Is a Huge Financial Obligation that Needs Further Study," *Style Weekly*, December 11, 2018.

201. Justin Griffin, "Breakdown of the City's Coliseum Deal Financial Projections," December 16, 2018, https://nocoliseum.com/breakdown-of-citys-overview.

202. Mark Robinson, "Coliseum Redevelopment Group Led by Dominion Energy CEO Wants City to Use Dominion Property Taxes for Project," *Richmond Times-Dispatch*, July 7, 2018; Mark Robinson, "Documents Offer Window into Stoney Administration's Negotiations on $1 Billion Private Redevelopment Proposal," *Richmond Times-Dispatch*, July 7, 2018.

203. Mark Robinson, "Stoney Endorses 'The Biggest Economic Development Project in Our City's History,' Backs $1.4 Billion Coliseum Redevelopment Proposal," *Richmond Times-Dispatch*, November 1, 2018.

204. Dominion Energy, "Who We Are," December 16, 2018, https://www.dominionenergy.com/about-us/who-we-are; Dominion Energy, "Financial Fundamentals – Annual Income Statement," December 16, 2018, https://investors.dominionenergy.com/financial-fundamentals/income-statement.

205. Yancey, *When Hell Froze Over*, 90.

206. Goldman, interview.

207. Beth Macy, *Factory Man: How One Furniture Maker Battled Offshoring, Stayed Local, and Helped Save an American Town* (Boston: Little, Brown and Company, 2014).

208. Editorial Board, "Stanley's Bold Bet on School Modernization Channels Francis Pickens Miller," *Roanoke Times*, August 19, 2018.

209. Editorial Board, "Stanley's Plan to Pay for Modernizing Virginia Schools," *Roanoke Times*, August 16, 2018.

210. Michael Martz, "Sen. Bill Stanley Announces Panel to Address Virginia's 'Obsolete' School Buildings," *Richmond Times-Dispatch*, April 17, 2018.

211. Ibid.

212. Justin Mattingly, "Virginia Senator Proposes Using Internet Sales Tax Windfall to Upgrade School Facilities," *Richmond Times-Dispatch*, August 16, 2018.

213. Editorial Board, "Stanley's Plan to Pay for Modernizing Virginia Schools," *Roanoke Times*, August 16, 2018.

214. Bill Stanley and Paul Goldman, "No New Taxes Needed: $3 Billion to Modernize Crumbling School Facilities," *Roanoke Times*, August 16, 2018.

215. Norman Leahy, "Bill Stanley's School Plan Shuffles the Partisan Deck," *Washington Post*, August 23, 2018.

216. Editorial Board, "Rural Virginia Needs to Raise a Ruckus Over Schools," *Roanoke Times*, September 28, 2018. Parentheses in original.

217. Mark Robinson, "Dissatisfied with Negotiations, Stoney Says Arena Redevelopment Plan Won't Go to Richmond City Council in September," *Richmond Times-Dispatch*, August 16, 2018.

218. Mark Robinson, "History Will Tell the Story," *Richmond Magazine*, December 28, 2016.

219. Jeremy Lazarus, "Goldman to Pursue New City Charter Change," *Richmond Free Press*, October 11, 2018.

220. Jeremy Lazarus, "Richmond Circuit Court Clears Way for Ballot Initiative on Schools vs. Coliseum," *Richmond Free Press*, October 18, 2018.

221. Brent Baldwin et al., "2018 Power List: Education," *Style Weekly*, August 28, 2018.

222. Levar Stoney, "More Money Leads to Better Schools, Stronger Students," *Virginian-Pilot*, October 21, 2018.

223. Mark Robinson, "Stoney Endorses 'The Biggest Economic Development Project in Our City's History,' Backs $1.4 Billion Coliseum Redevelopment Proposal," *Richmond Times-Dispatch*, November 1, 2018.

224. Justin Mattingly, "Stoney Unveils $600 Million Proposal for City Schools as Part of Coliseum Redevelopment," *Richmond Times-Dispatch*, November 16, 2018.

225. Wallenstein, *Cradle of America*, 15–24.

226. John Reid Blackwell, "'Our Kids Deserve Better': Marchers Converge on State Capitol to Demand More Money for Schools," *Richmond Times-Dispatch*, December 8, 2018.

227. Mark Robinson, "Against Stoney's Wishes, Richmond City Council Establishes Coliseum Redevelopment Commission," *Richmond Times-Dispatch*, December 18, 2018.

228. Josh Stanfield, "Majority of Richmond City Council Reject Dominion & Tom Farrell Money," *Blue Virginia*, January 14, 2019.

229. Jeremy Lazarus, "Pathetic," *Richmond Free Press*, January 18, 2019.

230. Robert Caro, *The Passage of Power: The Years of Lyndon Johnson*, vol. 4 (New York: Vintage, 2013), xiv. Italics in original.

Chapter 4

1. Robin Rudowitz, "Understanding How States Access the ACA Enhanced Medicaid Match Rates," Kaiser Family Foundation, September 29, 2014, https://www.kff.org/medicaid/issue-brief/understanding-how-states-access-the-aca-enhanced-medicaid-match-rates.

2. Karin Kapsidelis, "A Healthier State?," *Virginia Business*, August 30, 2018.

3. Rick Mayes and Benjamin Paul, "An Analysis of Political and Legal Debates Concerning Medicaid Expansion in Virginia," *University of Richmond Journal of Law and the Public Interest* (Fall 2014): 26–29.

4. Rudowitz, "Understanding How States Access."

5. Virginia Department of Planning & Budget, "Virginia's Budget: Frequently Asked Questions," July 16, 2018, http://dpb.virginia.gov/budget/faq.cfm.

6. Michael Paul Williams, "More About the Person, Less About the Dollar," *Richmond Times-Dispatch*, February 28, 2014.

7. Jeff Schapiro, "Part-Time Lawmakers and Their Full-Time Health Care," *Richmond Times-Dispatch*, February 23, 2014; Dave Ress, "Legislators Debating Medicaid Expansion Have Generous Insurance of Their Own," *Daily Press*, February 21, 2014.

8. Jeff Schapiro, "McAuliffe Learns His Job the Hard Way," *Richmond Times-Dispatch*, April 22, 2014.

9. Massey Whorley and Michael Cassidy, "Medicaid Expansion Would Pay for Itself," The Commonwealth Institute, August 2013, http://www.thecommonwealthinstitute.org/wp-content/uploads/2013/08/medex_pays_for_itself.pdf.

10. Michael Martz, "Va. Now Projects Medicaid Savings of $1 Billion Through 2022," *Richmond Times-Dispatch*, January 23, 2014.

11. Sean Gorman, "Landes Claim Medicaid Expansion Could Cost $1 Billion a Year Based on Shaky Assumption," *PolitiFact Virginia*, January 11, 2016.

12. Michael Martz, "High Stakes for Hospitals in Medicaid Fight," *Richmond Times-Dispatch*, January 16, 2014; Virginia Public Access Project, "Top Donors: All Years," https://www.vpap.org/money/top-donors/?year=all, 2019.

13. Michael Martz, "VCU, U.Va. Health Systems Urge State to Expand Medicaid," *Richmond Times-Dispatch*, January 30, 2014.

14. Whorley and Cassidy, "Medicaid Expansion."

15. Patrick Wilson, "Virginia Spends $6,500 Per Prison Inmate on Health Care Each Year. A New Report Shows the State Could Reduce that Cost," *Richmond Times-Dispatch*, November 13, 2018.

16. Michael Martz and Olympia Meola, "Coverage Gap Debate Hits Home," *Richmond Times-Dispatch*, March 16, 2014.

17. Tammie Smith, "Using Health Insurance on Hold for Some," *Richmond Times-Dispatch*, January 19, 2014.

18. Mayes and Paul, "An Analysis," 27, 31; Trip Gabriel, "Terry McAuliffe, Democrat, Is Elected Governor of Virginia in Tight Race," *New York Times*, November 5, 2013.

19. Jim Nolan, "Under Democrat Control, Senate Could Back Medicaid," *Richmond Times-Dispatch*, January 28, 2014.

20. Ballotpedia, "Virginia House of Delegates," https://ballotpedia.org/Virginia_House_of_Delegates, 2019.

21. Heather Sullivan, "Meet Virginia's New First Lady," WWBT, January 9, 2014.

22. Laura Vozzella, "Va. Gov. Terry McAuliffe to Remain Hospitalized for at Least Another Day," *Washington Post*, January 21, 2015; Laura Vozzella, "Virginia Gov. Terry McAuliffe Hospitalized After He Was Thrown from Horse in Africa," *Washington Post*, January 19, 2015; Travis Fain, "McAuliffe: That Horse Could Have Outrun a Lion," *Daily Press*, January 21, 2015.

23. Lynn Mitchell, "'Bob's for Jobs' Pays Off…Virginia Gets Northrup Grumman," *Washington Examiner*, April 28, 2010.

24. Laura Vozzella, "McAuliffe Invites Indiana Firms to 'Open and Welcoming' Virginia," *Washington Post*, March 30, 2015.

25. Patrick Wilson, "Virginia Governor Vetoes Anti-LGBT Bill on Live Radio," *Governing Magazine*, March 31, 2016.

26. SaraRose Martin and Jim Thomma, "Don't Pass 'Divisive' Proposals, McAuliffe Warns," *Southwest Times*, January 12, 2017.

27. Terry McAuliffe, "Inaugural Address," January 11, 2014, available at https://www.washingtonpost.com/local/virginia-politics/full-text-virginia-gov-terry-mcauliffes-inaugural-address/2014/01/11/f8a1c35e-7a0c-11e3-af7f-13bf0e9965f6_story.html?noredirect=on.

28. James Hohmann, "McAuliffe Offers Olive Branch to GOP," *Politico*, January 11, 2014; Terry McAuliffe, "Medicaid Expansion Means Quality Health Care for More Virginians," *Richmond Times-Dispatch*, February 2, 2014; Jeff Schapiro, "Next Few Months Likely to Be Intriguing," *Richmond Times-Dispatch*, January 1, 2014.

29. Terry McAuliffe and Lisa Lerer, "Forum: Sleep When You're Dead: Getting Things Done as a Governor," Harvard Institute of Politics, April 18, 2018, https://college.harvard.edu/sleep-when-you%E2%80%99re-dead-getting-things-done-governor.

30. Laura Vozzella, "Terry McAuliffe's Push to Expand Medicaid Rankles the GOP Lawmakers He Seeks to Woo," *Washington Post*, January 20, 2014.

31. Associated Press, "McAuliffe Reappoints Health Secretary," *Daily Progress*, December 18, 2013; Julian Walker, "McAuliffe Keeps Current Finance Secretary, Adds Staff," *Virginian-Pilot*, November 19, 2013.

32. Laura Vozzella, "At Executive Mansion, McAuliffe Puts Out the Welcome Mat," *Washington Post*, February 5, 2014; John Parkinson, "Freshman Lawmaker Tom Garrett Decides to Retire: 'I'm an Alcoholic'," ABC News, May 29, 2018.

33. Fredrick Kunkle and Laura Vozzella, "Virginia Lawmakers Approve Sweeping Transportation Plan," *Washington Post*, February 23, 2013.

34. Laura Vozzella, "Democrats Claim Win, GOP Says Not So Fast," *Washington Post*, February 23, 2013; Mayes and Paul, "An Analysis," 30.

35. Jeff Schapiro, "Little-Known Panel Obstacle in Health Fight," *Richmond Times-Dispatch*, April 9, 2014; Michael Laris and Laura Vozzella, "House and Senate in Virginia at Loggerheads Over Medicaid Expansion," *Washington Post*, February 20, 2014.

36. Michael Martz, "McDonnell Wants Review of Any Medicaid Expansion," *Richmond Times-Dispatch*, December 17, 2013.

37. Olympia Meola and Jim Nolan, "McAuliffe Urges Quick Work on Medicaid Expansion," *Richmond Times-Dispatch*, January 14, 2014.

38. Michael Martz and Olympia Meola, "McAuliffe, Lawmakers Clash Over Medicaid," *Richmond Times-Dispatch*, January 21, 2014.

39. Jeff Schapiro, "McAuliffe, GOP Honeymoon Ends Before It Begins," *Richmond Times-Dispatch*, February 9, 2014.

40. "It Is Official: Lynwood Lewis Wins 6th State Senate Seat After Recount," *DelMarVa Now*, January 1, 2014.

41. Virginia Constitution, Article V, Section 14, and Article IV, Section 11. There are other tie-breaking powers of the lieutenant governor that are still unsettled constitutional law but are beyond the scope of this chapter. See John Dinan, *The Virginia State Constitution*, Oxford Commentaries on the State Constitutions of the United States, 2nd ed. (Oxford, UK: Oxford University Press, 2014), 154–57.

42. Jim Nolan, "Under Democrat Control, Senate Could Back Medicaid," *Richmond Times-Dispatch*, January 28, 2014.

43. Jeff Schapiro, "Senate GOP May Not Be in the Wilderness Long," *Richmond Times-Dispatch*, February 2, 2014.

44. Michael Martz, "Senate Panel Backs New Private Insurance Marketplace," *Richmond Times-Dispatch*, February 4, 2014.

45. Michael Martz, "Senate Leaders Offer Option on Health Coverage," *Richmond Times-Dispatch*, February 7, 2014; Michael Laris and Laura Vozzella, "House and Senate in Virginia at Loggerheads Over Medicaid Expansion," *Washington Post*, February 20, 2014.

46. Markus Schmidt, "House GOP Leaders Maintain Stance Against Medicaid Expansion," *Richmond Times-Dispatch*, February 12, 2014.

47. Michael Martz, "State Chamber Touts Private Coverage Choice," *Richmond Times-Dispatch*, February 25, 2014.

48. Alan Suderman, "Medicaid Expansion Debate Good for Insurers," *Washington Examiner*, Associated Press, April 13, 2014; Michael Martz, "Community Hospitals on Front Line of Medicaid Battle," *Richmond Times-Dispatch*, April 19, 2014.

49. Bill Bolling, "Compromise: Elevate Policy Above Politics," *Richmond Times-Dispatch*, March 14, 2014; Olympia Meola and Michael Martz, "Goodwin, 3 Ex-McDonnell Aides Urge Health Care Fix," *Richmond Times-Dispatch*, March 5, 2014.

50. "Former Prince William Supervisors Chair Named President of Healthcare Association," *Inside NoVA*, April 10, 2014.

51. Martz, "State Chamber Touts Private Coverage."

52. Robert Burke, "Strained Relationship?," *Virginia Business*, April 29, 2014.

53. Jeff Schapiro, "Little-Known Panel Obstacle in Health Fight," *Richmond Times-Dispatch*, April 9, 2014.

54. Michael Martz, Olympia Meola, and Jim Nolan, "House, Senate Set Up Medicaid Showdown," *Richmond Times-Dispatch*, February 21, 2014.

55. Jim Nolan and Olympia Meola, "Legislators Dig In Over Medicaid Expansion," *Richmond Times-Dispatch*, February 26, 2014.

56. Olympia Meola, "Ingram, McAuliffe Clash Over Medicaid," *Richmond Times-Dispatch*, February 20, 2014.

57. Olympia Meola and Jim Nolan, "McAuliffe Expands Medicaid Push," *Richmond Times-Dispatch*, February 23, 2014; Olympia Meola and Michael Martz, "McAuliffe Presses Ahead on Medicaid," *Richmond Times-Dispatch*, March 6, 2014; Michael Sluss, "McAuliffe Uses Roanoke Valley Visit to Push More Medicaid," *Roanoke Times*, March 28, 2014; Michael Laris and Laura Vozzella, "In Va., Fight Over Medicaid Expansion Continues," *Washington Post*, February 24, 2014.

58. Michael Martz and Olympia Meola, "House Approves Own Budget Plan, Then Recesses," *Richmond Times-Dispatch*, March 25, 2014.

59. Jeff Schapiro, "'Two Years' Sent Shiver Through House GOP," *Richmond Times-Dispatch*, March 26, 2014; David Sherfinski, "Conflict Trumps Compromise in Virginia's Medicaid Expansion Debate," *Washington Times*, April 6, 2014.

60. Michael Martz and Jim Nolan, "Marketplace Virginia Is 'Probably Germane' to Budget," *Richmond Times-Dispatch*, April 15, 2014; Dave Ress, "Virginia's Budget Impasse Prompts Worrying Call from Wall Street," *Daily Press*, May 4, 2018.

61. Michael Laris and Laura Vozzella, "House and Senate in Virginia at Loggerheads Over Medicaid Expansion," *Washington Post*, February 20, 2014. Ellipsis in original.

62. Jim Nolan, "Poll: Virginia Voters Shift on Medicaid," *Richmond Times-Dispatch*, April 24, 2014.

63. Laris and Vozzella, "In Va."

64. Michael Martz, "McAuliffe: Budget Must Include Health Care Expansion," *Richmond Times-Dispatch*, March 1, 2014; Jim Nolan, "Medicaid Issue May Push Budget to the Brink," *Richmond Times-Dispatch*, April 27, 2014.

65. Associated Press, "Virginia State Sen. Phil Puckett Resigning," *Southwest Times* (VA), June 9, 2014.

66. Jim Nolan, "Republicans Take Control of Senate," *Richmond Times-Dispatch*, June 23, 2014.

67. Trip Gabriel, "Blocking Any Medicaid Expansion, Virginia Legislature Passes Budget Bill," *New York Times*, June 13, 2014.

68. Michael Martz and Jim Nolan, "Virginia Lawmakers Pass Budget that Thwarts Medicaid Expansion," *Richmond Times-Dispatch*, June 12, 2014.

69. Laura Vozzella and Jenna Portnoy, "Virginia Lawmakers Finalize Budget, Averting a Shutdown as GOP Thwarts McAuliffe Veto," *Washington Post*, June 23, 2014.

70. Jim Nolan, "Democratic Senator Puckett Resigns, Adding to State Budget Turmoil," *Richmond Times-Dispatch*, June 8, 2014.

71. Patrick Wilson, "Senator Chafin Pitches Sister for Anticipated Supreme Court Opening," *Richmond Times-Dispatch*, January 24, 2019; Amy Friedenberger, "Judge Teresa Chafin, Sister of Sen. Ben Chafin, Elected to Virginia Supreme Court," *Roanoke Times*, February 14, 2019.

72. Public Health Law Center, "Master Settlement Agreement," 2019, http://www.publichealthlawcenter.org/topics/tobacco-control/tobacco-control-litigation/master-settlement-agreement.

73. "Emails Show Unease Over Tobacco Job, Resignation," WHSV, June 27, 2014.

74. Jeff Schapiro, "McAuliffe, Others Pressed Puckett to Stay," *Richmond Times-Dispatch*, June 10, 2014; Laura Vozzella, "Puckett's Senate Exit Undid McAuliffe's Secret Plan to Pass Medicaid Expansion," *Washington Post*, November 22, 2014.

75. Laura Vozzella, "Warner Discussed Job for Puckett's Daughter," *Washington Post*, October 10, 2014.

76. Jim Nolan and Michael Martz, "Senate to Reconvene Thursday on Budget; Puckett Won't Take Tobacco Commission Post," *Richmond Times-Dispatch*, June 9, 2014.

77. Laura Vozzella, "Puckett's Senate Exit Undid McAuliffe's Secret Plan to Pass Medicaid Expansion," *Washington Post*, November 22, 2014.

78. Lowell Feld, "What the Puckett Resignation Scandal May Boil Down To," *Blue Virginia*, June 29, 2014.

79. Travis Fain, "Subpoenas Show Grand Jury Underway in Former Senator Puckett Case," *Daily Press*, June 25, 2014.

80. Vozzella, "Puckett's Senate Exit"; United States Department of Justice, "Thomas T. Cullen Sworn In as United States Attorney for the Western District of Virginia," March 30, 2018.

81. Alan Suderman, "Assembly Approves Former State Senator's Daughter to Judgeship," *Fredericksburg Free Lance-Star*, January 21, 2015.

82. Mark Hines, "Three Papers on the Factors that Influence State and Individual-Level Policy Support for Medicaid" (dissertation, Georgetown University, 2017), 66.

83. Feld, "Puckett Resignation."

84. Virginia Military Institute, "Watch Live as Corps Marches in Inaugural," January 12, 2018, https://www.vmi.edu/news/headlines/2017-2018/watch-live-as-corps-marches-in-inaugural.php.

85. Jenna Portnoy, "Ralph Northam, Va.'s Low-Key Lieutenant Governor, Juggles Politics and Pediatrics," *Washington Post*, July 27, 2014.

86. Ferit Nirappil, "What Virginia's Governor-Elect Ralph Northam (D) Promised During His Campaign," *Washington Post*, November 23, 2017.

87. Reid Wilson, "Dems Face Close Polls in Must-Win Virginia," *The Hill*, October 5, 2017; RealClearPolitics, "President Trump Job Approval in Virginia," 2019, https://www.realclearpolitics.com/epolls/approval_rating/president/va/president_trump_job_approval_in_virginia-6188.html.

88. Brock Vergakis and Bill Bartel, "Democrat Ralph Northam Wins Virginia's Hard-Fought Race for Governor," *Virginian-Pilot*, November 7, 2017.

89. Graham Moomaw, "Northam, McAuliffe Highlight Medicaid Expansion, Student Loan Debt, Absentee Voting as Top Priorities for Legislative Session," *Richmond Times-Dispatch*, January 9, 2018.

90. Michael Martz, "Virginia Hospitals Want Proposed Tax on Profits Out of Budget in Push to Expand Medicaid," *Richmond Times-Dispatch*, January 16, 2018.

91. Michael Laris and Laura Vozzella, "House and Senate in Virginia at Loggerheads Over Medicaid Expansion," *Washington Post*, February 20, 2014; Ian Simpson, "Control of Virginia State House at Stake as Recounts Begin," Reuters, December 13, 2017.

92. Ralph Northam, Gubernatorial Inaugural Address, January 13, 2018, available at https://www.richmond.com/news/virginia/government-politics/general-assembly/the-inaugural-address-of-gov-ralph-northam/article_f70a14bb-ef14-50eb-a3ca-804b003b70a2.html.

93. Michael Martz, "Northam Tells Legislators Medicaid Expansion Is 'a Matter of Basic Economic Justice'," *Richmond Times-Dispatch*, January 15, 2018.

94. Jeff Schapiro, "Era of Good Feeling? Not Yet," *Richmond Times-Dispatch*, January 20, 2018.

95. Michael Martz, "Virginia Senate Panel Defeats Legislation to Expand Medicaid," *Richmond Times-Dispatch*, January 25, 2018.

96. Michael Martz, "Cox Seeks 'Dialogue' with Northam on Medicaid but Demands Work Requirement," *Richmond Times-Dispatch*, January 29, 2018.

97. Michael Martz, "House Panel Adopts Work Rule for Medicaid, Dismisses State Fiscal Analysis," *Richmond Times-Dispatch*, January 30, 2018.

98. Jeff Schapiro, "Northam Rides to the Rescue — of Cox," *Richmond Times-Dispatch*, January 30, 2018.

99. Terry Kilgore, "The Next Step for Rebuilding Southwest Virginia's Economy," *Roanoke Times*, February 15, 2018.

100. See, e.g., Adam Searing, "Why Virginia Expanded Medicaid: Five Key Reasons," Georgetown University Health Policy Institute, Center for Children and Families, May 30, 2018, https://ccf.georgetown.edu/2018/05/30/why-virginia-expanded-medicaid-five-key-reasons; Abby Goodnough, "After Years of Trying, Virginia Finally Will Expand Medicaid," *New York Times*, May 30, 2018.

101. Norman Leahy, "GOP Resistance to Medicaid Expansion Cracks," *Bearing Drift*, April 11, 2018; Patrick Wilson and Michael Martz, "Republicans Facing Pressure from Left and Right in Virginia," *Richmond Times-Dispatch*, April 1, 2018.

102. Reema Amin and Dave Ress, "General Assembly Backs Budget, Medicaid Expansion," *Daily Press*, May 31, 2018.

103. Dave Ress, "Shad Plank: Personality in Politics, Primary Ballot Update and Medicaid Expansion," *Daily Press*, April 12, 2018.

104. Graham Moomaw, "Northam Calls Virginia Lawmakers Back to Richmond for April 11 Special Session on Budget," *Richmond Times-Dispatch*, March 13, 2018.

105. Alan Suderman, "Dominion Bill Advances, Helped by Shareholder Va. Lawmakers," WAVY, Associated Press, February 2, 2015.

106. Laura Vozzella, "A Key Virginia GOP State Senator Says He Is Willing to Break Ranks and Vote to Expand Medicaid," *Washington Post*, April 6, 2018; Frank Wagner, "Health Plan Could Help 2 Million Virginians," *Virginian-Pilot*, April 10, 2018; Editorial Board, "Senate GOP Leaders Hold Out Against the Inevitable," *Richmond Times-Dispatch*, April 27, 2018; Michael Martz,

"House Committee Adopts New Budget, with Changes for Medicaid Work Requirement, Insurance and Cash Reserve," *Richmond Times-Dispatch*, April 13, 2018; Michael Martz, "As Va. Budget Fight Resumes, Hospitals Balance Benefits of Expanding Medicaid, Cost of Tax to Pay for It," *Richmond Times-Dispatch*, May 13, 2018.

107. Jeff Schapiro, "For Some Republicans, Health Care Fight Not Over Yet," *Richmond Times-Dispatch*, May 30, 2018.

108. Norman Leahy, "The Medicaid Fallout for the Virginia Senate's Gang of Four," *Washington Post*, June 1, 2018.

109. Schapiro, "For Some Republicans"; Laura Vozzella, "Jill Vogel Embraces the Trump Agenda in Her Virginia Race," *Washington Post*, October 9, 2017.

110. Graham Moomaw, "For Va. House's Democratic Freshmen, Medicaid Expansion Vote Is Payoff to 2017 Campaigns," *Richmond Times-Dispatch*, May 30, 2018.

111. Michael Martz and Graham Moomaw, "Northam Signs Budget with Medicaid Expansion, Capping Five-Year Battle," *Richmond Times-Dispatch*, June 7, 2018.

112. Jeanine Martin, "Greene County GOP Censures Senator Emmett Hanger," *The Bull Elephant*, June 21, 2018; Virginia Public Access Project, "Hanger for Senate: Top Donors, 2016–2019," https://www.vpap.org/committees/124438/top_donors/?contrib_type=A&start_year=2016&end_year=2019.

113. Stephen Farnsworth and Jeremy Engel, "Ralph Northam's Excellent Timing," *Washington Post*, October 5, 2018.

Chapter 5

1. Martin Austermuhle, "Why Does Virginia Hold Elections in Off-Off Years?," WAMU, September 13, 2017.

2. Peter Wallenstein, *Cradle of America: A History of Virginia*, 2nd ed. (Lawrence: University of Kansas Press, 2014), 231.

3. Patrik Jonsson, "In Restoring Voting Rights to Felons, a Question of Redemption," *Christian Science Monitor*, April 23, 2016; Christopher Uggen, Sarah Shannon, and Jeff Manza, "State-Level Estimates of Felon Disenfranchisement in the United States, 2010," The Sentencing Project, July 12, 2012, available at http://www.sentencingproject.org/publications/state-level-estimates-of-felon-disenfranchisement-in-the-united-states-2010.

4. National Conference of State Legislatures, "Felon Voting Rights," April 30, 2017, available at http://www.ncsl.org/research/elections-and-campaigns/felon-voting-rights.aspx.

5. Dave Ress, "Records Show Marijuana Charges, Convictions Fall More Heavily on Black Virginians," *Daily Press*, July 29, 2018.

6. Alan Greenblatt, "Are Pardons Becoming More Politically Acceptable?," *Governing*, January 14, 2015; Bob Fredericks, "President Trump Backs Bipartisan Criminal Justice Reform Bill," *New York Post*, November 14, 2018; Natalie Andrews, "Senate Passes Landmark Criminal-Justice Overhaul Bill in Bipartisan Vote," *Wall Street Journal*, December 18, 2018.

7. Megan Patrick, "Socioeconomic Status and Substance Use Among Young Adults: A Comparison Across Constructs and Drugs," *Journal of Studies on Alcohol and Drugs* 73, no. 5 (September 2012): 772–82.

8. Timothy Coyne, "The Resurgence of Heroin: Benefiting from the Current Political Climate," *University of Richmond Public Interest Law Review* 20, no. 2 (2017): 185–202.

9. Ress, "Records Show Marijuana Charges."

10. Hannah Hartig and Abigail Geiger, "About 6 in 10 Americans Support Marijuana Legalization," Pew Research Center, October 8, 2018.

11. Julian Walker, "Voting Rights, Schools Top Governor's Annual Address," *Virginian-Pilot*, January 10, 2013.

12. Laura Vozzella, "House Panel Kills Felon Voting Bills," *Washington Post*, January 14, 2013.

13. Markus Schmidt, "Automatic Restoration of Felons' Rights Spiked," *Richmond Times-Dispatch*, February 12, 2013.

14. Errin Whack, "Va. Panel Announces Findings on Restoring Voting Rights of Former Felons," *Washington Post*, May 28, 2013.

15. Sean Gorman, "Cuccinelli U-Turns on Restoring Voting Rights to Non-Violent Felons," *PolitiFact*, June 3, 2013.

16. Errin Whack, "McDonnell to Expedite Rights Restoration Process for Non-Violent Felons in Virginia," *Washington Post*, May 29, 2013.

17. Errin Whack, "Va. Ramps Up Restoration of Voting Rights for Some Ex-Felons," *Washington Post*, July 15, 2013.

18. "McDonnell Says State Has Restored Rights of Record 6,800 Felons," *Richmond Times-Dispatch*, October 17, 2013; Associated Press, "Scooter Libby Gets Vote Rights Back," *Politico*, February 28, 2013.

19. Gary Robertson, "Virginia Ex-Governor's Law License Suspected After Corruption Conviction," Reuters, January 23, 2015.

20. George Brown, "McDonnell and the Criminalization of Politics," *Virginia Journal of Criminal Law* 5, no. 1 (2017): 1–37.

21. Julie Carey, Matthew Barakat, and Larry O'Dell, "McDonnell Trial: Virginia Health Official Witnessed Special Treatment," NBC Washington, August 7, 2014; Jim Nolan and Frank Green, "Health Secretary Did Not Believe Williams' Claims," *Richmond Times-Dispatch*, August 7, 2014.

22. See Virginia General Assembly HB 7, HB 556, HJ 48, all from 2014.

23. Whack, "McDonnell to Expedite Rights."

24. Michael Laris, "Voting-Rights Quest in Va. Will Become Easier for Ex-Prisoners Held on Serious Drug Charges," *Washington Post*, April 18, 2014; Office of the Governor, "Governor McAuliffe's Changes to Restoration of Rights Policy Receives Resounding Support," April 18, 2014.

25. Laris, "Voting-Rights Quest"; Jenna Portnoy, "In Virginia, Felon Voting Rights Mean a Simpler Path to Gun Ownership," *Washington Post*, May 20, 2016.

26. See Virginia General Assembly, 2015 HJ 491.

27. Alana Austin, "Governor McAuliffe Announces Reforms to Rights Restoration," WVIR, June 23, 2015.

28. Office of the Governor, "Governor McAuliffe Announces New Reforms to Restoration of Rights Process," June 23, 2015.

29. Jeff Schapiro, "McAuliffe Uses Executive Power to Paint Virginia Blue," *Richmond Times-Dispatch*, April 23, 2016.

30. Alan Suderman, "Virginia Governor Enables 200,000 Felons to Vote in November," *USA Today*, Associated Press, April 22, 2016.

31. Graham Moomaw, "McAuliffe Restores Voting Rights for 206k Ex-Felons; GOP Calls It Move to Boost Clinton," *Richmond Times-Dispatch*, April 22, 2016.

32. Sheryl Gay Stolberg and Erik Eckholm, "Virginia Governor Restores Voting Rights to Felons," *New York Times*, April 22, 2016.

33. Ben Campbell, interview with author, April 2, 2017.

34. Moomaw, "McAuliffe Restores Voting Rights."

35. Editors, "Virginia's McAuliffe Is Wrong on Felons' Voting," *National Review*, April 26, 2016; Jenna Portnoy, "In Virginia, Felon Voting Rights Mean a Simpler Path to Gun Ownership," *Washington Post*, May 20, 2016.

36. Alex Rohr, "Dozens of Felons Register to Vote in Lynchburg After McAuliffe's Controversial Executive Order," *Lynchburg News and Advance*, June 18, 2016.

37. Andy Kroll, "Terry McAuliffe Wants to Prove He's Not a Crony. But First He Has to Get Hillary Elected," *Washingtonian*, September 5, 2016.

38. Stolberg and Eckholm, "Virginia Governor Restores Voting Rights."

39. Dinan, *Virginia State Constitution*, 87–91.

40. Virginia Constitution, Article II, Section 1.

41. Virginia Constitution, Article V, Section 12.

42. Moomaw, "McAuliffe Restores Voting Rights."

43. "Attorney General Urges Court to Uphold Mass Restoration of Felons' Voting Rights," *Richmond Free Press*, July 8, 2016.

44. Whack, "Va. Panel Announces Findings."

45. Moomaw, "McAuliffe Restores Voting Rights."

46. Travis Fain, "Restored Felon Stats: Half White, 79 Percent Nonviolent," *Daily Press*, May 11, 2016.

47. Office of the Governor, "Analysis: Virginians Whose Voting Rights Have Been Restored Overwhelmingly Nonviolent, Completed Sentences More than a

Decade Ago," May 11, 2016. This undercounts the exact numbers, which were based on then-current records of about 163,000 out of 206,000 people. The news release describes its methodology.

48. Jenna Portnoy and Tom Jackman, "McAuliffe's Clemency Order Comes Under Scrutiny," *Washington Post*, June 2, 2016.

49. Laura Vozzella, "Virginia Pulls 132 Confined Sex Offenders from List of Eligible Voters," *Washington Post*, June 18, 2016.

50. Rohr, "Dozens of Felons Register."

51. Sheryl Gay Stolberg, "Virginia at Center of Racially Charged Fight Over the Right of Felons to Vote," *New York Times*, June 6, 2016.

52. Laura Vozzella, "GOP Sues to Block McAuliffe Order to Let 200,000 Virginia Felons Vote," *Washington Post*, May 23, 2016.

53. Graham Moomaw, "43 Va. Prosecutors File Brief Opposing McAuliffe Order on Felons' Rights," *Richmond Times-Dispatch*, June 17, 2016; Graham Moomaw, "After McAuliffe Order on Voting, Felons Try Faster Path to Gun Rights," *Richmond Times-Dispatch*, June 19, 2016.

54. *Howell v. McAuliffe*, Virginia Supreme Court, 2016.

55. Fenit Nirappil and Jenna Portnoy, "Va. High Court Invalidates McAuliffe's Order Restoring Felon Voting Rights," *Washington Post*, July 22, 2016.

56. "*Howell v. McAuliffe*," *Harvard Law Review* 130 (2017): 1970–77.

57. L. Michael Berman, "*Howell v. McAuliffe*," *University of Richmond Law Review* 52 (2017): 251–71.

58. Jenna Portnoy, "McAuliffe Promises to Dodge Court Ruling Against Sweeping Clemency Order," *Washington Post*, July 25, 2016.

59. Laura Vozzella, "McAuliffe Restores Voting Rights to 13,000 Felons," *Washington Post*, August 22, 2016.

60. Jon Kamp, "In Virginia, Gov. McAuliffe Wins Latest Republican Legal Challenge Over Voting Rights for Felons," *Wall Street Journal*, September 15, 2016.

61. Luke Rosiak, "Virginia Gov. Pardons 60,000 Felons, Enough to Swing Election," *Daily Caller*, November 6, 2016.

62. Laura Vozzella, "Va. Gov. McAuliffe Says He Has Broken U.S. Record for Restoring Voting Rights," *Washington Post*, April 27, 2017.

63. Dinan, *Virginia State Constitution*, 97.

64. Mechelle Hankerson, "How Much Will Redistricting Legal Battle Cost Virginians?," *Virginia Mercury*, August 17, 2018.

65. The 2010–16 history is reviewed in Thomas, *Virginia Politics & Government in a New Century*, 42–48, and some of the same sources are cited in this chapter.

66. Editorial Board, "Gerrymandering and Secrecy Add Up to Trouble," *Richmond Times-Dispatch*, May 9, 2015; Laura Vozzella, "Gillespie Took Partisan Mapmaking to a New Level. Try Turning That into a Bumper Sticker," *Washington Post*, October 31, 2017.

67. L. Douglas Wilder School of Government and Public Affairs, "Kaine Leads U.S. Senate Race by 23 Points, Wilder School Poll Shows," Virginia Commonwealth University, August 8, 2018.

68. Frank Newport, "Public Opinion and the Election 2000 Stalemate: A Summary," Gallup, November 20, 2000.

69. Wyatt Durrette, "If Politicians Were Angels, No Redistricting Reform Would Be Necessary," *Richmond Times-Dispatch*, September 24, 2018.

70. "Clinton Returns to Campaign Trail, for Virginia Gov Candidate," *Fox News*, October 4, 2017.

71. Monmouth University Polling Institute, "Virginia: Tight Race in CD07," Monmouth University, September 25, 2018.

72. Virginia Department of Elections, "Election Results: 2017 November General: Statewide," December 8, 2017, available at https://results.elections.virginia. gov/vaelections/2017%20November%20General/Site/Statewide.html.

73. Lowell Feld, "Optimism for 2019: Tim Kaine Won 26/40 Virginia State Senate Districts, 61/100 House of Delegates Districts," *Blue Virginia*, November 8, 2018.

74. Virginia Department of Elections, "Election Results: 2017 November General: General Assembly," December 8, 2017, available at https://results. elections.virginia.gov/vaelections/2017%20November%20General/Site/ GeneralAssembly.html.

75. James Moore and Wayne Slater, *Bush's Brain: How Karl Rove Made George W. Bush Presidential* (New York: Wiley, 2003).

76. Patricia Kilday Hart, "Between the Lines," *Texas Monthly*, January 2011.

77. Charles Lane and Dan Balz, "Justices Affirm GOP Map for Texas," *Washington Post*, June 29, 2006.

78. Karl Rove, "The GOP Targets State Legislatures," *Wall Street Journal*, March 4, 2010.

79. Olga Pierce, Justin Elliott, and Theodoric Meyer, "How Dark Money Helped Republicans Hold the House and Hurt Voters," *ProPublica*, December 21, 2012.

80. Laura Vozzella, "Gillespie Took Partisan Mapmaking to a New Level. Try Turning that into a Bumper Sticker," *Washington Post*, October 31, 2017.

81. Robin Young and David Daley, "'Gerrymandering on Steroids': How Republicans Stacked the Nation's Statehouses," *Here and Now*, WBUR, July 19, 2016.

82. Ryan Snow, "Legislative Control over Redistricting as Conflicts of Interest: Addressing the Problem of Partisan Gerrymandering Using State Conflicts of Interest Law," *University of Pennsylvania Law Review* 165 (2017): 147–64.

83. Robert Greenberger, "Gerrymandering Gets Focus," *Wall Street Journal*, December 4, 2003.

84. Ryan McDougle, "McAuliffe Jumps in on Democratic Gerrymandering Scheme," *Richmond Times-Dispatch*, February 4, 2017.

85. Vozzella, "Gillespie Took Partisan Mapmaking."
86. Brian Cannon and Ben Williams, "Slaying the Gerrymander: How Reform Will Happen in the Commonwealth," *Richmond Public Interest Law Review* 21, no. 1 (2017): 23–46.
87. Richard Wolf, "Supreme Court Upholds Virginia Redistricting," *USA Today*, May 23, 2016.
88. Rosalind Helderman, "In Fiesty Radio Interview, Saslaw Fights Back on Car Title Lending, Abortion Regulation," *Washington Post*, March 4, 2011.
89. Anita Kumar, "Va. Redistricting Deal Protects Incumbents and Punishes Challengers, Critics Say," *Washington Post*, April 2, 2011.
90. Rosalind Helderman and Anita Kumar, "Virginia Assembly Approves New Legislative Maps," *Washington Post*, April 7, 2011.
91. Virginia Constitution, Article II, Section 6.
92. *Vesalind v. Virginia State Board of Elections*, Circuit Court for the City of Richmond, Case No. CL15003886.
93. *Vesalind v. Virginia State Board of Elections*, Virginia Supreme Court, 2018.
94. United States Courts, "About: Supreme Court Procedures," 2019.
95. Nina Totenberg, "Supreme Court Considers Race, Politics, and Redistricting in 2 Cases," *All Things Considered*, National Public Radio, December 5, 2016.
96. Robert Barnes and Gregory Schneider, "Supreme Court Says Virginia Redistricting Must Be Reexamined for Racial Bias," *Washington Post*, March 1, 2017.
97. Rachel Weiner, "Court Strikes Down Virginia House Districts as Racial Gerrymandering," *Washington Post*, June 26, 2018.
98. Ned Oliver, "Explained: What Went Wrong with the 11 Disputed House Districts, Including a Republican Delegate's 'Murky Recollection' in Court," *Virginia Mercury*, August 30, 2018.
99. Graham Moomaw, "Expert Who Redrew Virginia's Congressional Map in 2015 Appointed to Draw New Va. House Districts," *Richmond Times-Dispatch*, October 18, 2018.
100. Graham Moomaw, "U.S. Supreme Court Agrees to Take up GOP Appeal in Va. Redistricting Case," *Richmond Times-Dispatch*, November 13, 2018.
101. Jenna Portnoy, "Special Prosecutor Investigating Possible Election Fraud in Rep. Scott Taylor's Race," *Washington Post*, August 7, 2018; Jane Harper and Victoria Bourne, "4 Dead People, 59 Fraudulent Signatures Found on Petitions Filed by Scott Taylor's Campaign," *Virginian-Pilot*, August 24, 2018; Dave Ress, "More Complaints of False Names on Petitions for Hampton Candidate," *Daily Press*, August 7, 2018.
102. Patrick Wilson, "Richmond Judge Finds 'Out-and-out Fraud' in Effort by Rep. Scott Taylor Staff to Get Independent on Ballot," *Richmond Times-Dispatch*, September 5, 2018.

103. Stephanie Akin, "Rep. Scott Taylor Falling Behind Challenger After Ballot Forgery Scandal, Democratic Poll Shows," *Roll Call*, September 18, 2018.

104. Joint Legislative Audit and Review Committee, *Operations and Performance of Virginia's Department of Elections*, September 10, 2018.

105. Graham Moomaw, "Review Finds Virginia Elections Agency Had Culture of 'Open Support for One Party Over the Other'," *Richmond Times-Dispatch*, September 10, 2018.

106. Joint Legislative Audit and Review Committee, *Operations and Performance*. See chapter 5.

107. Max Smith, "After Critical Report, Northam Says Va. Election Problems Won't Happen Again," WTOP, September 12, 2018.

108. Laura Vozzella and Ted Mellnik, "Va. Election Officials Assigned 26 Voters to the Wrong District. It Might've Cost Democrats a Pivotal Race," *Washington Post*, May 13, 2018.

Chapter 6

1. Peter Wallenstein, *Cradle of America: A History of Virginia*, 2nd ed. (Lawrence: University of Kansas Press, 2014), 24.

2. "Health of State Democracies: Virginia," Center for American Progress Action Fund, 2015, https://healthofstatedemocracies.org/states/virginia.html.

3. Dave Ress, "The Virginia Way, Part 8: Disclosure Rules Are Lax, and Reports Are Hard to Find," *Daily Press*, November 23, 2014.

4. Nancy Madsen, "Virginia Gets D Grade in 2015 State Integrity Investigation," Center for Public Integrity, November 12, 2015.

5. "Gender Parity by State," Represent Women, 2018.

6. Harry Enten, "Ranking the States from Most to Least Corrupt," *FiveThirtyEight*, January 23, 2015.

7. Laura Goren, "Virginia Is Exceptionally Unequal," Commonwealth Institute for Fiscal Analysis, February 23, 2016, http://thehalfsheet.org/post/139863776503/virginia-is-exceptionally-unequal.

8. "The Best and Worst States to Work in America," Oxfam, 2018.

9. Jennifer Davis McDaid, "Woman Suffrage in Virginia," Encyclopedia Virginia, October 26, 2018.

10. Frank Atkinson, "Virginia Can Show the Way, Again," *Richmond Times-Dispatch*, February 3, 2019.

11. James Branch Cabell, *Let Me Lie: Being in the Main an Ethnological Account of the Remarkable Commonwealth of Virginia and the Making of Its History* (Charlottesville: University of Virginia Press, 1947), 270.

12. Frederick Law Olmsted, *A Journey in the Back Country*, 1860. This is cited in Ben Campbell, *Richmond's Unhealed History* (Richmond, VA: Brandylane, 2012), 123–24.

13. "Term of the Senate, [26 June] 1787," *Founders Online*, National Archives, last modified June 13, 2018, http://founders.archives.gov/documents/Madison/01-10-02-0044. [Original source: Rutland, Robert, Charles Hobson, William Rachal, and Frederika J. Teute, eds., *The Papers of James Madison*, vol. 10, *27 May 1787–3 March 1788* (Chicago: University of Chicago Press, 1977),76–78.]

14. Campbell, *Richmond's Unhealed History*, 209.

15. Brent Tarter, "The Readjuster Party," *Encyclopedia Virginia*, Virginia Foundation for the Humanities, July 19, 2016.

16. Gregory Schneider, "'Campaign to Elect a Pipeline': Virginia's Most Powerful Company Ran Multi-Front Fight," *Washington Post*, November 29, 2017.

17. Patrick Wilson, "Lobbyists Take Changes to Gift Law in Stride," *Virginian-Pilot*, May 11, 2015.

18. Ben Campbell, interview with author, April 2, 2017.

19. Richard Gard, "Getting a Read on Ryan," *Virginia Magazine*, December 6, 2017.

20. James Ryan Inaugural Address, "Faith in the Unfinished Project," University of Virginia, October 19, 2018.

21. Ruth Serven Smith, "At Inauguration, Ryan Promises a UVa that Is 'Not Just Great, But Good'," *Daily Progress*, October 19, 2018.

22. 1 Peter 2:16, NIV.

23. K. Burnell Evans, "With Only $14 Million in Hand, Richmond School Leaders Aren't Sure How to Start Building a Better School District," *Richmond Times-Dispatch*, July 23, 2017.

Methodology

1. This appears to be a misquote: the correct quote is "wherever." See, e.g., National Archives, "From Thomas Jefferson to Richard Price, 8 January 1789," *Founders Online*, 2018, http://founders.archives.gov/documents/Jefferson/01-14-02-0196.

2. Jack Shafer, "Who Said It First? Journalism Is the 'First Rough Draft of History,'" *Slate*, August 30, 2010.

3. Thomas, *Virginia Politics*, 180.

4. Andrew Walworth, "'Moynihan': A Brilliant Portrait of a Political Rarity," RealClearPolitics, October 19, 2018.

INDEX

ABOUT THE AUTHOR

Mr. Thomas was born and raised in Richmond, Virginia. He attended college at the Duke University School of Engineering and graduate school at the Virginia Tech School of Public and International Affairs and the Tulane University School of Public Health. He is the author of *Virginia Politics & Government in a New Century: The Price of Power.*

Visit us at
www.historypress.com